Great Decisions, Perfect Timing

Divination Foundation Press, February 2015
0455 SW Hamilton Ct. Suite 601
Portland, OR 97239

Foreword by John Gray, PhD

Cover and interior by The Book Designers
Author photo by Miri Stebivka

www.Divination.com

EBook ISBN: 978-0-9884942-2-0
Print ISBN: 978-0-9884942-3-7

Great Decisions, Perfect Timing

CULTIVATING INTUITIVE INTELLIGENCE

PAUL O'BRIEN

FOREWORD BY John Gray, Ph.D.

Divination Foundation Press
Divination.com

For my grandson, Bryce,
and all future decision-makers.

CONTENTS

PART I — *Context and Resources*

Making decisions, especially important ones, can be stressful or even debilitating. Decision-making is becoming increasingly difficult, yet it is ever more crucial to do it creatively and effectively.

Avoid the pitfalls of premature commitment and all-or-nothing thinking. Learn techniques for better self-knowledge and base your sense of direction on what naturally fascinates you.

Carl Jung's Synchronicity Principle is a theory of relativity in the dimension of time, according to his friend, Albert Einstein. Consider how leveraging synchronicities to ride waves of change gives you a strategic advantage.

Jung's concept of the "collective unconscious" – also known as Infinite Intelligence – is our source of inspiration, energy, great ideas, and synchronicities. Learn how to access this reservoir of creative power any time you want.

PART II — *The Visionary Decision Making (VDM) Process*

The first two questions of Visionary Decision Making are "What is the vision that is motivating me to make a move?" and, thinking like a chess player, "What is the best next move, if any, for me to make?" Explore simple but effective logic techniques that help bring any problem or dilemma into focus.

Awakening the innate intuitive intelligence is the central lever of the Visionary Decision Making process. This chapter presents new ways to understand intuition by exploring the triune brain, along with meditation techniques to activate it.

FOREWORD

by JOHN GRAY,
author of *Men are From Mars, Women are from Venus*

Synchronicity is a term that the psychologist Carl Jung coined to describe the phenomenon of meaningful coincidence. We intuitively sense that events are more than just a coincidence when they serve as amazing twists of destiny that provide turning points in our lives. A common fruit of synchronicity is how we meet the right people at the right time. The term provides extra irony for me with regards to Paul O'Brien, because it describes our first meeting in more ways than one.

It was 1992 and I was on a book tour after *Men are From Mars, Women are From Venus* was published. Paul had just taped an interview with me for his Pathways radio show in Portland, Oregon. I thought he was an excellent interviewer and asked if radio was what he did for a living. He smiled and told me that he was a volunteer host for the community radio station (a public service he has continued for 30 years). He also shared that he had recently left a position as a software executive to start a "quirky" Macintosh software company. Being an early Mac user, this intrigued me, and I inquired as to the type of software he was producing.

When I learned that his first product was an interactive version of the I Ching for the Macintosh named *Synchronicity*, I almost fell out of my chair. "*You* developed the *Synchronicity* program?" Surprised by my reaction, he replied, "You've heard of it?" I said, "Yes, I own it, and my wife and I love it. I can hardly believe that

I am meeting the guy who developed the *Synchronicity* program for my Mac!" Paul replied, "Well, it's amazing for me to realize that I have been listening to your cassettes on relationships for years – not knowing who *you* were... and now I discover that you are one of my first customers ... this is almost *too much* synchronicity!" We shared a good laugh over it.

My wife Bonnie and I had used different versions of the I Ching as an aid to decision-making since the 1970s and found the Taoist divination system to be a source of wisdom. Around 1991, we tried out Paul's new software as a possibly engaging new way to consult it. In addition to taking all the busy work out of casting an I Ching reading (the recording and calculating of lines, etc.), the program contained an elegant, modern, and non-sexist version of the ancient text, which was composed by Paul.

The program's combination of poetic text and multimedia was groundbreaking in 1990, but *Synchronicity* would only prove to be the opening act in Paul's entrepreneurial adventure. Focusing on a mission to provide universal access to authentic divination systems, he eventually gave the world do-it-yourself I Ching and Tarot readings via the Internet. In the process he also created what turned into the largest astrology and numerology website, which became the exclusive provider of horoscopes and divination features for AOL, Google, Beliefnet, and other large websites.

Great Decisions, Perfect Timing: Cultivating Intuitive Intelligence includes the story of how Paul made the strange but strategic decisions that led to a fascinating business success that was based on staying true to his unique creative vision against all odds. Beyond the highly entertaining personal anecdotes, the book provides an unconventional toolkit that is grounded in timeless wisdom, designed to help you improve your odds at finding success in your own way by upgrading your decision-making and improving your timing. His visionary approach to decision-making revolves around Jung's *Synchronicity Principle*, which Jung had discovered based on his own fascination with the I Ching, and which describes the essence of perfect timing.

I have long noticed how synchronicity plays a huge role in relationships, especially for people who are destined to become partners. It certainly played a prominent part in my connecting with my wife, Bonnie, over 35 years ago. In an amazing twist of fate that occurred a couple of years before we even met, I was assigned the task of taking care of her needs – specifically some health needs – under the direction of our spiritual teacher. She was pregnant and needed special things to be procured, errands to be run, etc. I was a monk at the time and had not even met her. But as a result of synchronicity, I was helping provide for my future wife's needs years *before* we met!

If life is elegant, synchronicity explains why. As Paul puts it, from the synchronistic point of view, there are no accidents. The way Bonnie and I came together is just one example of the mystical ways that people who are destined to be together can and do find each other. In 30 years of relationship counseling, I have heard so many simply amazing stories of how long-term partners have met. More often than not, a meaningful coincidence – or synchronicity – is at the start of it.

Timing has also played a major role in my career as an author and teacher, but as this book explains, synchronicity doesn't operate in a linear fashion. This is where two key components of his "Visionary Decision Making" system – self-discovery and intuitive intelligence – come to the forefront.

In 1983 I was a relationship counselor and starting to speak about the ideas that would later coalesce in *Men are From Mars, Women are From Venus*. I wrote my first book in 1989, entitled *Men, Women and Relationships*. It revealed a way of approaching and enriching relationships between men and women, based on appreciating our differences as well as our similarities. To highlight any differences, real as they may be, was "politically incorrect" in the 1980s. As timing would have it, this first book of mine came out one month after Deborah Tannen's bestseller, *You Just Don't Understand*. Although her analysis was quite different, it was academically grounded. The popularity of her book created a much wider discussion around the different ways that women and men communicate.

Even though her book overshadowing mine seemed like a setback at the time, it turned out that a scientifically oriented and academic book was necessary to launch a serious discussion about gender differences. A year later *Men are From Mars, Women are*

From Venus came out and went on to become one of the biggest best sellers of all time. In the inscrutable way that synchronicity operates – as Paul describes in this profound book – what ended up looking like perfect timing was aided by a setback that seemed terrible at the time, but which turned out to be a blessing in disguise. As we adopt new beliefs around intuitive intelligence and cultivate what Paul calls a "synchronistic lifestyle," we can better hold on to our visions. We will know there is a reason for everything – including frustrated plans and apparent setbacks – even if we don't understand those reasons right away.

In this book, Paul O'Brien shares his hard-won wisdom along with timeless principles on how to awaken intuitive intelligence to improve your results in any area of life. Over the past twenty-five years, Paul's modern version of the I Ching has helped hundreds of thousands of people – via software, the Internet, an ebook version, and a smartphone app. Now *Great Decisions, Perfect Timing: Cultivating Intuitive Intelligence* provides a more expansive toolkit to put the knowledge of synchronicity, the power of archetypes, and the elegant mindfulness of intuition to work for you. If you give them a chance, the principles and practices taught in this book will help you manifest happiness, success, and, of course, love!

INTRODUCTION

We are drowning in information, while starving for wisdom.
The world henceforth will be run by people able to put together
the right information at the right time, think critically about
it, and make important choices wisely. —E. O. WILSON[1]

Have you ever passed up something that was good, hoping that something perfect would come along? Did you ever miss an exceptional opportunity because your timing was off? Do you find it difficult to tell the difference between a risk worth taking and wishful thinking? Making great decisions with perfect timing is not easy... and you are not alone if you have experienced any of these situations. In fact, the story of my entrepreneurial career and evolving sense of mission perfectly illustrates risks worth taking and the critical role of timing.

In 1988, I had an established career as a software marketing specialist, having advanced from the position of office secretary at a college computer center to VP of Marketing in 15 years. I had developed professional product marketing skills, but I felt an inner stirring, a longing to make a living marketing more creative – as opposed to high-tech – products that I personally cared about.

One day, inspired by a reading from the *Book of Changes* – a reflective intuitive decision-making aid that I had learned to appreciate – I made a decision to invest my savings to produce a multimedia version of that ancient divination system. I believed that by developing an interactive version of this tool that I had used since I was a teenager, I might bring intuitive decision-making support to others via a more engaging presentation of the I Ching, which had only existed (for thousands of years) in book form. I had no reason to believe that an interactive program based on a system of Taoist wisdom could ever become very profitable, but the idea fascinated me so much I didn't concern myself with bottom line calculations. At first, it was an experiment and purely a labor of love.

Though I had never been in charge of producing software, let alone multimedia – which was just becoming possible with the advent of graphical computers like the Macintosh – I did understand the personal software business. And in addition to my interest in Taoist philosophy and practices, I had long been fascinated by the potentials of interactive multimedia to educate and enlighten, as well as entertain.

The Book of Changes, or *I Ching*, was developed in China 3,000 years ago to help emperors and military leaders make strategic decisions. Now, I was fully aware that a computer-assisted I Ching was too esoteric to attract a publisher or investors. Yet I couldn't bring myself to set the idea aside. I was enthralled by the intersection of two powerful fascinations – the workings of an ancient Chinese oracle and the potential of interactive media – that a hybrid fascination with the idea of creating an interactive version of the I Ching was born in me and practically took on a life of its own. The outcome would be the first divination program ever published, as well as one of the first multimedia titles for consumers, years before CD-ROM technology was available.

With the help of a grad student programmer and a friend who was an artist, I used my savings to finance the creation of a prototype while I continued at my job. A couple of months later, when the prototype was somewhat functional, I was so pleased with how well it worked that I decided to complete, package it, and bring it to market, even though that would require risking the rest of my savings and potentially my career. I could only hope that the resulting product would appeal to enough people to keep a little business afloat until I could figure out how to market it widely or create more popular products that also meant something to me. It all started in my basement.

Now, I know what you're thinking: the story of a guy with an idea starting a company in his basement (or garage) seems familiar.

What made this situation unique, however, was the extraordinary degree to which the fulfillment of my plan was driven by personal fascination and how much it would depend upon an agile intuition and a willingness to make bold decisions. Instead of focusing on raising money to capture market share, my approach depended on noticing subtle signs and trusting my sense of timing. Since I was so driven by a creative vision that inspired me, I named the company Visionary Software.

As a "bootstrap entrepreneur" without backers, I realized that it was absolutely critical to make the right moves at the right time. With limited credit, I would face the imminent possibility of running out of cash and going bankrupt for a long time. For my fledgling software enterprise to survive as an ongoing business, exceptional decision-making was going to be absolutely necessary. Everything was on the line. There was no room for major missteps.

The program was called *Synchronicity*, titled after Carl Jung's famous principle that explained how authentic divination systems like the I Ching work. Though the English translation of *I Ching* is *Book of Changes*, it has always been more than a book. It is a divination system designed to stimulate intuition for strategic decision-making and change management.

Ironically, even though Jung's *Synchronicity Principle* is all about timing, my timing in producing I Ching software in 1989 turned out to be far from perfect. As much as I may have wanted such a program for my own enjoyment and use, most people familiar with the I Ching simply did not buy software in those days before email and the worldwide web. There was no market for multimedia, especially since CD-ROMs were not yet in use, which meant the program required installation from multiple floppy disks. To make matters worse, just about the only people who bought software at that time were engineers or financial analysts – who had little awareness of, or interest in, divination.

In spite of being born too soon, *Synchronicity* managed to become a minor cult hit in Macintosh circles, if only because it was cute and unusual. Even so, after all my fervent marketing efforts, it became clear that the survival of the new business would require reaching a much broader audience. So, I hustled to keep the startup afloat by quickly developing more mainstream programs in the area of time management. Curiosity and enthusiasm originally propelled the first project, but I had a larger vision that I thought of as *creative freedom*. My modest definition of this concept was just to be able to make a living doing something I cared about.

Following my interest in the perfection of timing, I developed a priority management program called *First Things First*, which enjoyed much broader popularity, and cash-flow from sales was able to keep the growing operation afloat. After five more years of month-to-month struggle, I handed the reins to a management team, three business experts with MBAs who promised that they would raise money and expand *First Things First* into a world-class time-management package for Windows as well as Mac (they didn't care about my beloved *Synchronicity*). As it turned out, their total failure to raise money, as well as their own lavish spending, bankrupted the company. In the process, I lost everything that I had built – except the ownership of the original *Synchronicity* program, which (in a prescient move) I had legally assigned to myself (without objection).

The failure of my first entrepreneurial venture was disheartening, but at least I still had the rights to my original creation. Several thousand people had used *Synchronicity*; many had never seen anything like it and sent heartfelt thank-you letters. I even bumped into some people who, when they realized that I was the author of it, admitted they had pirated the program and handed me a couple of twenty dollar bills on the spot! The appreciation from such people encouraged me to hold on to the vision of such a product... and my dream of creative freedom.

When the World Wide Web came into popular use five years after the demise of Visionary Software, my first company, I saw a new opportunity to resurrect the original vision using CD-ROMs. This new delivery platform made it possible to deliver a rich multimedia experience... for both Mac and Windows. So, for the second time around, I used every dollar I had socked away as a consultant to turn *Synchronicity* into a graphically and musically rich CD-ROM. Around that time, I happened to interview a Tarot scholar on my Pathways radio show. Through that interview, I came to understand that authentic Tarot (not the psychic mind-reading variety) operates on the same Synchronicity Principle as the

I Ching, only with a different set of archetypes. With her scholarly help, I produced a database of Tarot interpretation text and spent a year developing a media-rich, do-it-yourself Tarot reading CD-ROM to double our company's product line.

A couple of years after we had put up a website to market the two CD-ROMs, we noticed that people were banging on a little multimedia sampler we had put on the website to help market the CD-ROMs, but in spite of the popularity of the sampler (based on clicks), sales were not increasing very much. The interactive bit, however, was going viral with thousands of people playing it over and over. This was a signal to me that we were meant to be in the Internet business rather than just using web to sell CD-ROMs. We needed to build a "pay-to-play" ecommerce website, which was quite an expensive proposition.

Through a most unlikely sequence of synchronicities – and after being laughed off by two banks – one nerdy little middle-aged banker with a comb-over, wearing a polyester suit and driving a Ford Pinto, did all the paperwork for us to get an SBA loan to build a website to sell do-it-yourself I Ching and Tarot readings on a one-off basis. (Now, who would have ever imagined a large regional bank – or any bank, for that matter – financing an I Ching and Tarot reading website?)

Once we had procured the 7-year loan, the process of building the pay-to-play ecommerce site took almost a year, during which time we invented our own web currency, which we called "Karma Coins," to allow people to make micropayments (i.e. amounts too small for a credit card). This idea just made sense to me, but it was a revolutionary concept at the time. All in all, my entrepreneurial juices were flowing again, and this time around, the timing felt a little better, as I brought my creative and marketing skills to bear all over again as a bootstrap entrepreneur.

After a few more years of plugging away – at one point re-mortgaging my home to make payroll – I added astrology to the mix and negotiated some syndication deals with the largest Internet portals, including AOL and Google, who needed the "fresh daily content" of a well-written horoscope. As a result of such major affiliations, huge volumes of traffic began flowing to our small but rapidly growing Oregon-based website. After that, it was only a couple of years before our site had acquired millions of registered members. Approximately two percent of our members bought a reading or a report product, which was a notable direct-marketing feat – and highly profitable. Ever loathe to being in debt, we paid off the entire SBA loan in 2 years.

The original *Synchronicity* program had evolved into a multi-faceted divination website offering astrology, numerology, and Tarot, as well as the I Ching. These online experiences were not only creative and authentic, but also became wildly popular – especially with women who, following the advent of the world-wide web and email services, had started to use computers in large numbers. After fifteen years of pursuing my dream and struggling to make ends meet, my creative endeavors had begun to produce exceptional returns. Nobody, including myself, had ever believed it would be possible for an esoteric program like *Synchronicity* to morph into a profitable business. It seemed foolhardy enough to imagine that such a niche product could support me and my son, let alone a staff of people.

Even though accumulation of wealth had never been my goal, our enterprise was becoming downright lucrative! This second time around, my little startup was growing fast and far exceeding my original concept of creative freedom. I was receiving much more income than I had ever made as an executive or consultant, and our products were touching the lives of millions. This felt like success to me, creatively and financially.

By the time our website was attracting over 40 million Internet pageviews a month in 2006, the company had been winning growth awards for a couple of years. It was around this time that large media firms like Disney and Barnes & Noble began to take notice and came sniffing around. They could see the massive traffic, they could sense the high profit margins, and they were interested in acquiring the company. Such attention was flattering, but I would hear none of it... at first. I loved this little business that had grown to support twenty-five employees, six million registered members and hundreds of thousands of customers. We had no debt or nervous investors. I felt pride that the business was winning awards as well as making millions of dollars. I was having a gratifying time developing new products and running a prospering business. After so much grueling labor, I felt a strong affection for my "babies," the offspring of my creative imagination. The last thing I wanted was to sell them off, now that they were amply repaying my sacrifices and labors of love.

The company's success had more than fulfilled my vision of making a living doing something I cared about. I had succeeded beyond my initial dream, and as a result of self-financing with savings and "sweat equity" – and the help of a serendipitous bank loan – I had no investors to answer to. I had neither "exit strategy" nor any perceived need for one. Just keeping the business afloat had provided enough motivation for me to work extremely long hours for a long time, but those days of killer stress were over now.

At this point, I was entering my fifties. I had put in a couple of decades of 70-80 hour weeks, and I was beginning to tire of it. It was also getting tiresome to stay ahead of copycat competitors who were duplicating every creative move we made.

Although I was fatigued from so many years of long hours, I still felt young and energetic, and the traditional idea of retirement held no meaning for me. I started to imagine how I could be even more creative if I were free of the pressures of running a business – with the burdens of taking care of employees, customers, budgets, and deadlines. I had worked for non-profits in the past and was interested in how I might promulgate new ideas, as well as books and interactive media, to promote personal and cultural evolution. I knew that I liked to write and speak publicly; I enjoyed consulting and mentoring. I didn't have time to explore these interests while building or running a business. If I was able to sell the company for a high enough price, I could have the freedom to pursue creative endeavors at my own pace in a non-profit format for the rest of my life. A new vision was incubating within me.

The year was 2006. After the implosion of the dot-com bubble, the markets were beginning to re-stabilize. The number of new companies going public with an IPO – which had dropped 90 percent since 1999 – was starting to rise again. My intuition told me that if I could sell the company during this window of opportunity, the timing might be right to get a good price. It was certainly an option to be considered. On the other hand, my emotional attachment to the company and our millions of subscribers would make letting go of it an incredibly difficult decision. Besides, the company was making serious profits and there was no *need* to sell it. However, I knew my strongest passions were more philosophical and philanthropic than acquisitive or managerial, and I was open to considering a big change.

Even though I was conflicted, I felt called upon to make a pivotal decision that would have huge consequences for the rest of my life. I knew from experience that windows of opportunity don't stay open long and that timing is always a critical factor.

Fortunately I had some help for making major decisions, including the I Ching itself. After meditating on my dilemma, I cast an I Ching reading on the subject and got the reading, "Breakthrough," which pointed to deliberately making a big change. After meditating on this for a couple of days, I decided I would accept the right offer if I could get my "number" – an amount large enough to support creative freedom for the rest of my life. With the stipulation that no employees would have to move or lose their job, I would let go of my attachment to the company and give it over to new owners who could send my beloved creations into even wider distribution.

Retaining an investment bank to find a compatible buyer was the first order of business. I wanted a firm that understood new media, one that could locate a buyer who could realize the future potential of what I had created and put its resources behind continuing growth. Because of the esoteric nature of my products and services, I knew that finding the right match would take a minor miracle. But it would only take one, and after years of studying the I Ching, I had come to appreciate the miraculous power of synchronicity.

To complicate the process further, I came to the conclusion that I needed to be the one who would negotiate the terms of the deal – a stance that was anathema to the investment bankers. They were practically livid. But this was going to be the biggest deal of my life, and I would not allow a broker to set, or even propose, the price or the terms. In spite of enormous (and vociferous) pressure from the bankers that I had retained who, like all brokers, were more worried about there being *no* deal rather than whether it would be the best possible deal, I stuck to my guns. This was not easy – I had to summon my inner warrior to stand up to the experts this time around – but it turned out to be a visionary decision.

Drawing upon my own internal resources, feeling strong as a non-desperate seller, trusting intuitive guidance, and sticking with my decision to be the one who negotiated the terms, I managed to get twice my "number" – much to the bankers' happy surprise, their commissions skyrocketing. The timing of the sale was January 2007, which turned out to be excellent – with corporate valuations as high as they had been since the dot-com era seven years earlier and shortly before the financial crash of 2008, which was still months away.

Creative freedom, my dream for decades, had come home in a much bigger way than I had ever imagined. Faced with an abundance of creative opportunities that I would now be free to explore, I realized how limited my original vision had been. But I was entirely grateful for it. And my first act after selling the company was to set up the non-profit Divination Foundation as a way to enjoy the much greater creative freedom of being able to produce and contribute good works without the need to make a profit.

In this book, it is my hope to share valuable lessons and skills that I learned and mastered over decades, which culminated in a personal victory in the area of livelihood, so that you may more easily achieve your definition of success – whatever it is – in any area of life. My particular success involved an entrepreneurial venture. Yours might pertain to another important realm – relationship, family, spiritual development, or artistic expression. No matter what you are trying to achieve or attain, skillful decision-making and timing will be critical.

Understanding your strengths and weaknesses is an unending process of self-discovery and creative evolution. Real success depends on being true to what fascinates you. Living from a place of authenticity and learning to access creative powers will help you better manage change, feel the confidence to take risks that can grow you, and open to greater grace, creativity, contentment, and wisdom.

While my story may seem like a fluke – perhaps the result of some "good karma" – there is more to it than that. Forty years of trial-and-error has gone into developing the Visionary Decision

Making (VDM) approach that I was developing for myself – and, unwittingly, for this book. The art of VDM has been central to my unfolding destiny in this lifetime, and it can work wonders for you, too. Any motivated person can learn and master the concepts, skills and philosophical approach of VDM and apply them for the achievement of success or happiness in any and every area of life – including career, education, love, family, and personal finance.

This book is intended to help you notice those make-or-break moments when intuition is the key to knowing what you need to do next. The skills herein will help you reawaken and tune up your natural intuitive sensitivity. You will learn to harness new beliefs that change the way you see and approach situations and relationships. Once you learn how to activate intuitive intelligence when you need it most, you will more quickly realize visions that are in alignment with who you are. The main secret to achieving the abundance and joy you deserve is becoming clear about what your heart desires and making the right moves at the right time.

On a practical level, the philosophy and techniques of VDM can help you decide when to have a difficult conversation, what risks are likely to pay off (financially or emotionally), or how to invest wisely, get that dream assignment or create the lasting relationship you always wanted. Learn how to prioritize the decisions you should take up now and determine which ones to put on the back burner for the time being. By learning to recognize fruitful turning-point opportunities and identify when they are ripe for decisive action, you can approach them with clarity of vision and greater self-confidence.

There is no formula for strategic decision-making, because you can't force intuition or make creative decisions through willpower alone. In order to do your best, you need to learn how to produce the conditions in which the intuitive sense is able to receive clear signals. You also need to attain the mastery of skill sets that you can call upon when a turning point arises.

This book is divided into three parts. Part I explores the increasing importance of decision-making skill, reveals the key concepts that support Visionary Decision Making and the creative resources that seem hidden but are always available.

Part II describes the techniques and practices of the Visionary

Decision Making process: focusing on a strategic vision; understanding how our "triune brain" affects decision-making and how to work with it; activating your intuitive antenna; tapping collective wisdom via an authentic divination system; utilizing the power of archetypes; executing a plan at the right time; persevering in your pursuit of results; and achieving levels of mastery. These skills provide reliable ways to develop and support our mysterious faculty of intuitive receptivity.

Part III explores the Visionary Decision Making philosophy and approach to life, which includes learning how to upgrade your belief system, experiment with more visionary beliefs and create a synchronistic lifestyle. The result will be a new perspective and experience of life – marked by the grace, confidence and wisdom that flow from an empowered and creative way of approaching change while staying true to what inspires you.

Although developing good habits is important, intuitive intelligence requires more than following a formula or set of rules. The VDM path is more like learning how to dance. When it comes to making the right moves at the right time, your dance partner is life itself or what can be referred to as your destiny. The more you pay attention and practice VDM skills, the better you will become at sensing the unique rhythm of your life, while you make moves with a masterful sense of timing.

Throughout the book, you'll find short practices designed to increase self-knowledge or activate your intuition. These exercises will help you develop VDM skills and become more keenly aware of psychological resources at your disposal. VDM skills will become habits that support you and provide stability on the road to a more meaningful, harmonious, and abundant life. You can perform the exercises as you encounter them or come back to them at any time. For your convenience, they are compiled in Appendix A and can also be downloaded (and customized as needed) from the web page indicated in the appendix.

May this book offer you a better sense of how *you* can develop your intuitive instinct and, as you become more sensitive to it, improve your judgment and timing!

PART I

Context and Resources

CHAPTER 1

Decisions, Decisions

Life is the sum of all your choices. –ALBERT CAMUS

As you may have inferred from my story in the Introduction, change is a constant in life – maybe the only constant there is – and sudden change is not unusual. Opportunities arise and, along with them, conflicting interests and tradeoffs. In my case, all of a sudden the option of solidifying a secure career was competing with a new and exciting vocational opportunity. Anything can happen. You could be offered a higher-paying position, but in a field you find less exciting. Or an employer might tell you that you need to relocate to a different city to keep your job. You could be laid off from a job that you really like or offered a promotion to a position that you won't. Someone you love could announce that your relationship needs to change, pronto.

Whatever the case, each of us will have to deal with unexpected changes of a significant nature. During the course of a lifetime, we will face turning points and dilemmas that call for making strategic choices that may substantially alter our lives, our bank accounts, and our futures. In order to achieve success and personal fulfillment, we need to be ready when major challenges and new opportunities arise.

How we make such decisions is more critical to our personal freedom, abundance, and joy than any other thing humans can do.

If our decisions are made well, they will lead to skillful actions executed at the right time, they will put us in position to take advantage of significant opportunities. Because of their long-term ramifications, strategic decisions require the most forward-thinking, or "visionary," approach.

Making important decisions can be stressful and even debilitating. In their efforts to cope with the difficulty of it, people range between impulsiveness to overanalytical procrastination. We indulge in all-or-nothing thinking, focus too much on the details, or tell ourselves that we need to wait for more information. Creative potential can be hamstrung by the ego's preoccupation with past regrets and future fears.

The good news is that there are ways we can learn to improve our decision-making in a hectic, complex world where making the right moves at the right time has become increasingly difficult. That is what this book is all about.

Jeff Bezos, founder of Amazon.com, gave a commencement talk at Princeton University a few years ago, in which he emphasized the central importance of decision-making in life: "I will hazard a prediction that when you are 80 years old and, in a quiet moment of reflection, narrating for only yourself the most personal version of your life story, the telling that will be most compact and meaningful will be the series of choices you have made. In the end, we are our choices."[2]

The concept is straightforward – good decisions made now will set up even better future decisions. Conversely, bad decisions lead to more of the same. When you make shortsighted choices, you jeopardize access to resources and find yourself in even more desperate straits. Bad decisions will hem you in until you feel trapped. If you make ill-considered choices long enough, you will lose your freedom – perhaps physically as well as psychologically. On the other hand, if you consistently make more skillful choices, effective decision-making becomes even easier and steadily supports your learning and eventual success. To gain such an advantage, all you have to do is develop skills and practices that help you make better decisions!

There are three levels of decision-making – mundane, tactical, and strategic. Most of the choices we make each day are mundane and without much consequence. Tactical decisions have to do with the different ways that we implement a strategy, but it's the strategic decisions that alter the direction of a person's life or a business and determine its future. The primary focus of Visionary Decision Making is the major strategic choice-points that influence and determine one's career, as well as important relationships, personal growth, business dealings, or politics. Unlike mundane choices, major decisions of a personal, organizational, or societal nature require a deliberative process that is informed by logic and guided by intuitive intelligence.

These days we have instant access to virtually unlimited information and our understanding of human psychology is also evolving rapidly. With an amazing capacity to envision and intuit, plus an array of powerful resources at our disposal, one might assume that human beings would have become excellent at strategic decision-making by now. After all, we are the only species that can visualize different possible outcomes from different possible choices that we might make. Unfortunately, most of us have lost the intuitive sensitivity we were born with and don't even know that we lost it or realize the importance of the loss. Nevertheless, once we wake up to what we are missing, we can cultivate the ability to reconnect with our intuitive instincts. Indeed, we must do so, if we want to improve the decision-making that is vital to success and happiness.

Our Modern Decision-Making Crisis

There is nothing more frightful than ignorance in action.
—J. W. VON GOETHE (1749-1832)

In today's society, the average person makes thousands of mundane decisions every day. Driving a car, we choose to go this way or that. We select a brand of toothpaste in the supermarket or appetizers from a menu. We decide which movie to watch or magazine to read. Most of these choices we make out of habit or impulsively. Unlike strategic choices, they are not very stressful because hardly anything is at stake.

Having too many choices, however, can tax us to such an extent that we lose some of our ability to see and think clearly. Alvin Toffler named the problem "overchoice" in the book *Future Shock* written in 1970, long before change had accelerated to anything near current levels.[3] Toffler had the foresight to envision a world where too many choices, coupled with accelerated change, would cause life to become more stressful rather than liberating. More than forty years later, we are living in that world. The Chinese curse, "May you live in interesting times," has come true with a vengeance!

There are many ways to make bad decisions. It's easy to make them prematurely or impulsively if our mind is under the influence of fear, anxiety, overeagerness, or fatigue. Procrastinators, on the other hand, put off the decision-making process as a way of coping with the stress. Overanalytical types wait for yet more information, forgetting how easy it is to miss out on windows of opportunity before they realize the time has passed.

Fear of failure adds considerable stress to the equation. Suppose, you wonder, the decision you make turns out to have been a monumental mistake. Not only will you have to suffer the consequences, you'll get the blame for having made it! If you leave the decision to someone else and things go wrong, you can blame them. But decisions made by others will never help you develop confidence in your intuitive intelligence. No matter what the reason, not showing up is to cast a vote. If you try to avoid the stressful work of decision-making by being passive or delegating your power, that is a decision too – and one that could boomerang with unintended and unwanted consequences.

Too Much Information

Modern technology delivers an overabundance of information to consider. Theoretically, more data should augment our understanding of a situation, increase our options, and improve our ability to make skillful choices. If we were a tireless computer, this might be true. Paradoxically for us, an overabundance of information increases the difficulty of good decision-making.

These days our minds are bobbing in a vast sea of information, while bombarded on all sides by advertising, opinion shows, magazines, email newsletters, websites, email, text messages, and tweets. It is virtually impossible to sort out so much information in the hopes of finding something useful.

How can we tell good information from bad? What information should we trust? Given today's accelerated rate of change, tuning into the right information at the right time is a vital if short-lived opportunity. Constantly bombarded by conflicting messages, it's difficult to tell the reliable from the bogus. To make matters worse, current information becomes obsolete more quickly, so even currently pertinent information has a shorter "shelf life." For this reason alone, an agile intuition is required from the start and throughout – if only to decide which information to trust, in order to sort the wheat from the massive preponderance of chaff.

Logic and intuition are both important, but the VDM process is more art than science. It's closer to painting or sculpting than figuring out a formula or reverse engineering. Sometimes the results of our artful efforts are good, other times less so. And like any work of art, strategic decision-making requires a certain amount of *work*, something most people would prefer to minimize or avoid altogether. Long-range decisions require a broader perspective based on higher levels of insight and wisdom, making the process more rigorous.

A factor impacting the quality of important decision-making is what *The New York Times* described as "decision fatigue" – the decline of careful attention when people are called upon to make too many decisions in a limited amount of time.[4] A new kind of stress occurs when the brain is not capable of sorting an abundance of data. Instantaneous communication technologies – like cell phones, text messages, and email – add an exaggerated sense of urgency and the pressure to make decisions more quickly. Another person's expectations of rapid decision-making on our part can add to the pressure to pull the trigger without having done sufficient homework or due diligence.

Consider the Collective Good

Our need for improved decision-making is personal, but on a crowded planet, it is critical for society, too. Our human tribe has incredible capacities for cooperation, communication, empathy, and love, but we are in desperate need of superior leadership, which relies above all on improved decision-making. The survival of our planet depends on whether or not the leaders we hire or elect will make long-term decisions that are for our collective good.

Throughout history, societies have delegated the responsibility for sweeping decisions to sovereigns, presidents, experts, priests, and oracles. Decision-making is the primary activity for which we richly compensate political leaders and CEOs. Talented decision-makers command the highest pay scale, and if they contribute to or protect the collective good, they deserve it. A president deals with international diplomacy in a way that affects world peace; a CEO makes a strategic move that affects an entire market; and a pension fund manager decides to sell short causing ripple effects throughout the economy. Making these kinds of decisions – the crux of good government – deserves lots of support.

Big decisions have big consequences; such is the nature of global change and the connected world in which we live. Some decisions at a societal level could materially impact life on this planet for thousands of years. Even if you are not a leader in a position to make such decisions, you will be affected. We all have a tremendous stake in how wisely our leaders deliberate the choices we face in these critical times. Unfortunately, with all the false advertising that goes into elections (at least here in America), there is no guarantee that our business leaders, elected politicians or representatives will be visionary decision-makers.

With the growing complexity of today's global problems – as populations grow and consume finite resources – we need enlightened decision-making more than ever. The materialistic obsession of 19th and 20th century capitalism was based on an illusion of unlimited frontiers and resources, but we need to upgrade that belief system. Consideration of the common good is an ethical standard for governing society. Likewise, in order to be in alignment with our own good, each of us needs to consider the common good in *all* of our decision-making.

President George W. Bush famously declared himself, "the Decider." In spite of his humorous phrasing, as executive director of our government, he was correct. His number one responsibility was to make decisions for the citizens of the country, decisions that affect billions of lives around the planet. Every one of us is the "decider" in our personal realm. As an adult, the conscious part of you is the CEO of your life, whether you like having the responsibility for the choices you make or not. No matter what your position in society, the most important aspect of your job in this lifetime is to make critical decisions for yourself and those who depend on you.

Complexity and Creative Opportunities

There is a bright side to the tidal wave of information that is rendering decision-making more difficult. An age characterized by massive change invites greater inventiveness and produces an abundance of new opportunities.

Complexity can work to your advantage if you develop a keen intuition that is able to perceive large underlying patterns. This is the superb talent of hugely successful entrepreneurs such as Steve Jobs. Personally, I had a chance to become a successful entrepreneur by dint of entering the complex and rapidly changing field of software at the right time and being intuitive enough to envision future possibilities. (Obviously, Jobs operated on a much broader scale than my esoteric multimedia company, but the principle is the same.)

In every decision, there are risks. Sometimes we can roughly calculate the odds for and against our chances of attaining an outcome that we desire. Sometimes that is difficult. Either way, strategic decision-making involves taking a chance on a major change or transformation and is always something of a gamble. As Eileen Shapiro, author of *Make Your Own Luck*, wrote: "Humans are gambling animals. We all gamble, all the time. Every time we act, we invest time, or reputation, or effort, or money with no guarantee that the results that we seek, no matter how likely they may seem, will occur as we have planned – or as we will desire when the results occur."[5]

One could say that a goal of developing a better intuition is to improve your odds across the board. While I can't guarantee specific results from adopting the philosophy and practicing the skills presented in this book, I can promise that, if you do, your odds of succeeding at whatever you set out to do will increase dramatically. Will you lose some bets? Of course. Will there be setbacks? Of course, but even your mistakes will become less costly as your decision-making becomes more conscious.

Good decisions require a responsible attitude, the practice of specific skills, and coordination between logic and intuition. If you understood the dynamics of my story in the Introduction to this book, you know exactly what I mean.

The Visionary Decision Making Process

Making visionary decisions skillfully is the secret to success in every area of life. It requires more than logical analysis of pros and cons combined with courage and positive thinking. Farsighted decision-making also depends upon intuition, imagination, timing, receptivity, attitude, and commitment. Whether you are naturally better at offense or defense, your perspective, belief system, and attitude will determine the quality of the decisions you make and ultimately the extent to which you fulfill your destiny.

Visionary Decision Making (VDM) is a way to consciously resolve major choice-points and dilemmas that come your way, and make bold decisions that are in alignment with who you really are.

The VDM process requires the interplay of intuition and logic, a mix of imagination and introspection. It taps new sources of information that have always been available (but underused) to help you creatively make the changes that will manifest your highest ideals.

It's tempting to believe that to get what you want, all you have to do is form a mental picture of it in your head. Indeed, some best-selling books and DVDs on the "secrets" of material success offer such a simplistic formula, but manifestation is not as easy as strongly desiring something and obsessing on fantasies about it. Although intuition has never been fully understood – and even though the results of Visionary Decision Making may seem miraculous – the skillful use of intuition is not magic. We may not fully understand or yet be able to empirically prove how intuition works. However, like electricity, we can harness it and put it to good use.

The Visionary Decision Making process goes beyond visualization, attraction, affirmations, and obsessively focusing on what you want. It requires coming to a decision, committing to an action, and making the best move at the right time. This is the only reliable path to achieving success in any area of life. By taking the trouble to awaken and engage your hard-to-get intuitive sense, you greatly improve the odds of achieving a positive outcome, regardless of what you focus on.

CHAPTER 2

What Fascinates You

Respond to every call that excites your spirit. —RUMI

You are born to certain parents at a certain time in a certain place, and this sets up your challenges and opportunities in this lifetime. The unfolding of your destiny results from a synergy between the hand you were dealt and the quality of the decisions you make – in other words, the way you play your cards. Luckily our destiny is not determined by fate alone. You have freedom of choice as to *how* you play your cards. Your success and happiness depend on exercising this power and making wise decisions.

Making great decisions starts with knowing whom you are, a process of self-discovery that begins when you are born and, hopefully, never ends. Mature self-knowledge benefits from a process of introspection that looks closely at your personal history – including major lessons you've learned, the nature of your strongest interests, your unique mix of talents, and your set of values. Knowing these things will help you become clear about your calling – what it is that you are meant to do and contribute in this lifetime. This clarity does not come easy, of course – because of a multitude of tasks and distractions, but also because our priorities shift as we grow, learn, and evolve.

Three Stages of Life

A human life can be divided into three stages, and each stage offers particular kinds of decisions to make and a different ordering of priorities as we change and grow. Knowing your current priorities is a vital aspect of self-knowledge and important to review, no matter what stage you are in.

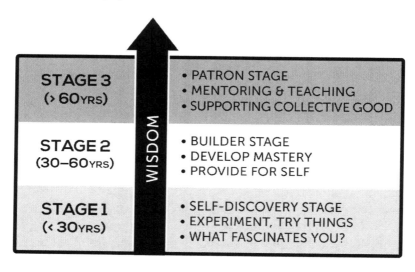

STAGE 3
(> 60YRS)
- PATRON STAGE
- MENTORING & TEACHING
- SUPPORTING COLLECTIVE GOOD

STAGE 2
(30–60YRS)
- BUILDER STAGE
- DEVELOP MASTERY
- PROVIDE FOR SELF

STAGE 1
(< 30YRS)
- SELF-DISCOVERY STAGE
- EXPERIMENT, TRY THINGS
- WHAT FASCINATES YOU?

WISDOM

VDM STAGES OF LIFE

Ideally, self-discovery continues throughout a lifetime, but it is a central function of Stage One – which is all about learning who you are, what you are good at, and what you like to do – mostly by experimenting through trial and error. This stage encompasses the first thirty or so years of life.

Unless children are damaged by neglect or abuse, curiosity and a passion for learning come naturally to the young. My early childhood illustrated this in a funny way. One bright morning when I was four and a half, I hopped onto the school bus with my five-year-old friend who was going off to kindergarten (this was in a safer day and age where little kids typically took school buses on their own). Not knowing where I had disappeared to, my mother reported me missing, and the police went searching. Eventually, the police found me – much to everyone's surprise – sitting on the floor with the rest of the children in a kindergarten class, having a wide-eyed, interested time. The teacher hadn't noticed that I wasn't a member of the class!

The only strategic decision that young adults between the ages of eighteen and twenty-nine most consistently need to make is simply what to try next. It is only natural to want to explore compelling interests, passions, or fascinations, and that is exactly what we should do in our twenties. As long as curiosity-driven pursuits cause no harm to yourself or others, Stage One is meant for honoring your naturally inquisitive nature and giving yourself permission to experiment as widely as you are inclined.

Satisfying curiosity is fun – and it should be – but we seriously curtail it by putting pressure on young adults to specialize. College students very often feel excessive pressure, beyond their maturity level, to make long-term decisions like committing to a career before they know whom they are. It's not uncommon for students to believe there is something wrong with them if they can't confidently declare what they want to be when they grow up, let alone decisively choose a major. To make matters worse, comparing themselves with young media celebrities in entertainment, sports, or business can be dispiriting. Without permission to try all kinds of things, young people easily become self-critical, second-guess themselves, and dampen their own natural curiosity as a result of misguided social pressures.

It is an exceptional phenomenon when a gifted child gets started very young on what will become his or her career (take Mozart, for instance). Even in modern societies where children are afforded a large education, this is extremely rare. There are not many like the world-class violinist Itzhak Perlman, who smashed the toy violin he was given as a young boy because he knew he needed to play a real one (eventually a Stradivarius). Most of us are not such prodigies that we get in touch with a deep level of fascination that early in life... and if we did these days, we'd probably be forced to take medications for acting out! But even if we have been denied chances as a child to be adventurous in our own way, we will have ample opportunities to make meaningful self-discoveries during Stage One.

The brain's neocortex doesn't stop developing until the age of 26, and young people should be free to explore their natural interests for at least the entire time that their brain is growing. As long as it's not harmful, having permission to follow what motivates you allows character to develop in harmony with your natural interests. If the pressure to make huge decisions you are not psychologically or emotionally prepared for weighs you down, self-discovery is very difficult, if not impossible. A good example is a 19-year-old deciding to take on a tremendous amount of personal debt for the sake of entering a profession that may turn out to be unsuited to her or his temperament. The crushing burden of servicing extreme indebtedness can make it impossible to have enough time or energy to discover new things or experiment with developing interests that are not related to one's current job or career path. This kind of burden will impact one's entire life!

Stage Two, which generally does not start before age 30, is the phase of building, being productive, and accomplishing mastery. Making a commitment to doing something you have an aptitude for launches this stage. The focus is on building a career or family (or both) and accumulating the resources needed to provide for yourself and others. Your priorities reorder in favor of creating a stable platform for yourself and your family group or tribe. At this stage, you accomplish things. You gain mastery at your craft or calling by being of service in your natural way and becoming truly productive. Fulfillment and great joy is found in contributing energy and expertise toward building something for yourself and those who may depend on you.

This is followed by Stage Three, the Sponsor or Patron Stage, which starts around age 60 (or a bit later in this age of extended active lifespans) and which is characterized by a shift from building and providing security to giving back wisdom, support and creating a legacy. Gradually, the provider of the builder stage evolves into generous giving for the sake of future generations, pursuing philanthropic endeavors and in some cases serving as a wise elder. In Stage Three, one might be drawn to mentoring receptive younger folk and helping them clarify their Stage One and Stage Two decision-making. Great joy can come from the exercise of generously providing guidance and material support to younger people who will receive it.

The Visionary Decision Making approach works best when calibrated to your current stage of life. It's important to put off making lifelong commitments in Stage One until you know yourself. Although Stage One decisions can be strategically important, it is advisable to save long-term commitments for Stage Two, when you know and are ready to focus on what fascinates you. Only then will you be sufficiently engaged and inspired to put in all the work of building a productive career, family, or intimate partnership. This will give you a wealth of knowledge and resources for providing in Stage Two and eventually graduating to Stage Three.

> Astrology provides a basis for the VDM stages of life – the orbit of the planet Saturn, which is the archetype for coming to terms with reality and being accountable for decisions you have made (your karma). When Saturn completes its orbit and comes back to the position in the sky it held the moment you were born, astrologers refer to this event as your "Saturn return." Its occurrence approximately every 29.5 years is considered a significant passage, roughly coinciding with VDM's three stages.

Fascinations Point the Way

The fascinations that you discover during Stage One are especially important keys to self-knowledge. A *fascination* is defined as something that "casts a spell or enchants." Beyond appealing to your curiosity, it is something that attracts and delights you. This is human nature. Babies are fascinated by lots of things because everything is utterly new. By the time you are a young adult, fewer things fascinate you, but the ones that inspire you the most will be an outgrowth of your temperament and aptitudes. Your strongest interests have the potential to enchant you and lead you down a path toward fulfillment of your personal destiny. As Joseph Campbell wrote, "Follow your bliss and don't be afraid, and doors will open where you didn't know they were going to be."[6]

Two fascinations that were foremost – and ultimately life changing – occurred when I was in college. As a teenager in the

San Francisco Bay area, I had come of age during a tumultuous time. Anti-Vietnam War protests caused riots at the University of California where I was a student for nine quarters straight. A cultural revolution was in full swing. Being independent for the first time and feeling flush with personal freedom, anything and everything seemed possible in a rapidly changing world. One day on campus, I perked up when an attractive coed offered to show me an ancient tome called the *Book of Changes* (*I Ching* in Chinese), which she claimed would provide insights and timely advice about any problem I asked of it. I tried not to let my skepticism show.

The company of this pleasant girl appealed to me, even if that involved playing some silly (or so I thought) fortune-telling game. When she asked me to write down something I needed advice about, I played along by scribbling a few words that didn't hold any real significance for me. While I could have been intrigued by the idea of an ancient book that was an oracle, at the time I was trying to humor her. She asked me to focus on my question (which I could not) and had me toss three coins six times. After she decoded my coin tosses into a six-line pattern, or "hexagram," we looked up the chapter and "changing lines" that corresponded to the pattern I had tossed.

My first I Ching reading was Hexagram No.4 entitled "Youthful Folly," which refers to the lack of respect that an immature student has for the teacher. This seemed to be a flat-out dismissal of my flippant query and caught me off guard. At the age of nineteen, I knew nothing of divination systems or Jungian psychology. I was expecting some kind of Magic Eight Ball that I could have a good laugh about. Instead, the I Ching ignored my frivolous query and reflected my shallowness with some sound advice about the need to straighten up. "Youthful Folly" was an accurate description of my life at that time: cutting classes, smoking pot, and trying to get with girls. The way it was accurately mirroring my attitude and energy, the I Ching caught my attention. I asked her if I could try casting another reading. I wanted to see what it would come up with next.

Once again, I wrote down something that didn't have any real import for me, but my intention was more serious. This time I was testing the oracle, rather than just toying with it. Once again, the I Ching ignored my disingenuous query and came back with a reading, "Questioning the sincerity of the seeker." Hmm. When

I had made fun of it, it had made fun of me. Now, when I tested it, it tested me back! Because of the way the I Ching reflected my energy, I began to intuitively understand that the meaning and value of an I Ching reading is derived not from predictions or specific instructions, which I had assumed would be the case, but from reading *between* the lines. Thus began a personal fascination with – and eventually a reverence for – what turned out to be a powerful and useful intuitive decision-making aid.

A few years later, at the age of 23, I was thunderstruck by a second fascination – the cutting-edge technology of computer software. In those days, most people didn't know what software was. The first personal computer kits were a few years away. Apple didn't exist. Programming courses at the university relied on feeding punch cards into huge computers. Web pages and public email would not arrive for another twenty years.

My friend Jack was the programmer for a small non-profit computer center attached to the University of Oregon in Eugene. He was in charge of the center's "minicomputer," a machine with gigantic magnetic tape drives and only one small terminal the size of an oscilloscope. Despite its immense size, it was called "mini" because it merely filled a room, whereas IBM mainframes in those days took up entire floors. Minicomputers were cutting-edge technology at the time, even though for $150,000 (in 1975 dollars), they had less computing power than an iPhone today!

Jack and I would go to the computer center late at night to play one of the earliest computer games called *SpaceWar*, which was developed for minicomputers by programmers at MIT. Playing that primitive game on a huge computer was my introduction to the phenomenon of software.

Fascinated by the interactive aspect of software, I saw programming as a new form of creativity that might eventually support educational and personal development, which were strong interests of mine. I was able to envision computers delivering sophisticated entertainment and educational content fifteen years before the first graphics-based computer (the Macintosh), and twenty years before CD-ROMs made such a notion viable. Based on my visions of such a future in the works, I felt a powerful desire to enter this nascent industry.

I had dropped out of college rather than go into debt, but with Jack's help, I was hired as the office secretary at the computer center on the basis of my typing speed (word processing was still ten years off). Making the decision to take a secretarial job that paid less than I had been making as a foreign car mechanic turned out to be a visionary decision, and proved to be a pivotal step on the path of my career destiny.

Marsha Sinetar wrote a book entitled, *Do What You Love, The Money Will Follow*. The title says it all.[7] When you discover and follow your fascinations, good things happen, including the activation of your intuition and, as per Joseph Campbell, the experience of bliss. For the second time in my life, I had stumbled upon a personal game-changer. Along with the I Ching, interactive software was a fascination that passionately resonated with me.

As I took a serious interest in the intersection between two "technologies" – one ancient, one new – I became aware of a significant historical connection between them. Gottfried Leibniz, who "discovered" binary mathematics in 1666, found confirmation for his theories in the I Ching's binary system. Leibniz was impressed by its representation of the universe as a progression of combinations of dualistic polarities (yin and yang) that could flip from one state to the other. Heartened by his insights about how the I Ching was based on a binary system, Leibniz refined his mathematical model, which transposed the Arabic 10 digit numeral system – one that Europe had not fully adopted until the 10th century – into a binary system of ones and zeros. Although there was little practical use for it at the time, modern information theory and the basis for how computers and software work were derived from Leibniz's formulations.

Developing the intersection between my two fascinations – software and the I Ching – led to the invention of divination software fifteen years later, which could not be construed as a shrewd move even at that time. My impulse to go for it was supported by the I Ching, intuition, and meditation, so I decided to honor my passion and see where it might lead, like Joseph Campbell had recommended. I made the visionary decision to listen to my heart and its natural interests, despite all the inherent risks. I went against the advice of everyone I knew and "followed my bliss."

Self-Knowledge and Risk Tolerance

How you play your cards in life is related to how you strike a balance between freedom and security. Knowing where you land on the security-versus-risk spectrum is essential for conscious risk-taking.

When I started my own business in 1988, I was able to tolerate a higher level of insecurity than the average single parent. My risk-tolerance supported pursuing my dream of creative freedom – the idea that I could get my needs met and be creative at the same time. Even though the financial risks were daunting, I had the internal "safety net" of knowing that I could always return to the software industry if I failed at my entrepreneurial venture. As I learned, a combination of your innate resourcefulness and skills you develop is the only real security and it is a security that nobody can ever take from you. The best way to gain such inner security is to work toward mastering marketable skills, and this is a process that hopefully can happen to some extent via any of the various jobs we have to do along the way just to pay the rent. (In my case, I started as a secretary in a field I was interested in and gained a ton of real-world experience at marketing by helping my boss.)

Of course, human beings want both security and freedom, and everyone has to deal with some tension between these paradoxical needs. So... where would you currently peg yourself on the security-freedom spectrum? No matter what level of risk you are ready to take, whether your destiny is to be an entrepreneur or an artist, or even if you chose to provide your services, abilities, and intelligence to and through a large corporation – your time and energy are yours alone to give. No matter what form your contribution takes, in the final analysis, you work for yourself. Accept that responsibility right now. You are the executive decision-maker (or CEO, or whatever archetype you like best for the executive function) of your individual life, and this means that you have decisions to make. That is your top job. You are called upon to bring your conscious mind to bear on the decision-making responsibility that you have to yourself and yours. If you merely think of yourself as a victim of circumstances, you will invariably (and inadvertently) give your power away.

What Does Success Mean to You?

A general definition of success is getting what you want. Unless you are playing a competitive game, and the experience of winning means that much to you, success should not come at the expense of anyone else. Although money is a medium of exchange and a way to measure wealth, success is not all about the accumulation of wealth. Who you are and what you want defines success for you. This is only possible once you become clear about something you want to do that is in alignment with your temperament and spirit.

Your definition of success will change over time. For instance, having begun Stage Three of life, I feel less of a desire to compete for rewards or status. My desire for freedom of thought and expression is as strong as ever, but my focus is on cultivating wisdom and doing what I can to help humanity make paradigm shifts that produce a positive, healing difference in the world.

There is no right or wrong to any of this. As long as something is not harmful, your desires boil down to doing whatever is going to reduce suffering or increase joy.

If you increase happiness for yourself and others, you are a success – even if you are performing a humble service that few people notice. The ancient Taoist sages, who understood the flow of yin and yang in the cycles of nature and culture, were modest and did not feel a need to call attention to themselves. They were not trying to prove that they were special. They found contentment by staying in harmony with the rhythms of nature. Their decisions and timing were effortless and skillful. In terms of contentment or freedom from suffering or personal satisfaction, they were a success too.

Society equates success with money, because money can be spent on so many desirable things – security, success, status, power, freedom, luxury and pleasure. But money is none of these; it is a technology of exchange that makes it easier for humans to trade possessions, time, energy and labor for the things they need or want. Money that is earned and accumulated can be thought of as *stored labor* – a compensation for strategic and strenuous efforts already made. This, in turn, confers a greater power for supporting what's truly valuable and helping others. As Charles Eisenstein, the author of *Sacred Economy*, points out, true wealth is "a function of one's generosity and not one's accumulation; it is the manifestation of abundance, not scarcity."

By turning valuable labors into a medium that can be spent later, money is an offshoot of the invention of private property, a phenomenon that did not arise in earnest until our species moved out of the forest and settled down in agricultural communities between 5,000 and 7,000 years ago. The appropriation and ownership of private property changed everything.

Anthropologists estimate that nomadic hunter-gatherer tribes consisted of no more than 150 individuals who shared everything communally. To strive for special status or to compete with your extended family was considered bad form and could ultimately be cause for ostracism. Between 5,000 and 8,000 years ago, the new agriculturist settlers organized permanent communities and built dwellings that were divided up on the basis of family units, giving rise to the separation and privatization of property. In fact, marriage was originally an agreement between men, with women and children as property. Men created laws and political structures, along with written language, which was first used to keep track of property and enforce property laws.

As Steven Taylor shows in his profound book, *The Fall: The Insanity of the Ego in Human History and the Dawning of A New Era*[8], this monumental paradigm shift included the demotion of females, who are reckoned to have been equals during the hunter-gatherer period that lasted millions of years. The building of city-states gave rise to empires, monotheistic religions and large-scale wars. This huge transformation of human society may have taken place over a span of some one or two thousand years, but considering that modern Homo sapiens has been around for at least 200,000 years, the change happened very quickly in the grand scope of things. The result of the agricultural revolution was that, in the process of this "fall," the patriarchal society that has prevailed ever since has been marked by a value system that is predominantly ego-driven and possessive.

It didn't have to be this way, but putting patriarchy's hierarchy of values aside, "success" – as I use the term – is *not* synonymous with the accumulation of wealth or power over others. In our media-saturated world, you don't have to look far to realize that there are legions of miserable rich people who never feel they have enough power or security. What kind of success is that? On the other hand, there are people whom I consider successful that others would dismiss as paupers. My cousin Lennie is a case in point.

Lennie is a retired barbershop owner, even though he occasionally cuts hair for extra cash. Otherwise, he lives off the grid as much as possible. He hunts, fishes, and gardens around the solar-assisted house and trout ponds that he built with the help of friends. He makes guitars, writes songs, and performs at events, often for free. I visit him every other summer on the shores of Lake Leelanau in Michigan, a fresh water wonderland where all four of my grandparents and both of my parents were born. Lennie lives his life with passion; he's doing what he has chosen to do, and he loves his life. If this is not a measure of true success, I don't know what is. Real success only depends upon fulfilling one's personal priorities.

Success does not mean the same thing to everybody. Seeking status and trying to "keep up with the Joneses" will not bring you closer to your heart's desires or support the clarity necessary to realize what would fulfill you. Many desires are operating at the same time, with new ones arising all the time. There is no shortage of things that have the power to distract the mind. Just be clear about what is most important to you, including your vision for yourself if you have one.

Once you identify your true values – once you have analyzed where you are putting your time, energy, and money – don't fight them. Go with your strengths. As my story demonstrated, if you put energy into your passions, you will be rewarded with success, one way or the other. If you are trying to live up to the expectations of others, make the decision to let go of that now. Remember that you are the CEO of your life. It's time to know yourself and start making decisions that align with your personal values.

Hierarchy of Values

It's normal to get confused about what your real values are when you think in terms of who you would like to be – or think you *should* be – rather than discovering who you naturally are. It's a mistake to identify with inherited or adopted beliefs about what *should* be important to you. One practical and logically quantifiable way to measure your real values is to analyze and quantify how you spend your time, energy, and money.

Dr. John Demartini developed an approach that I find helpful. In the *Demartini Value Definition Process*[9], he reveals a method to increase and maintain awareness of one's ever-shifting "hierarchy of values" – the things we want and the priorities we give to active interests and desires.

Demartini uses the word "values" in a specific, practical, and measurable way. In his system, values are not prioritized by how they align with ideals, moral codes, or entrenched beliefs. He teaches a way to identify your real values by analyzing how much time, energy, money, and thought you actually invest in them: make a list of your current four or five major activities or preoccupations. Once you have created this list, keep it as a file on your computer or smartphone, or keep a small printed copy in your wallet or purse. The idea is that you can glance at your list to always remind yourself of your top current values. Edit and refine it as you become more and more clear about your unique hierarchy of values.

Using Demartini's method is not complicated, but it can be challenging to get clear about priorities because of emotional factors and conflicts of interest. For instance, you might spend more of your time working at your job than anything else. According to Demartini's system, this would make working for a living one of your highest values. Even if you don't like your job, you do value being employed – enough to show up at a job you don't like! The job provides something (a paycheck) you need and value highly as a means to an end. Taking care of your needs – as well as, possibly, those of others close to you – by making a steady living is naturally a top priority for most adults. Whether you love your current job or not, making a living is highly important.

Things can get complicated when major life passages cause a reshuffling of top priorities. For example, a woman who has invested years of her time and energy being a good mother will experience massive changes when her youngest child leaves home. She thinks less about mothering and more about plans to take classes, start a business, play music, or take up painting. The children who move out of the family home will also think and act differently. Instead of continuing to be dependent on someone else and preoccupied with the carefree fun of childhood, they will begin experimenting with and developing the skills they need to take care of themselves and make their own way in the world. If and when they become parents themselves, providing for their children will become a strong value. Priorities, like fascinations, change as we proceed through the three stages of life.

Getting Clear About Your Path

As we have seen, when it comes to doing what will make you happy, you need to be clear about what you want the most, and how it relates to your stage of life. Freedom will be within reach if you begin the path of decision-making from a place of such authenticity.

The American social philosopher Eric Hoffer observed, "When people are free to do as they please, they usually imitate each other." As true as this seems, it is almost tragic. Compared to any other nation or civilization from the past, citizens of the modern world have a tremendous amount of freedom. The problem is that with so many choices, most people only have a vague idea of what they really want.

As philosopher Ken Keyes pointed out, many people say, "I don't know what I want, but I'm damn sure this isn't it!" While it is easy to identify with this sentiment, this stance will never help you move forward in manifesting desires or life goals. A negative framework can provide useful information, but in order to succeed you must go beyond knowing what you *don't* want. You need to identify and target what you *do* want, to manifest your dream. Commit yourself to knowing what it is, and then taking the risk of going for it.

When I was in my late 20s, I attended an encounter group. I remember sharing that I would like to have what I want, but unfortunately was not clear about what that was. The group leader's advice was short and succinct: "Get clear!" That was all he said.

The Importance of Desire

The role of desire is widely misunderstood. I grew up thinking that my desires were "selfish," and some traditions seem to teach that desire is inherently wrong or evil, or at best a source of temptation. In Buddhism, for example, the second of the Four Noble Truths is often mistranslated as, "Suffering is caused by desire." But in reality the original word *tanha* (often translated as "desire") has a much more nuanced meaning than our word "desire." In the original Pali language, *tanha* means an intense yearning for the continuation of pleasure (or the cessation of pain). It implies an intense emotional attachment, which is much more compelling than just a desire or preference. The words "craving" or "addiction" – which can be defined as desire plus an emotional demand – offer more precise translations of *tanha*.

The Buddhist teaching is not that we should live a life free of desires or be totally detached. On the contrary, wisdom means knowing what to care about and making skillful decisions around strategic visions. Without desire, progress toward anything (including the state of mental freedom called "enlightenment") is impossible. Desire is natural and necessary for movement and growth. The etymology of the word is the Latin *sideris*, – or "of the stars" – which reminds us that desire is a signal that comes from above, including nudges from what I like to refer to as "Infinite Intelligence" toward a higher calling (we explore the nature of Infinite Intelligence in Chapter 4). As my story in the Introduction to this book demonstrated, following one's creative desires can turn out to be a very positive thing. So how do we go about identifying our most authentic desires in order to have lodestars that guide us on our journey?

Before we go further, let's clarify that the kind of desires under discussion here are more about *doing* than about *having* or *consuming*. Sometimes, when I ask people to define their desires, the answer involves buying something or taking a vacation. Of course, there is nothing wrong with shopping or travel or other pleasure-oriented consumption. But for the sake of personal fulfillment, we focus on the desire to *do* rather than *have* – to contribute in a way that is in alignment with our nature and satisfying for us.

Productivity is a natural human desire and the essence of Stage Two. It is only in modern – and some would say decadent – times that so many people have come to identify as consumers first, rather than producers (an attitude only exacerbated by a careless attitude toward debt). From the VDM point of view, this is a psychological malaise that demotivates people from achieving goals that are worthy of them, accomplishing meaningful things, and making a difference in the world.

An authentic desire engages both the mind and the heart. If a desire does not involve the heart, it is probably ego-inspired. On the other hand, if you experience a purely emotional desire, this too is out of balance. You want to avoid completely over-riding logic, or elevating a strong feeling to a leadership role it isn't qualified to fill. A coordinated intersection between head and heart, however, is a synchronicity that supports your intu-itive sense and can provide trustworthy guidance. For instance, if the desire to practice law is based on a talent for argumen-tation (a logical alignment), combined with a desire to defend women against violence (a heart alignment), the chances of being inspired to become a lawyer would increase exponentially. Can you think of things you do, or might do, that represent an inter-section between your heart and head?

The heart is not just a locus of feelings. It is the center of what is now widely referred to as *emotional intelligence*. This is not a new idea. Ancient peoples believed that the heart was the real cen-ter of a human being. The Egyptians went to great lengths to pre-serve the heart with their highly developed embalming skills, but they threw away the brain. The Egyptians may have been limited in their understanding of biomechanics, but they certainly knew the heart is more than just a pump. Like most indigenous cultures, they considered it to be a spiritual center of the body.

In traditional Ayurvedic medicine of India, the heart center is the location of one of the "chakras," or energy centers of the body. The heart center is in the middle of the seven chakras, ruling love and courage. It takes courage to love, a courage that propels us beyond concern for just our own self-interests or ego. In French, the word for heart is *coeur*, the root of the word "courage" in English.

Love can be a high-level risk, but it is well worth it. What you love inspires you to learn and evolve, expanding your capacity for success and joy. This is the way of co-creating a life with the help of Infinite Intelligence. Doing what you love or what you are good at (usually something you like to do) plays a critical role by supporting our fascinations and heartfelt desires. Inspiration and intuition acting in concert produces the most profound desire, which is the magnetic force behind the famous "Law of Attraction," wherein the object of your heart's desire is drawn to you.

For the sake of VDM, self-discovery is coming to know what you love and getting clear about what you want to do in life. In order to make the passage from Stage One of self-discovery to Stage Two of contributing and accomplishing, you must determine and maintain awareness of what you want to do the *most*. These top value desires are what carry the most *meaning* for you, which is the essence of personal wisdom and key to the Visionary Decision Making process.

We Attract What We Focus On

The Law of Attraction is a concept that was reintroduced in best-selling books and movies like *The Secret*. Although the concept has been around for over 100 years, the power of focus is relevant to modern decision-making and our desire to creatively manage change.

The Law of Attraction is based on the premise that what you expect is what you get. The mind exerts a magnetic attraction on whatever it focuses on, whether it is a worry, fear, or other imaginative thought that you're dwelling on. Once a person gets focused on a certain viewpoint, her or his personal subconscious does everything it can to find evidence to prove that idea or perspective is *right*, no matter how wrong it may be. I'm sure you've had an experience of noticing something you don't like (my boss is so picky, my housemate is so messy, etc.), and then for days you see a million reasons that your point of view is correct. You may start noticing every time your partner leaves a drinking glass lying around, but overlook the fact that he picked up your dry cleaning or washed your car.

Not only do we strongly tend to see what we expect to see, but we also attract and receive what we expect, because the bias of attention attracts our focus. This means that even when you concentrate on things you *don't* want, the very act of paying attention to these negative aspects draws them closer. Like it or not, our thinking minds are like magnets that are always attracting something. We can either attract what we want by focusing on it, or we can attract what we don't want by focusing on that.

The game of golf elegantly illustrates this dynamic. Although swinging a golf club is an athletic skill, the game has a very large mental component. To make a good swing in golf, you need to be relaxed and focused at the same time – a kind of synchronicity. Both of these mental states can be impacted by the considerable time there is for thinking between each shot. Your thoughts and attitude will have a major impact on your next swing and its outcome. One of the first lessons of the inner game of golf is to focus on the target, not the hazards. The best shots are inspired by a clear vision of where you want the ball to go – not where you don't want it to go or are afraid it *might* go. Focusing on hazards is the worst thing you can do in golf (or in life). Any golfer can tell you that dwelling on the ponds and sand traps will invariably skew a shot to fly right into them. In golf – as in life – what you focus on is what you get.

Being aware of what you don't want can be helpful at times, but unless there is a real and present danger, focus instead on what you *do* want. Where we put our attention is an immediate and important decision that we make on a moment-to-moment basis. How you phrase your goals makes a difference to your ability to stay focused on them, even if they only reside in your memory. Aside from writing your goals down, sharing them with a friend can help you with mental clarity and reduce tendencies toward fearful or negative thinking.

You Can't Have It All, Baby

There is an old saying, "You can do anything you want, but not everything you want." Choosing where to spend your time and energy is critical to achieving success. Stay aware of your hierarchy of values, so the most important activities get the attention they deserve in the face of so many competing distractions. Finding your calling happens by following your interests and values, not by combing the classifieds to find a franchising opportunity or coming up with a business plan designed to make lots of money. Devotion to inspiration and the flow of creative power will help you discover your true livelihood and your path to destiny.

Once you are clear about what you want, making progress will depend on clear goals, decisive commitments to reaching them, and making the right moves at the right time. This involves letting go of "lesser affections" that would compete for attention and distract you – things you may like a lot, but don't have the time, energy, or resources to invest in. The sacrificing of some lesser affections is generally essential to making progress toward a strategic vision. It's interesting to note that the word "decide" comes from the Latin *cedere,* which translates as "to cut off."

Knowing who you are and maintaining an awareness of your highest priorities is central to making visionary decisions. In Part II, we get down to the nitty-gritty of how to begin the Visionary Decision Making process.

CHAPTER 3

The Psychology of Perfect Timing

*I am open to the guidance of synchronicity, and do not
let expectations hinder my path.* —THE DALAI LAMA

W e consider ourselves lucky when events unfold the way
that we want or when we are in the right place at the
right time. The experience isn't only pleasant – it also
feels meaningful. Human beings thrive on understanding not only
how things happen, but *why*.

The idea that things happen randomly has always been too difficult for humans to accept. We crave some explanation of why, when, and how things happen, even though we usually aren't able to understand the reasons until some time after the fact... if ever. Nevertheless, we are wired to look for explanations. The human mind has an innate need for meaning.

Ancient Greek and Roman cosmologies included many deities – a goddess named Destiny and the Fates, for instance – who were believed to have powerful influence over the lives of mortals. Their divine intervention included help in the form of good things that would happen if you were favored by the gods. Compared to imagining a totally chaotic universe, these kinds of beliefs provided human beings some feeling of order and reassurance. Today, our traditional approach to the sacred – which had historically been associated with deities and temples of worship, rituals, and holy days – has lost its meaning for us and has been misdirected into more secular forms of adoration such as the passionate pursuit of status, power, or romance. There's an interesting angle on this by Robert Johnson, author of *We: Understanding the Psychology of Romantic Love*, who makes the point that love of the divine has been replaced by a modern obsession with romantic love (placing unwieldy demands on intimate partnerships in the process).[10]

Rather than ascribing events to any sort of divine intervention, strictly rational types assume a weak position relative to change to the extent that they believe in a random universe ruled by chance. Being a helpless pawn in the cosmic casino is not a particularly empowering or reassuring point of view. The religious traditions of the East, including Hinduism and Buddhism, take a spiritual but nontheistic approach to the question of why things happen. One of their principle tenets is the impersonal *Law of Karma*. Essentially, this means, "What goes around comes around," or as the same idea is put in the Christian world, "as you sow, so shall you reap." From a karmic point of view, your intentions, attitude, and actions influence how the universe will respond to you and the returns you will get. According to concepts of cosmic justice, we each ultimately get what we deserve, good and bad. The Greek Fates operated in a somewhat similar manner.

Our sense of meaning atrophies when the culture's belief systems become obsolete or start to break down. Without a stable operating system of beliefs that continues to make sense and work well, people lack an important psychological support structure, and they struggle more to discern whether a certain course of action is in their best interests or not. This can lead to despair and impulsive decision-making. In social and political spheres, it lends itself to the rise of tyranny by dominator thought-police, who forcefully appoint themselves to tell us the meaning of things in terms that are to their advantage but to our detriment.

We are not gaining the knowledge and personal power to create our own sense of meaning, which makes it easier to accept and skillfully deal with major changes, no matter how challenging or disruptive they may be. When we find meaning in our lives, we feel a healthy sense of personal power.

The Visionary Decision Making paradigm strikes a blow for

personal freedom in all of this. It focuses on the fact that when we are equipped with sophisticated psychological knowledge and in tune with who we really are, we are much more than victims of fate or the pawns of other people. We are free to take part in shaping our own destinies, even though it is an effort that requires faith in ourselves as well as significant personal efforts.

Even the most cynical people enjoy getting what they want, but it is the rare person who knows how to manifest good fortune with consistency. With the right understanding and skills, you can now learn how to improve your odds greatly by developing a better sense of timing. In this chapter, we explore Carl Jung's sophisticated take on being in sync with change. We consider this one of his greatest discoveries, one that provides a breakthrough for understanding the phenomenon of perfect timing, one that helps us make sense of things and grow, rather than shrink, ourselves.

The Synchronicity Principle

Jung provided the world with sophisticated ways to understand the human mind, the meaning of an individual's life, and the way things happen. Foremost among these was the *Synchronicity Principle*, which posits that things have a relationship in time as well as space. Synchronicity can be defined as the coincidence of two or more events that are not related by cause-and-effect, but which occur together in a meaningful way, even though the connection may seem mysterious to us. In psychological terms, however, we sense that it is a *meaningful coincidence* – partly because it shakes us up. In the VDM paradigm, we take a synchronicity as a sign that something important is trying to happen.

Carl Jung's impact on the field of psychology was enormous. He is famous for highlighting the concept of extroverted and introverted personality types, which led to the development of the popular Myers-Briggs personality test. He was one of the foremost analyzers of dream symbolism, an art that he enhanced with the exercise of "active imagination" (a technique his friend, Albert Einstein, naturally excelled at). In addition to his empirical work as a clinical psychiatrist, he spent decades studying Eastern and

Western philosophies, mythologies, and divination systems, as well as sociology, literature, and the arts. Jung's range of knowledge and intellectual fluency was broad and deep, and his contribution to furthering a deeper understanding of most of these areas was prodigious.

The Synchronicity Principle described a confluence of events in the dimension of time where, as Jung put it, "Things arising in the particular moment of time all share the characteristics of that moment."[11] Synchronicity is an intersection of an individual's conscious mind with a vastly larger collective reservoir of consciousness (which is as of yet unconscious as far as the individual is concerned) that surrounds it. David Richo, a Jungian psychotherapist, writes: "Meaningfulness happens when an event or experience in conscious life puts us in contact with unconscious forces that lead us to a fulfillment of our destiny. Our destiny is anything that leads to birth, death, finding a life purpose, or awakening to spiritual consciousness. Coincidence is a bond between two hitherto unconnected realities. Synchronicity joins something going on outside us with something happening inside us."[12]

Intuition is an instinct that can bring conscious awareness to what was unconscious, in its ability to perceive coincidental connections as well as ferret out their meaning. As you start noticing synchronicities, you can train yourself to understand what they mean for you. In their own subtle way, synchronicities can serve as a gentle alarm that wakes you up to your intuitive sensitivity and the meaning in your life.

The Interconnected World

Although Jung was the first scientist to focus on the phenomenon of timing and the meaningfulness of amazing coincidence, the idea behind his Synchronicity Principle had been widely held for centuries. Human beings have long noted that events tend to cluster in time, as evidenced by folk sayings like, "Good things happen in threes." Long before the 17th century, when Newton enthroned causality – the notion that every effect has a definite traceable cause – as the central principle of science, many cultures took synchronicity very seriously, particularly in the East. Human actions were not viewed simply as an expression of one's will or any single cause, but as an element in the context of an exquisitely interconnected universe.

In ancient Buddhist teachings, the concept of "co-dependent origination" held that no part of the universe has an independent existence separate from everything else. All the parts are inter-connected and depend upon the whole for an identity. This aware-ness comes naturally to indigenous peoples, where no tribal elder would consider a significant undertaking without examining the congruence of that action with respect to the context of his com-munity, as well as the timing of it. As Jungian analyst and author Robert Hopcke writes about indigenous spirituality: "To act, within this worldview, is a humble, careful process. This way of thinking, in which one's subjective experience of interconnection with the world is more important than individual mastery over the environment through cause-and-effect, is a mode of living which accommodates the reality of meaningful chance quite easily."[13]

What we call synchronicities were taken as "signs and omens" in native cultures (also as recorded in the Torah, or Old Testament). Ironically, we are now learning what indigenous peoples have always known – the value of recognizing significant portents and an ability to sense their meaning in the long-term, and garner a better sense of direction in the short-term. It's ironic that modern psychology came to this understanding at the same time as the physical sciences were going to the extreme of splitting atoms.

20th Century Physics and Psychology on Parallel Tracks

It is a meaningful coincidence that Carl Jung closely observed the phenomenal discoveries of the new physics by his friends Albert Einstein and Wolfgang Pauli at the same time that he was study-ing the mythology and cultures of the world and coming up with the Synchronicity Principle.

Jung's discovery of the psychological relationship between tim-ing and meaning paralleled the new discoveries of the new physics

– and both recognized the limits of causality in our understanding of the universe. Until the early 20th century, the bedrock of scientific method since Newton had been an absolute faith in *causality* – the idea that every effect has a cause that eventually can be identified, traced, and understood in a logical way. This fundamental belief was basic to the scientific worldview, but this ideological hegemony started to crack with Einstein's Theory of Relativity and new discoveries in quantum physics in the early 20th century.

Quantum mechanics dealt with the existence of subatomic particles – or waves, depending upon how they were observed – that seemed to flicker in and out of existence and which could be observed to be in more than one place at the same time. To make things even more disorienting, Einstein's Theory of Relativity described a reality in which time moved faster or slower depending on velocity. This was all very challenging – and still remains challenging for most of us – disturbing the comfort that humans derive from causality as a concept our senses can observe in normal affairs and easily understand.

Around the same time that his friends were shaking up physics with proofs of acausal behavior in the subatomic realm, and in one of his phases of profound visionary insight, Jung came up with the Synchronicity Principle, which was just as counterintuitive and challenging to the psychology establishment. It all started with him noticing acausal phenomena arising in the experiences and dreams of his patients, whereby he came to realize that synchronicity was a bonafide psychological phenomenon. Like the new physics, his psychology was iconoclastic, breaking free of the limitations of the cause-and-effect paradigm. This is not to say that Jung denied all cause-and-effect in the psychological realm. Rather, he pointed out that there are categories of personal experience in which a dynamic of synchronicity transcends the normal operations of cause-and-effect.

The radical discoveries in subatomic physics and psychology upset the highly mechanical model of the universe that had held sway since Newton's era. These radical theories (mathematically proven in physics) challenged the prevailing linear concept of time, which had only been amplified by the invention of mechanical clocks and the subordination of human activities to them. Even now, scientific experimentation disregards the dimension of time. It is assumed that a controlled experiment will turn out the same whether you do it Tuesday at noon or in the middle of Saturday night. In science, timing is never a part of the equation.

Einstein was Jung's occasional dinner guest in the 1920s. According to Jung's letters, Einstein was supportive of Jung's formulation of the synchronicity theory, noting how it might be considered a theory of relativity as applied to the dimension of time. Jung wrote, "It was Einstein who first started me off thinking about a possible relativity of time as well as space, and their psychic conditionality. More than thirty years later, this stimulus led to my relation with the physicist Professor W. Pauli and to my thesis of psychological synchronicity."[14]

From a traditional scientific point of view, the synchronicity principle was absurd, a form of magical thinking. But it made more sense when viewed alongside the radical new discoveries of subatomic physics. Jung's theory of synchronicity got further indirect supported from Werner Heisenberg's proof of the Uncertainty Principle in 1927. Heisenberg posited that the *position* and the *velocity* of a subatomic particle could not be simultaneously measured, because at the subatomic level, the act of perceiving or measuring affects and changes that which is being perceived. In other words, an exact objective measurement of anything – including physical reality – is rendered impossible.

For those who perceive synchronicity, it's not that big a stretch to appreciate how everything that happens in a given situation at a given time participates with, and affects, everything else in that situation – including the consciousness of the perceiver. In fact, this is one way to define the Synchronicity Principle.

In 1997 I had the privilege to videotape an interview with the late Terence McKenna for inclusion on the multimedia *Oracle of Changes* CD-ROM.[15] McKenna was an American philosopher, ethno botanist, lecturer, and author. He spoke and wrote about a variety of subjects, including plant-based entheogens, shamanism, metaphysics, alchemy, language, culture, technology, and the origins of human consciousness. He also formulated a concept about the nature of time based on fractal patterns he discovered in the formation of the hexagrams of the I Ching, which he dubbed "novelty theory." It was his interest in both technology and the I Ching that brought us together. He was one of the smartest people I have ever interviewed.

In the interview, McKenna explained the essential difference between the focus of Western science and that of the ancient Chinese. Western science had successfully focused on what things are made of and how things work, which led to outstanding breakthroughs and inventions that have greatly benefitted humankind. McKenna pointed out that the Chinese civilization had also made formidable scientific advances, but that the wise men of this much older civilization were interested in answering a different question, which was: *how do things go together in time?* To the highly civilized Chinese, how things go together in time was important for all kinds of reasons. Good timing was essential for emperors and kings to keep order in the kingdom, conduct meaningful rituals, and know when to launch political moves, campaigns, and major enterprises. Even now, timing is a critical factor in extremely important areas of life where logic is of limited help – such as relationships, negotiations, and interventions of all kinds – as well as the scheduling of social customs, marriages, and other important events.

Synchronicity as Perfect Timing

When it comes to inventions, it's easy to see how innovation involves the synchronicity of two or more disciplines or technologies intersecting in a creative moment where things come together in a novel and surprising way. (In my case it was the intersection of I Ching and software.) According to a timing all its own, Infinite Intelligence dynamically generates synchronicities, like a metaphysical lightning storm. If we are on the lookout for them, amazing coincidences will occasionally flash into our consciousness along with symbols that we intuitively know are too relevant to be totally accidental or meaningless.

Synchronicities are happening constantly, even if the vast majority are too mundane to warrant special attention. In the sense that in every moment, a multi-faceted convergence of factors is coming together at the same time, synchronicity is a definition of the universe's perfect timing. And, indeed, according to a synchronistic point of view, everything happens in its own good time, even if it may not seem like it from the ego's point of view. From a cosmic perspective, synchronicity means that there are no accidents, not even down to the tiniest detail. According to this vantage point, everything happens for a reason and is unfolding perfectly according to a pattern, plan, or laws, even if the plan is inscrutable to human logic, and the laws are still to be understood in human terms. Of course Infinite Intelligence would operate according to a creative pattern that is beyond the rational human mind! After all, it takes all of interconnected reality into account, and proves a fertile resource from which new ideas and events arise like bubbles in a seething cauldron.

Because they are acausal by definition (i.e., outside the bounds of cause and effect) synchronicities are not amenable to measurement and scientific proof any more than trying to get a fix on a subatomic particle or wave. On the other hand, the belief that everything happens for a reason – that there is a divine order beyond sensory appearances – can never be disproved and is actually psychologically useful. From a practical point of view – and in alignment with the theme of this book – accepting the inscrutability of life's evolutionary dynamic, while availing ourselves of whatever meaning is currently accessible by our limited minds, will help us to make better decisions.

Let's humbly accept that it's not our job to fully understand the reasons things are unfolding the way they are right now. Maybe we'll get it in a few months, or a few years, or maybe not at all in this lifetime. Our primary task in the here-and-now is to take note of a synchronicity, act *as if* there is a good reason (even if we don't know what it is), and try to glean a sense of direction so that we can better answer the immediate and more vital question of what is our best next move. In the VDM approach, we use a belief in synchronicity as an operating assumption, choosing to accept the mystical patterns of destiny and learn how to let ourselves find support and guidance in the significant signals coming our way.

Even in the case of disappointing experiences, we derive benefit from the synchronistic point of view. It can be calming and healing to assume that cosmic timing is at work and that an intelligent force is clearing the way for something better to come. It may be humbling to accept that we are not capable of fully understanding the big picture, but despite the occasional conceits of science, it is true. Nevertheless, we can still take advantage of meaningful signs and omens that appear in the form of the synchronicities and dream symbols, which can be helpful when we are going through transitional periods of great change.

The Dreamlike Aspect of Synchronicity

The Synchronicity Principle suggests that there are no accidents and that synchronicity is actually the way of things, and operating all the time. In this paradigm, events unfold according to some higher order, even if it is beyond our ability to understand the cosmic blueprint. Viewing the world through synchronistic eyes perceives the underlying web of connectedness that weaves itself through nature and human lives. This is not about wishful thinking or even imaginative interpretation, but analogous to being inside of a dream while being aware that it *is* a dream. According to lucid dreaming experts, the awareness that we are dreaming allows us to imbibe the dream world and its lessons.

As lucid dreamers know, changing our perspective within a dream doesn't cause it to become a dream. It had always been a dream; we just hadn't recognized it as such. In a similar way, when we realize that we live in a synchronistic universe by becoming aware of meaning in coincidences and other signals, the universe reveals its synchronistic structure more vividly.

In his clinical practice, Jung had his patients record their dreams and daily experiences to become aware of strange symbols, archetypes, and any special coincidences. Under the old paradigm, these would have probably been overlooked, dismissed as mere chance or, worse, as mental garbage. As Jung developed a point of view that was tuned to and expectant of synchronicity, meaningful coincidences were perceived more often, stimulating more new insights. And all of this happened quite naturally.

The more you are on the lookout for synchronicities, the more of them you will certainly notice. Synchronicities, like the symbolic representations in your dreams, are not really separate from the dreamer. The events may seem external, but the meaning and ultimate impact is internal and intimate, and needs the awareness and attention of you, the perceiver. Once you become lucid in this waking dream of normal life and become more aware of the fact that you are living in a synchronistic universe, your life will reflect the rich fabric of that reality back to you in a clear way. Recognizing the synchronistic matrix that provides a substratum for your experiences will empower you to be a creative, cooperative, and active partner in your own awakening and process of personal development.

Jung's exploration of the phenomenon of meaningful coincidence was one of his great contributions to our self-understanding. It helps us see human life as an interconnected web of subjective and objective experiences with synchronicity providing a link between the two. In one of his letters to Jung, the physicist Wolfgang Pauli referred to the Synchronicity Principle as Jung's "spiritual testament." Although he was not a religious person, in synchronicity, Jung acknowledged creative power at work in human nature.[16]

Tracking and Cultivating Your Synchronicities

Becoming aware of synchronicities as they happen is a huge advantage for the visionary decision-maker. Learning to notice and leverage synchronicities supports a holistic and creative perspective where timing is not only considered, but is recognized as a vital factor. The development of great timing depends on paying more respect to the dimension of time, in order to become more aware of special intersections, and then schedule the strategic moves you might make according to their meaning and sequence. A consideration of how things best go together in time will help you make better plans, clarify situations, and realize when a new direction should be taken.

The experience of synchronicity is an opportunity to receive useful timing information from beyond the limits of normal linear thinking. Since it's easy to overlook synchronicities when you are in a hurry, we need to slow down to consider possible meaning in coincidental happenings. Keeping a Synchronicity Journal is one way to do this and will help you take full advantage of signs and omens that the universe provides.

Whether you go with paper or make a digital file, make a point to record all your meaningful coincidences – as well as dreams, hunches and good ideas – that occur every day. If you use such an electronic device, I recommend setting up a Synchronicity Journal file on your smartphone, tablet, or computer. Make a habit of entering all the synchronicities that seem meaningful, whether you are sure or can fully understand their meaning yet or not.

Just knowing that you are keeping such a journal will cause you to notice synchronicities more often, which is a positive effect of setting up and maintaining one. And you will be able to more quickly capture the moment when a profound coincidence happens. Your physical sense of a "gut feeling" or that "feeling in your bones" will become sharper and more refined as you hone your intuitive sense.

The synchronicities that you record will change your perspective and lead to new insights, new relationships, and new opportunities. This is the expansive way that creative spirals work. The deeper meaning of your ideas, the real significance of the people you meet, and new potentialities will become clearer as you go back and look them over. I suggest adding reflections and insights once a week or so, as you attain a deeper understanding of the meanings over time. This will help you to expand your consciousness beyond the level and preoccupations of ego.

Synchronicity may reveal the universe's perfect timing, but we humans will never fully comprehend it. Nor will we ever achieve perfection in our decision-making or timing. Nevertheless, even a slight improvement in our ability to notice and leverage synchronicities will produce better decisions and timing, along with all the advantages and opportunities that these will produce. Even slightly increasing your awareness of synchronicity works on your behalf like compound interest, building on itself to make your life more abundant and meaningful. In Part II of this book, we explore practices that you can employ to take greater advantage of synchronicity awareness. In the meantime, let's take a look at other resources that Jung's research uncovered, which are available to help us on our journey to success, greater meaning and fulfillment.

CHAPTER 4

The Resource of Infinite Intelligence

We live in the lap of an immense intelligence that, when we are in its presence, we realize that it is far beyond our human mind.
—RALPH WALDO EMERSON

In the early 20th century, Napoleon Hill, the famous motivational teacher and author of the best seller, *Think and Grow Rich*, interviewed five hundred of the most successful people in America. He concluded that, without exception, an ability to access a level of intelligence transcending personal consciousness was pivotal to their monumental success. He referred to the universal resource, which he said those successful leaders had learned to tap, as "Infinite Intelligence."[17]

In the 19th century, American philosopher Ralph Waldo Emerson penned an essay entitled, "The Over-Soul," about how all of our creative potential comes from connecting to a larger field of consciousness, which envelops us even when we are not aware of its presence. Emerson was among many philosophers who tried to identify this power. He called it Universal Mind or Superconscious Mind.[18]

Carl Jung's research confirmed the intuitions of Hill and Emerson, but he characterized the vast reservoir of creative potentials as a "collective unconscious." It is wholly unconscious, that is, until we become conscious of parts of it, but the real point for our purposes is that there is this vast extension of the personal unconscious that we can become aware of, which contains creative powers that we can access and take advantage of with our conscious mind.

The collective unconscious is a shared reservoir of patterns, symbols, creative ideas, and energetic dynamisms that can intersect and operate through the personal unconscious. Sigmund Freud had promoted the idea of the personal unconscious mind as a kind of vault stuffed with repressed thoughts and feelings, but Jung was the first psychologist to explore an unconscious connection to a non-personal repository of mythologies and archetypal themes that affect everyone. (Chapter 7 shows how archetypes can be put to good use.)

Unlike psychological complexes and phobias – which are reactions to personal experience and conditioning – the contents of the collective unconscious, according to Jung, have their origin in a shared cultural heredity that influences the evolution of our culture and species. "The collective unconscious is ... the mighty deposit of ancestral experience accumulated over millions of years," Jung wrote. "Because the collective unconscious is, in the last analysis, a deposit of world-processes embedded in the structure of the brain and in the sympathetic nervous system, it constitutes in its totality a sort of timeless and eternal world image which counterbalances our conscious, momentary picture of the world."[19]

It is "collective" because it belongs to and is available to everyone, and operates through us all to different degrees depending upon our awareness of it. It stimulates our personal unconscious by means of dreams and synchronicities, whether we become conscious of those unconscious connections or not. As Jung put it, "I have chosen the term 'collective' because this part of the unconscious is not personal but universal; in contrast to the personal psyche, it has contents and modes of behavior that are more or less the same everywhere and in all individuals."[20]

As evidence for a collective unconscious, Jung noted that major elements of patients' dreams did not refer to their actual experiences or relationships. In fact, much of the material that appeared in dreams was strange to patients and had no connection to their personal experience at all. "It is a fatal mistake to regard the human psyche as a purely personal affair and to explain it exclusively from a personal point of view," he wrote.[21] Even when they could not personally relate to the content of their own dreams, patients could still discover meaning in them – sometimes even transformational meaning. Jung pointed to a broad, impersonal dimension of mind that operates both within and beyond the scope of an individual's life.

Freud had treated the unconscious as a kind of personal toxic waste dump, but for Jung it was a creative gold mine. By pointing out the existence of a wider collective aspect of the unconscious, Jung provided a psychological explanation of heretofore-unexplainable factors like creativity, intuition, and consciousness. Jung saw enormous power and potential in the collective unconscious:

> *[The collective unconscious] is of absolutely revolutionary significance in that it could radically alter our view of the world. Even if no more than the perceptions taking place in such a second psychic system were carried over into ego-consciousness, we should have the possibility of enormously extending the bounds of our mental horizon.[22]*

Jung's revelation of the collective unconscious as the psychic inheritance of all humankind transformed our understanding of self and its relationship to the world. Beyond just investigating ways to cure the mentally ill, his scientific curiosity was exploring humanity's psychological and spiritual potential – with huge ramifications for creativity and leadership, informed and supported as they are by muses, heroic characters, and other archetypes.

A Powerful Resource for Expanding Horizons

The term "Infinite Intelligence" appeals to me as one description of the collective unconscious, because I am focusing on it here as an unlimited resource of inspiration, energy, great ideas, and synchronistic signals that inform decision-making and good timing. From a practical point of view, it doesn't matter whether you think of connecting with this cosmic intelligence as psychological self-actualization or spiritual practice. Either approach supports the expansion of consciousness – in contrast to a reliance on current beliefs.

Consciously accessing this resource of great ideas and creative inspiration is what differentiates Visionary Decision Making from reactive decision-making that is characterized by small-minded goals, defensive responses, and limited options.

Infinite Intelligence can be thought of as a potential extension of personal consciousness, analogous to an online "cloud," where vast information is stored in a cosmic server. As we explore in detail in Chapter 6, you can use your intuition to make a "wireless connection" and tap into this cloud to download information in the form of impressions, flashes of insight, and inspiration. Although it is always available to you to inform or stimulate your imagination, the information in this collective reservoir is not owned or controlled by you, any individual, or government agency.

Infinite Intelligence has three characteristics that support the VDM process: it is the origin of all great ideas; it is the source of personal and creative power; and it is the energy field generating synchronicities and meaning. It is the intuitive decision-maker's largest and most supportive asset, and it's always there for you. All you have to do is make a connection and tap into it!

Source of Great Ideas and Inspirations

When we come up with new ideas, we love to think that they originated with us. We "thought them up," we own them. But what we consider to be our thoughts only seem like "ours," because we have identified with and invested in them.

Anyone who learns meditation quickly comes to realize that the thoughts that pop onto our field of attention do not originate with us, if only because they come uninvited. Even if they seem terribly familiar, this is because we made a nest for them in the past, by dwelling on them. Meditation, which is generally practiced as a way to transcend the personal mind in favor of a more cosmic consciousness, teaches us to let go of thoughts as they arise and merely note their passing. Even so, thoughts will continue to arise in the mind's field of attention of their own accord. Even though a meditator is choosing not to actively engage with or think about them, they still come – out of habit or streaming from the collective unconscious. From the point of view of the letting-go exercise that is traditional meditation, thoughts are a nuisance. From a VDM point of view, however, thoughts in the form of creative insights can have value, even if they occur when you are meditating (perhaps *especially* when you are meditating... we will look at how to take advantage of this in Chapter 6).

Everyone knows that Thomas Edison invented the lightbulb, right? Yes, but so did at least 23 other inventors. Two of them even sued over the patent rights, since their prototypes were so similar. This is an extremely common experience. In fact a study in 1960 led sociology professor Robert Merton to declare, "The pattern of independent multiple discoveries in science is in principle the dominant pattern, rather than a subsidiary one."[23]

While such concurrent insights may seem disconnected and merely coincidental, the concept of the collective unconscious provides the explanation that we are all plugged into the same creative power source. The difference is based on how and where an individual has focused her or his intuitive antenna, and how sensitive it is. A good idea is one whose time has come. It is an evolved thought form picked up by individuals whose intuitive sense is receptive and ready. Great ideas, emanating from Infinite Intelligence, can arise in many ways such as dreams, good advice from advisors, meditation, or an authentic divination system like the I Ching.

The fact that we are the recipients – and not really the inventors – of great ideas is elegantly expressed by Bob Proctor, author of *You Were Born Rich,* who wrote, "I am grateful for the idea that has used me."[24] It's as if every idea, from the lightbulb to the Slinky, already circulated within the universe, along with an astounding number of other new ones. Finding your "muse," or guiding creative spirit, is part of becoming a visionary decision-maker. Everyone is creative in his or her own way – it's just a matter of tapping into your personal talents and connecting with Infinite Intelligence.

The Reservoir of Creative Power Contains Archetypes

Infinite Intelligence – Jung's collective unconscious – is an unlimited creative resource that is always available to everyone. It can be thought of as a wellspring of energy and psychic power that you can access to strengthen intuition and from which to receive ideas and inspirations. It is the province of archetypes, which are symbols, instinctual patterns of behavior, and powerful personality dynamics. These "figures and movements" (as Jung put it) are universal human models of personality or patterns of behavior.

Archetypes have been expressed in the hopes, dreams, fears, and desires of humanity across cultures and throughout time, in the form of myths, deities, heroes, and demons. For example, the "mother figure" archetype is psychologically active in individuals who may not be mothers but who otherwise manifest traits of nurturing, etc. One way to think of an archetype is as a generic version of a personality type, which can inform or reinforce aspects of an individual personality.

The concept of archetypes has been around since Plato and the Greeks as well as the more ancient cultures of India and China. Carl Jung brought new interest to the subject when he introduced it as an important element of psychology in 1919. For our purposes, invoking archetypes, particularly archetypes of creativity and power, helps you trust your intuition and turn on your personal power, both vital to superior decision-making (we learn how to do this in Chapter 7).

With the support of many archetypes – each powerful in a different way – you can facilitate significant changes in your career, relationships, and entire life. After you learn how to invoke the power of various archetypes that are particularly useful for VDM in Chapter 7, some will seem more natural to you than others based on your personality traits. In fact, archetypes operating in and through your unconscious have heretofore helped to shape your personality and character.

When you know how to tap into the power of Infinite intelligence, it becomes *your* power on loan – to channel through your attitude, thoughts, and actions. Throughout the ages, people have relied on rulers, priests, gurus, and other middlemen to mediate with archetypal gods on their behalf. Now every intelligent individual has access to the knowledge to go there directly. Creative energy is always flowing through and around you. In order to leverage it, all you need to do is consciously connect to what has been unconscious. Your physical self and your breathing are, together, an excellent touchstone to help you maintain a more conscious connection with nature and spirit. Infinite Intelligence will provide support, safety, and security once you learn to be receptive and open to the inspirations and ideas that are picked up by your intuitive sense.

Our Relationship to Infinite Intelligence

Visionary Decision Making challenges us to extend the bounds of our mental horizons and reach for creative powers that would be individually beyond any one of us. We are each part of the "world mind," according to Jung, so the creative powers of Infinite Intelligence are always present and available for our conscious connection. And it's not that hard to connect – just paying attention and maintaining awareness of the connection makes up 80 percent of the required effort. A spiritual and creative dimension is always there for us to access, but connecting to Infinite Intelligence is still up to us.

The skill that allows us to pay attention to Infinite Intelligence is called mindfulness, which we learn how to produce in Chapter 6. Without mindfulness, we may miss creative solutions, as well as subtle timing signals that pop up in the form of synchronicities. Obviously, this is a different orientation to Infinite Intelligence than monotheistic religions teach. Rather than imagining an omniscient God that watches over us and pays attention to us as if we are children begging for treats, VDM's psychological and spiritual development point of view would have us tap into the creative powers of Infinite Intelligence and cooperate with them.

Making life-changing decisions is more work than just asking God (or consulting a divination system, for that matter) for direction, to give you what you need, or tell you what to do. You are required to exercise free will and cooperate as a co-creator, as a partner in the unfolding pattern of your life and destiny, as an intuitive channeler of Infinite Intelligence. Use your head and heart and intuition. Be willing to do the work of paying attention, making your own decisions, and undertaking the risks that bold decisions entail. Once you develop a habit of tapping Infinite Intelligence to inform your important decision-making, your attitude and your future will automatically begin to improve.

The Divine

Even though Jung – in the service of psychology, which he considered a science – was careful to use secular terminology when referring to the collective unconscious, many observers like myself consider it to also be a *spiritual* resource. After all, it is a realm populated by archetypes including divine beings. It's fine to personalize the divine in your own mind, if that's what you prefer. The important thing is to remember that your decisions affect the unfolding of your destiny more than anything you can imagine the Fates or God have in store for you.

For one year that I lived in India, I observed that everyone had complete freedom to relate to his or her own preferred representation of the divine. In the open-minded Hindu culture, it seemed natural to have conversations about God or the spiritual dimension of life with just about anyone – even a stranger on a bus – without a hint of conflict. Some Hindus have affection for Krishna while others favor Shiva, Vishnu, or Ganesh; some even prefer Jesus as their favorite deity.

Most Buddhists, in contrast, perceive the divine in an impersonal way – as a resource of creative power that they can tap anytime, a concept relatively similar to the collective unconscious. Taoists also conceive of divine power as an impersonal repository of Infinite Intelligence, rather than a patriarchal Creator-God who controls or judges his creation. Like Buddhists, the Taoists related to the divine as an impersonal resource that is always on tap. They referred to it simply as "Nature."

Each individual is entitled to his or her unique conception of the ineffable divine realm. When I was a struggling bootstrap entrepreneur and people would ask me if I had investors (which in the normal sense I did not), I would reflect on Infinite Intelligence and smile, saying, "My backer has infinite resources."

Ultimately, it is not important how you choose to conceive of or visualize the realm of Infinite Intelligence; just remember it is a supportive resource that is always there for you. Through it, our intuitive sense has access to unlimited information at a moment's notice. Tuning in to this dimension of higher consciousness will enable you to take advantage of ideas, recognize good timing, and make more enlightened decisions.

PART II

The Visionary Decision Making Process

CHAPTER 5

Your Strategic Vision

You've got to think about big things while you're doing small things, so that all the small things go in the right direction. —ALVIN TOFFLER

T he Visionary Decision Making process comes into play once you are clear about a strategic vision that will inspire you to make a bold or life-changing move when the time is right. Certainly, depending on the values at stake, few decisions are so strategic. Potential life-changers may coincide with major passages or transitions in life, but exceptional opportunities for change arise only occasionally and are impossible to precisely predict.

A vision is "strategic" for you if it is based on what is most important to you as an individual at this stage in your life. A strategic vision can lead to a strategic goal. Whatever they may be, goals that are strategic need to be clearly envisioned. Logic can help us clarify.

A strategic vision and goal that you become committed to will require making what I refer to as *visionary decisions.* Such transformative decisions are rooted in the depths of your being and are an active expression of who you have discovered yourself to be. The focus could be in any area of life: finding a partner, experiencing a higher level of health or shifting to a more fulfilling career. It might involve something that you are inspired to achieve even if it requires hard work. It could be the result of a recurring vision that is in alignment with strong interests or talents.

If some thought or type of opportunity keeps arising or, conversely, if conditions in an area of life become chronically unpleasant, these could be patterns that are trying to tell you that it is time to make a profound change. A visionary decision isn't about the form or the details as much as the level of personal meaning that making a shift holds for you.

In my story in the Introduction, my strategic vision was in the arena of livelihood - my dream of making a living doing something creative and meaningful to me. After fifteen years of cultivating business and marketing skills at day-jobs that paid the rent, my vision was ready to be realized. In my case, this eventually took the form of developing a new kind of software that leveraged ancient wisdom to help people make more intuitive decisions.

Once you know who you are – your most important values, and what inspires you – the central driving questions of Visionary Decision Making are the "what" questions, as in, "What is my vision of making a move?" and, as in a game of chess, "What is the best next move to make?"

Board games like Chess and Go are excellent ways to practice strategic thinking. These games rely on the moves you decide to make, such as trying to get into the most advantageous position, or making tactical responses to shifts in position by the other player (i.e. circumstances outside yourself). The depth of your calculations depends on the strength of your logic in analyzing possible moves, along with your intuition in anticipating what the other player will do.

Set Your Intention

The first step in the process of formulating a strategic vision is to identify the problem, dilemma or opportunity and frame it as a specific objective that you can focus on. Getting clear about the issue that needs to be decided starts by asking, "What is the most beneficial thing to do that is good for me and also in alignment with the good of all?"

Whatever your vision, write it down and play with it, revise the wording of it until it makes complete sense to you and you can define it clearly. Such a clarification process is empowering in itself. If you become aware that you're making some mountain out of some molehill – or you are overthinking something or "sweating the small stuff" – you can let it go and redirect your energy in a more productive direction.

Define your vision and consider *what* decision you need to make, or dilemma you need to resolve, in order to move toward your vision. Before you seek any definitive answer, commit yourself to an open-minded and creative frame of mind around what's possible. Rather than approaching the situation as merely a problem to be solved, reframe it as a learning opportunity to be seized.

It helps to be in an environment that supports clarity and peace of mind, as both your inner mindset and outer setting are important. You can't make an effective decision of any importance when you're distracted. Conflicts of interest, wanting too many things at once, and random distractions drain attention and potency. For example, you can hardly help but be disturbed if you are in a traffic jam behind a truck with a broken exhaust system spewing toxins. When faced with a visionary decision, you need to be in a place where you can focus!

Comfortably settling within yourself and your environment supports confidence that there *will* be signs. Tap into the belief that you will be provided with the clues and information you need to attain your objective. Remember that you will come to understand what any given dilemma or choice-point means for you, and that you will eventually see the best course of action. Don't expect a miraculous windfall to deliver your goal into your lap. Prepare to notice clues in the form of meaningful coincidences by maintaining your conscious intention to perceive signals that can help guide you.

The Power of Logic

The Visionary Decision Making process is primarily driven by intuition, but the use of logic to do some focusing homework plays an important role. Some of the worst decisions are purely emotional or knee-jerk reactions to jarring events that have not allowed logic enough space and time to weigh in. Even though relying on logic all by itself is not sufficient for the most important decisions, logical analysis can help you position yourself for making the best choice from an array of options.

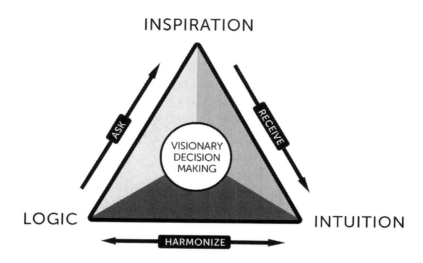

A wise mentor long ago counseled me against black-and-white thinking by reminding me that *there are more than two solutions to any problem.* This is an excellent adage to remember whenever you are thinking in all-or-nothing terms. Do your best to recognize all your options and apply a dose of logic as an antidote to getting carried away by strong emotions. That is logic's job and its rightful role. Wishful thinkers abandon logic at their own risk!

Of Two Minds

Humans have the largest neocortex-to-brain ratio of any mammal and this has supported the evolution of our capacity to reason, which is generally associated with the left hemisphere of the neocortex. Roger Sperry, one of the neurobiologists who pioneered split-brain studies (and won a Nobel Prize for it), demonstrated that the two hemisphere's – which physically appear almost identical – are "two separate realms of conscious awareness; two sensing, perceiving, thinking and remembering systems."[25]

Logical problem solving is a function of the left frontal lobe of the neocortex, sometimes loosely referred to as the "left brain." New discoveries in brain imaging have shown that the conscious, rational functions of thinking, planning, writing, etc., are based in the left frontal lobe for most people. The other half – the right hemisphere of the neocortex – is the locus of older, more instinctive forms of intelligence, including emotional and intuitive intelligence. It's almost as if we have two independent brains, each with their own memory and units of storage. These two halves of the neocortex can be at odds – and often are – or they can work it out like two political parties in a divided government.

Intuition is a process of sensing patterns and perceiving new connections. It is rooted in a synergy between the right brain and the limbic brain (more on this in the next chapter). Logic is a process of taking things apart and analyzing them in order to figure out what they're made of or how they work. Such "reverse engineering" can certainly play a useful role in creativity. Once you take something apart and figure out how it works, it can be possible to reassemble the pieces in a new configuration to serve a different purpose. Countless modern innovations have been the result of this approach that is generally the province of the left brain. Human engineering, which has changed everything from farming to transportation to medical cures, has enhanced the survival of our species, even as the overuse or misuse of technology threatens our ongoing existence.

The left brain – the hemisphere that stores information in the form of words, thoughts, ideas, plans, etc. – has played a huge positive role in the development of human culture in the past 5,000 years, especially since the Renaissance and the birth of scientific method. And, for the purpose of decision-making, logic provides a useful filter that helps distill options through comparative evaluation and a process of elimination. It helps us differentiate between the far-sighted decision rather than the impulsive or emotional one. In an information-saturated world where we have so many more choices, a logical comparing and sorting ability is critical.

Facts vs. Biases

Facts provide a basis for logical deduction. Facts are determined by observation and measurement, which is why fields like science, engineering, and law are characterized by adherence to logic. Emotions and relationship dynamics, on the other hand, cannot be measured or quantified, which is why it's impossible to be totally scientific when it comes to decisions about politics or love affairs or timing in general. All manner of important areas in life cannot be empirically measured.

There is a tendency to create our own reality by choosing to ignore facts that don't fit the way we'd like to see things, and exaggerating observations that affirm our biases or a desired point of view. In its most innocent form, this is referred to as "belief bias," and it's an extremely widespread phenomenon, and often negatively inclined. Psychologist Dan Staso was quoted saying, "Negative beliefs cause us to filter out information long before it reaches our conscious mind. This system of false beliefs filters in information that is consistent with our long-held assumptions and filters out information that contradicts those beliefs. The results include: failure to see or create opportunities; reluctance to utilize resources that are easily available or to assert oneself in situations that could lead to new possibilities; failure to believe others when they offer support; and refusal to accept help from those who could make a difference."[26]

In some cases, belief bias can lead to risky and dangerous delusions. One example is the reality of humanmade climate change that is killing life on the planet and causing sea levels to rise. There is abundant evidence for humanmade climate change. Peer-reviewed climate scientists almost unanimously agree that the drastic changes in weather, rising sea levels, and melting snowpacks are the result of air pollution from massive increases in the burning of coal and oil since the early days of the industrial revolution in the 19th century. However, there are a handful of scientists who take a contrary position, based on "research" funded by carbon-based energy companies who have been in denial about the harmful potential of their products. The unwanted mountain of scientific evidence is totally ignored while self-serving investigations proceed along "logical" lines to generate the desired conclusion.

It can be difficult to know if something is fact or merely strong opinion – especially in a networked age where people so easily have the capacity to loudly and anonymously broadcast opinions and represent them as facts, without being accountable for evidence or sources. Reality-based logic is a powerful decision-making aid, but we need to bear in mind how thin the line between facts and opinions can be... and how challenging it is, given our biases, to tell the difference.

To become exceptional decision-makers, we must be ready and willing to question everything – using our intuition, a baked-in form of which is known as "common sense." We often formulate opinions based on our perceptions of possible facts, and we often need to accept expert evidence that is beyond our ability to figure out for ourselves. If we use our intuition and would rather our beliefs were based on reality rather than comfort, convenience or fantasies, this is not a problem. But in a world rife with cultural regression into political and religious fundamentalism, we have to be especially careful before pledging allegiance to any opinion from professional rabble-rousers, political or religious. When people become unquestioningly devoted to a belief system, they propagate self-serving beliefs and make terrible decisions – often by doing what they are told by self-serving leaders!

Chaos Theory Reveals a Higher Order of Logic

In the 1960s, a new field of scientific study known as "chaos theory" was developed by meteorologist Edward Lorenz to help account for non-linear patterns in weather prediction. In its broadest sense, chaos theory demonstrates that apparent disorder is largely a matter of perspective. If we step back far enough – or step up close enough – unseen patterns emerge. Since it was formulated, chaos theory has had applications in physics, engineering, economics, biology, and philosophy, as well as meteorology. It is a good example of the dynamic of a decision-making process that allows for meaning in events that on the surface only seem to be happening randomly.

Chaos theory is an example of a change in perspective that takes us beyond the black-and-white thinking that has been epidemic in human society. True, in many areas of education – like arithmetic, for example – there are specific right and wrong answers. In the entirely logical domain of mathematics, linear thinking works just fine. Chaos theory is a much more nuanced and inclusive way of looking at reality and how things work – whether it's the motion of clouds and galaxies or the trajectory of a baseball (or, perhaps, even the dynamics of an intimate relationship).

Assuming a new point of view requires intuitive big-picture pattern recognition. Just as we discern the subtle patterns in clouds, tree roots, or shorelines, we intuitively understand that our lives and our minds are also a pattern of nature. This insight provides a new level of confidence in our ability to use intuition to make sense of larger patterns, including the shape and trajectory of our own lives.

The Logic of the Greater Good

We have all heard English poet John Donne's 400-year-old expression, "No man is an island." On our modern and crowded planet, we are more interconnected than ever before, but we're not feeling it. Too many people operate egocentrically, as if there were enough space on Earth to wall themselves off with their family in their own "private Idaho." Such a self-centered definition of "independence" is, at this point, a throw-back. It represents a lower rung on the ladder of humanity's cultural evolution. In America at the time of this writing, a fierce strain of self-interested hyper-independence is as strong as ever.

In the 18th century, when economics was just becoming a formal discipline, philosopher Adam Smith proposed that the "wealth of nations" increases when individual citizens further their self-interest. Smith coined the metaphor of an "invisible hand": an unconscious positive effect on the macro level that results when each person acts for his or her own personal benefit. According to the thesis, if you do what's best for yourself, and I do what's best for myself – and each person acts rationally in his or her own best interests – the results will be positive for society as a whole.

There are several problems with this, beginning with the fact that, as we have seen, people are not rational decision-makers on the whole. Furthermore, it is often the case that the interests of one individual conflict with those of another. According to the pure self-interest ethic, in such a situation an economic "survival of the fittest" principle then comes into play. The markets will determine the individual winners and the losers, but society as a whole will benefit and the wealth of nations will increase. All of this is fine, theoretically, especially when frontiers and natural resources seem to be infinite. Indeed, they seemed that way when Adam Smith formulated this theory. But now we know that our collective resources are limited.

At the same time that we are facing shrinking resources, we are all more interconnected than most people are conscious of. Modern physics has proven it with the "butterfly effect" (coined by Edward Lorenz), which is named after a useful metaphor. The butterfly effect stipulates that a tiny action in one place (such as the flap of a butterfly's wings in Brazil) can be part of the cause of a larger effect in a different place (like a tornado in Texas). The point is that every action benefits (or damages) the global system as a whole. If you understand our common interconnection, you realize that a capitalist fantasy of unregulated self-interest is a dangerous idea masquerading as fair and altruistic. There is such a thing as getting too good a deal and when you do, it will come back to bite you. A primary task for logic is the process of eliminating options that violate your ethical or spiritual standards.

Tragedy of the Commons

A zero-sum, win-lose mentality never yields long-term positive results in interactions between individuals, businesses, or nations. The reason for this was elegantly explained by Garrett Hardin, an ecologist and professor at the University of California at Santa Barbara, in a 1968 article titled, "The Tragedy of the Commons," published in the journal *Science*.[27]

His basic concept is simple: *using a limited but shared resource selfishly will hurt everyone – including oneself.* In the example he uses, Hardin describes a village of herdsmen whose sheep share a common pasture for grazing. Each herdsman will realize a short-term advantage when unilaterally acquiring and adding animals to his herd, despite the impacts on the shared resource. Eventually the long-term overexploitation by such self-interested individuals leads to the deterioration and destruction of the entire pasture and all the animals, causing huge losses for everyone, including the self-centered individuals themselves. This is a great way of explaining why win-lose always turns out to be lose-lose.

The Tragedy of the Commons shows that when it comes to common resources, we are interdependent, whether we like it or not. On a crowded planet with billions of human beings making excessive demands on limited resources, we can no longer afford to make decisions based solely on individual short-term benefits. Our long-term interests are inextricably bound with the common good. We ultimately do not benefit as individuals if we disregard the interests of others – and not just family and friends. This is not naïve altruism. Considering what we know now, it's pragmatism; it's been scientifically demonstrated and it is logical common sense.

Consideration of the collective good, which includes our personal good, is an important filter for the visionary decision-maker. This principle is elegantly expressed by the Sanskrit word *ahimsa*, a three-thousand-year-old term that translates as "harmlessness." *Ahimsa* is descriptive of choices and actions that consider the collective good rather than indifference or carelessness with regard to it. It's an idea that is reflected in the core teachings of all the great religions, from the Golden Rule of Christianity and Islam to the karmic law of cause-and-effect taught by Hinduism and Buddhism. Whatever you call it, it's in your best interests to cultivate an understanding of an ethic of harmlessness for your own sake.

A growing awareness of our interconnectedness is why, even in intellectually rigorous settings such as the Harvard Business School, more attention is being paid to teaching the ethical aspects of decision-making. Does the choice you're considering support you in becoming your best self and also have a positive affect on others? Is there anyone who could be harmed by you acting on behalf of your personal interests or furthering your competitive advantage?

A logical filter for the highest quality decision-making sounds something like this: If something that I desire would bring any kind of harm to anyone else, (beyond a simple competitive disadvantage within the rules of a game), I choose to disregard it as a viable option. It's that simple. But when self-interest is involved, simple is not necessarily the same as easy!

The Use of Logic in Visionary Decision Making

VDM requires a well-balanced, holistic, and focused approach that includes logic. By itself, logic is usually not enough to resolve human dilemmas – especially in categories like relationships, negotiations, or all matters of timing – but logic still plays a part in the process. Let's review important ways that logic supports the process of strategic decision-making:

• *Testing and reaffirming highest priorities.* Getting clear about your hierarchy of priorities is essential. It's imperative to know how they are ordered at this point in time, while recognizing desires and tendencies that can distract you from pursuing what is more important. Demartini's Hierarchy of Values technique (described in Chapter 2) is a superb way to logically analyze how you spend your energy and what you spend the most time thinking about. However you get there, you need to refine what's important to you from a practical perspective. Whatever is most important gets the highest priority, but priorities shift during different periods of a person's (or business') life.

• *Sacrificing a lesser for the greater.* Although it's not a popular concept, sacrifice or renunciation has to play a part in prioritization. When you are aware of all your choices, you also become more aware of the fact that you will have to give up something, that you may be called upon to sacrifice a lesser good for the greater. This lesser good may still be attractive – very appealing in its way – but in focusing on what you need most, "shiny objects" lose their luster and power over you. Giving up something lesser makes room for something better. Back in the 1970s, there was an advertising slogan: "You can have it all, baby!" A bold promise, but not true. You may be able to have *anything* you want, but not *everything* you want.

• *Helping strong emotions to calm down.* Don't expect to be objective when you're angry, frightened, or emotionally overwrought. Even an over-the-top joyful feeling makes it impossible to be objective. Bear in mind this counter-intuitive rule: No matter how it feels – good or bad – *the stronger the emotion, the less you can trust it as a guide to action!* Do not let your decision-making be influenced by how strongly you feel about something or how much you fear something. The strength of a feeling is not an indicator of intuitive activity. Intuitive impressions usually present with a more subdued signal strength. Strength of emotional reaction, therefore, is not a trustworthy basis for making decisions or significant choices. Things are never as good – or as bad – as they seem. Always put off important decision-making until your feelings calm down.

• *Enlarging the scope of your options.* Sometimes it looks like there are no good options. More often it seems that there are two choices, usually some variation of "fight or flight." This is quintessential black-and-white thinking, a widespread habit that adversely affects decision-making for most people. As my advisor told me, there are always more than two solutions. I find this idea to be a useful reminder when I feel pulled by two opposing choices. Consider a wider field of possibilities and find a third alternative, even if it is simply to let things pass and do nothing for the time being.

• *Sorting and comparing your two or three better options.* Sorting the relative value of your best options weeds out the less appealing ones until you reduce the set to your two or three best options. For this purpose, many people use a logical process made famous by the American philosopher Benjamin Franklin: listing "pros and cons." This approach is based on the idea that various elements in the mix can be weighed against one another. So a certain item in the "pros" column can cancel an item in the "cons" column when they are of equal weight. Similarly, two small "pro" items might cancel a single large "con."

For some choices, the consideration of pros and cons will work well enough. If you're dealing with abstract or emotional decisions, however, Franklin's system has a serious psychological shortcoming, known as "loss aversion." The fear of losing generally feels stronger than the allure of potential gain, because fear is more urgently motivating than optimism or faith (and for good reason, since it's in the jungle that the fear response of fight-or-flight evolved). In other words, the impact of "cons" – negative possibilities that we fear could happen – is generally a stronger influence on us than the positive resonance of positive potentials.

A Better Logical Process -
The Weighted Pros Technique

In order to balance out the emotional impact of loss aversion – which is the greater impact that fear of losing has over the hope of winning – I use a variation of Ben Franklin's "Pros and Cons" technique that I call "Weighted Pros." It is a practical approach that can usefully be applied in every major decision-making situation. When faced with a strategic decision, create a simple table with your three best options across the top. For example, if your decision has to do with finding the right place to live, you might boil it down to three options like this:
  • rent downtown condo
  • buy house in suburbs
  • housesit for friends
  Instead of listing pros and cons next to each of the options, list only its advantages. There are two reasons for only listing positives

and not tallying the negatives. First of all, a con is usually an inversion of one of the pros of what is one of the alternative choices. On an emotional level, the pro of one choice can seem more compelling when viewed as a con of another. It just seems to be easier for the human mind to focus on what it doesn't want rather than what it does want. We need to make a concerted effort to counteract that tendency and take the fear element out of the calculations. Give each of the positives a weighted value on a scale of 1-10 (10 being the highest positive score), and then add up the total values for each column. The option that offers the highest value is likely to be your best logical choice.

The Weighted Pros technique is a simple but excellent way to use logic to evaluate the options in any situation, and a good place to begin a strategic decision-making process. There may be times where nothing more than this level of logical sorting will be needed to make the best decision, but not when it comes to major strategic decisions.

Limitations of Logic in Decision-Making

The economist Herbert Simon won a Nobel Prize for his work on decision-making and problem solving. His work showed how, in complex situations, facts and information pile up so quickly that a decision-making process relying just on logic becomes unreliable and virtually impossible. To counter this, Simon studied the development of intuition as a form of pattern recognition that develops over years of experience in a wide variety of circumstances. Intuition – a process that operates outside the bounds of pure logic – proved to be an important tool for arriving at the optimal decision. All told, Simon's work on "bounded rationality" is a powerful endorsement of intuitive decision-making, while recognizing the important role of rational analysis.[28]

As we have seen, a logic-based approach is the classical model of decision-making and works well with measurable phenomena, but it cannot take on the subjective realms of morality, society, love, politics, creativity, and spiritual development. Often choices we are called upon to make cannot be adequately defined in logical terms, partly because there are too many variables. To make matters worse, even the information we currently accept as true now has a shorter shelf life. Rapid change makes the best current information (and thus our beliefs) obsolete more quickly than ever. Certainly, having good information to weigh and analyze is a vital component of great decision-making. However, in a world where there is too much information – and no easy way to prove which bits are reliable or true – intuition is required just to decide which information to trust!

The analytical process is only as good as the information that is available. As Gary Klein, a business authority on decision-making and author of *Sources of Power: How People Make Decisions,* puts it so perfectly, "Analysis has a proper role as a supporting tool for making intuitive decisions. When time and the necessary information are available, analysis can help uncover cues and patterns. It can sometimes help evaluate a decision. But it cannot replace the intuition that is at the center of the decision-making process."[29]

Another possible problem is that many logical decision-makers have a tendency to delay decision-making while they await more information. In some cases, this is a form of procrastination. The unfortunate result of many an info-gathering delay is that a promising window of opportunity is missed. Gerd Gigerenzer, a German psychologist who has studied rationality in decision-making, said: "The trick is not to amass information, but to discard it: to know intuitively what one doesn't need to know."[30] The trick is to use logic to clearly define and focus on your strategic vision and any goals that flow from it.

It is understandable that humanity has revered reason for the last several centuries, but as my story and this book attests, we are foolish if we ignore the wisdom of instinctive right brain intelligence. When it comes to strategic decisions of utmost personal or organizational importance, using logic is important, but depending on logic alone for strategic decision-making will not produce the best results. As Blaise Pascal wrote, "Reason's last step is recognizing that an infinity of things surpass it." After you have applied the filters of logic, it's time to open up to the parts of your mind that go beyond the reach of logical analysis in order to release your intuitive intelligence.

CHAPTER 6

Intuitive Intelligence

The intuitive mind is a sacred gift and the rational mind is a faithful servant. We have created a society that honors the servant and has forgotten the gift. —ALBERT EINSTEIN

I often tell my friends: When you don't know what to do, do nothing. Get quiet so you can hear the still, small voice – your inner GPS guiding you to true North. —OPRAH WINFREY

We have all been given the sacred gift that Einstein and Oprah refer to. Cultivating our intuitive intelligence and mastering the art of putting it to good use is at the heart of the Visionary Decision Making process.

The Oxford English Dictionary defines intuition as, "The ability to acquire knowledge without inference or the use of reason." Intuition is a holistic and non-verbal instinct that receives information directly, without interference from the conscious mind, which in turn finds it mysterious. In fact, the conscious mind often misses out on the value of the intuitive intelligence altogether, because until its impressions are noted and translated by our left brain with its verbal intelligence and put into thoughts and words, the conscious mind basically can't take advantage of intuitive perceptions.

The direct reception of information by the intuition is something that cannot be forced into action like logical analysis. It depends on being open and receptive to a spontaneous flow of impressions, insights, ideas, synchronicities, hunches, and inspirations that come to you. Intuitive intelligence has an ability to take in whole patterns, the interconnections of which may not be logically comprehensible, even if the parts are. Unfortunately for the conscious mind – the inner CEO – the intuitive information that you receive does not always get translated into ideas and words that your left brain can catalog for use in strategic planning and conscious decision-making.

> Carl Jung was the first psychologist to deeply investigate intuition. In *Psychological Types* (1923), Jung described intuition as "a perception of realities which are not known to the conscious mind, and which comes to us through the unconscious."[31] Intuition is not merely a perception, he said, but a creative process that has the capacity to inspire. Jung noted that the mind requires intuition to function at maximum performance and that our dreams, so rich in symbolic value, cannot be interpreted without the use of intuitive imagination.

Intuition is a very subtle instinct compared to the five physical senses, although it can piggyback on one or the other of them in order to be perceived – in the form of a sensation, feeling, image, or as a quiet voice. Intuition can stimulate a timely impulse to make a move in a specific direction, to avoid an action, or sometimes to simply let circumstances change and do nothing at all. An intuitive perception is a mystical experience that can take shape as a thought or a vision, or be physically felt, as in a "gut feeling." One might say, "I knew it in my bones," "I had a hunch that just felt right" or "Somehow in a flash it just became clear to me."

Intuition is what helps us to read between the lines of dreams or sessions of active imagination in order to ferret out the meaning and personal relevance of symbols and archetypes that show up. Intuitive perceptions are like sparks that bridge the gap between the *receptivity* of a stable grounded mind (Earth) and the spontaneous lightning of *creative power* (Heaven). When information is taken in via intuition, it can produce the "aha" type of moment that presents a new idea, point of view, or sense of direction. To further understand the role of intuition, let's briefly consider the complex interplay between the parts of the human brain.

The Older Right Hemisphere of the Neocortex

Human beings have a "triune brain" that consists of three parts – the reptilian brain or brain stem (responsible for instincts); the mammalian or limbic brain (which among other things controls emotions); and a large neocortex with left and right hemispheres. As Dr. Caron Goode notes, "The neocortex is the thinking brain, choosing information we should listen to and act on from the reservoir of our memory."[32] I would add that, in addition to memories, this selection process applies to new information in the form of non-verbal impressions that make it across the connective tissues from the right brain, having been received there via our intuitive instinct.

> Einstein's quote at the beginning of this chapter asserting that the rational mind ought to support the intuitive mind is notable because of his background as a physicist. Einstein also said, "Intuition makes us look at unrelated facts and then think about them until they can all be brought together under one law. To look for related facts means holding onto what one has instead of searching for new facts. Intuition is the father of new knowledge, while empiricism is nothing but an accumulation of old knowledge. Intuition, not intellect, is the 'open sesame' of yourself."[33] I recommend the book *The Right Brain and the Limbic Unconscious: Emotion, Forgotten Memories, Self-Deception, Bad Relationships* by R. Joseph for further reading on the connection between intuition and both the right hemisphere of the neocortex and the limbic brain.[34]

Dr. Roger Sperry's Nobel Prize winning split-brain research "...gave a physical basis to the ability to work with images, intuition, and holistic thinking in the right brain hemisphere."[35] Further research proved that people whose right hemisphere has been seriously damaged lack the sensitivity to felt energies, instincts, and nuances innate to normal humans and mammals.[36] We are naturally wired for intuitive information.

One way to visualize this "sixth sense" is as a sensitive little antenna that is able to receive subtle frequencies that provide an immediate sense of what's happening or about to happen. The more practiced you become at using your right brain's intuitive antenna, the more trustworthy it will prove to be. With practice, and the greater sense of confidence that will naturally result, the insights you receive will become more and more accurate.

It is not so easy for us to access our intuitive sensations because of the structure of our brain. Psychiatrists and authors Thomas Lewis and Fari Amini describe it, "The swirling interactions of humanity's three brains are like the shuttling of cups in a shell game. ...Because people are most aware of the verbal, rational part of their brains, they assume that every part of their mind should be amenable to the pressure of argument and will. Not so. Words, good ideas, and logic mean nothing to at least two brains out of three."[37] To complicate matters further, memories are stored in the two halves of the neocortex in quite different ways.

For the perception of patterns that we refer to as intuitive, the personal unconscious (right brain) must be free to make a "wireless" connection with the collective unconscious (a.k.a., Infinite Intelligence). This first phase of intuitive perception is for the holistic, non-verbal right brain to perceive synchronicities, hunches, and flashes of insight, and take note of them in the form of images, impressions, and feelings states – which are stored as non-verbal information in the right brain's private memory.

In order to be useful to the conscious mind, left brain processing of these impressions, images, etc., needs to take place. The two halves of the neocortex are connected by a dense highway of fibers called the corpus callosum, which itself is not fully developed until age 10 or so. If the left brain has sufficient access to information coming from the unconscious – the right brain – the left brain can take note of and translate intuitive impressions and images into terms it can formulate, plan around, and put to good use.

Although it is an oversimplification, intuitive impressions stored in the right brain need to be made conscious so they can be deciphered by the left brain in order to be useful to us. We need to help the left brain recognize, receive, and translate impressions picked up by intuition, rather than disregard them or censor them according to its own stored memories, which include biases and old beliefs. The task is to make it a point to convert intuitive impressions, feelings, and images into thoughts and ideas that can be used in conscious decision-making and creative pursuits. This is where archetypes, dreams, and divination can play a helpful role. Once the left brain is able to successfully translate intuition's perceptions, our hunches start to prove more reliable, if not prescient.

For visionary success, logical analysis needs to follow perception, rather than govern it. Allowing creative synapses to fire *before* logical processing becomes too involved will lead to the most far-reaching discoveries and decisions. Scientific visionaries like Einstein and Jung and neurobiologists like Roger Perry understood this. Ironically, Western science as a whole has glorified logic at the expense of anything that does not conform to measurement and analysis. While logic performs an important filtering function by helping to sort options, breakthrough decisions are always driven by intuition. An overreliance on logical analysis will derail the intuitive mind's ability to receive signals and contribute its valuable sense of things.

Education's bias toward logic persists despite numerous studies that show that even the successful leaders and executives rely heavily on intuitive decision-making. A recent report by Applied Predictive Technologies found that 73 percent of respondents trust their own intuition for decision-making. Even among decision-makers who said they were data-driven, more than two-thirds (68 percent) said they trusted their intuition in the decision-making process.[38]

Unfortunately, we cannot just make intuition happen; like relaxation and meditation, it involves a "letting-go" dynamic that cannot be forced. Since the intuitive mind operates outside the realm of cause-and-effect, it is impossible to come up with a logical or linear formula for its activation. Later in this chapter, we will explore some powerful practices that we can do to invite more intuitive insights into our life and decision-making. Before we go there, let's review the major ways intuition is going to be most useful to us.

Applications of Intuition

Intuitive intelligence helps in any area of life, but it is especially notable in the areas of creativity, empathy, and spirituality. And, of course, strategic decision-making.

Creativity: Artistic expression is a form of intuitive intelligence that combines with an artistic technique that can be learned. Those who work in the creative arts and who are able to give free rein to fantasies and imagination, invariably test out as highly intuitive. One function of intuition is to find the patterns within, or to make sense of, symbolic content, some of which can come via dreams. A well-known example of art coming through dreaming is the Beatles' song, "Yesterday," the melody of which came to Paul McCartney in his sleep. Fantasy has also played a role in phenomenal scientific discoveries and technological innovations. For instance, the familiar double helix structure of the DNA molecule was revealed to Nobel Prize winner James Watson in a dream featuring spiral staircases. Dr. Caron Goode also notes that, "Brain mapping using EEG topography found that creativity and intuition are associated with theta waves usually linked with daydreaming or fantasizing ... intuitive ability is finally recognized as the fuel behind innovation, creative thinking, inspiration, and psychic experiences."[39]

Empathy: Empathy is a form of intuitive intelligence that allows us to perceive subtle feelings and pick up on what is going on within the mind and heart of another human being – even when that other person may not be aware of it. You can say that empathy is the ability to understand another's feelings from the inside out.

"Limbic resonance" is a term used to describe the ability of the people closest to us to influence our nervous system and brain chemistry – in other words, our ability to feel each other's feelings and read each other's minds, in a sense. The authors of *A General Theory of Love* describe this phenomenon using the example that "women who spend time together frequently find their menstrual cycles coming into spontaneous alignment. This harmonious, hormonal communion demonstrates a bodily connection that is limbic in nature, because close friends achieve synchrony more readily than those who merely room together."[40]

People who are most limbically resonant are generally more empathic. Empathic compassion inspires us to provide emotional and physical support. This form of intuitive intelligence is innate to all humans and needs to be encouraged, especially since we are such social animals.

Spirituality: Everyone is endowed with a mystical capacity, even if many people never become aware of it. Intuition is vital to the experience of the spiritual dimension, which is about our relationship to God, Spirit, the Universe, or whatever we choose to call what philosopher Alan Watts once referred to as the "Ultimate Ground of Being." Philosophically, intuition gives us a clearer view of the broadest patterns, and what requires greater broad-mindedness than an appreciation of the complexities of an infinite universe. Once we know and accept our humble place in the cosmic scheme of things, we can better appreciate the synchronistic perfection of our lives. On a personal level, spiritual perception can give us a psychological sense of freedom from existential suffering, infusing us with feelings of calm and clarity to know we are part of something so beautiful and grand.

Decision-making: The complexity of our problems, and the scope of our creative potential, exceeds logic's processing capability, which is why intuitive intelligence is essential for Visionary Decision Making. Maintaining a high level of receptivity to intuitive intelligence also requires a commitment to decipher what is meaningful. Insights and inspiration – the happy fruits of an active intuition – provide direction and awareness of new opportunities. Intuition used for decision-making is similar to the interpersonal limbic resonance noted above. In this case, however, you can think of it as limbic resonance with Infinite Intelligence.

Timing: Timing is the secret sauce of the most successful strategic decisions. Arriving at a conclusion and committing oneself is hard enough – and that process, as we saw in the last chapter, is aided by logic. But your odds of producing a successful outcome also depend greatly on whether you choose the right timing to execute a decision. Deciding *what* should be your best move may be largely intuitive, but deciding *when* to make that move is *entirely* intuitive. (Chapter 9 explores the sublime skill of good timing and how to know when to execute important decisions.)

Obstacles to Intuitive Reception

As we can see from the above, there are plenty of ways to benefit from intuitive intelligence, but we need to give it the freedom that it needs to operate. Since intuition is not something we can force to happen, a large part of intuitive awakening involves identifying, then letting go of, obstacles and destructive tendencies that block the delicate antenna's ability to receive and store impressions that could be useful to the conscious mind.

Static on the line. Obsessive thinking or sensory distractions that compete for our attention obstruct the receptive capacity of intuition. Subtle signals that intuition can profit by are also drowned out by interference within the mind – the noise of the internal chattering mind, which Indian yogis have humorously referred to for thousands of years as the "monkey brain." As noted earlier, receiving signals from the reservoir of Infinite Intelligence is like downloading information via a wireless network. In order to be able to do this, you need a clear connection – one that does not have too much static interference or other downloading going on at the same time.

Addictions. Emotion-backed cravings of the ego lead to compulsive habits or addictions, which create blind spots and place exhausting demands on consciousness. Addiction can be thought of as a craving or emotional attachment that is out of balance and becomes a cause of hardship or suffering. All the energy we expend trying to satisfy the seemingly insatiable appetites of ego – which may simply be trying to protect us by compensating for deep needs for love that were not met in early childhood – keeps us from being able to make an intuitive connection. When there is an addictive level of emotional attachment, even getting and possessing the object of desire produces suffering – if only in the form of anxiety over the prospect of losing it or running out. An addict has difficulty tapping into intuition in the face of his or her obsessions, which results in a downward spiral of fewer good choices until the person is desperate and trapped.

Trauma. Physical or emotional trauma throws the intuitive antenna out of whack. Whether it's a result of a personal or family tragedy, health crisis, or some other event that turns your world upside down, trauma will certainly override intuitive sensitivity. It is advisable never to make a strategic decision during or immediately following a traumatic event, which can be emotionally overwhelming for a protracted period of "post-traumatic stress" depending upon the severity of the event and personality factors.

Intuitive intelligence that you would otherwise have had access to isn't readily available until you have processed the trauma and become free from its impact. If you have been seriously traumatized, put off having to make strategic decisions until you recover your best level of emotional and psychological balance.

Emotional Blockages

The limbic brain, as we noted earlier, is the source of most of our emotions. Perhaps the biggest blocks to intuition's clear reception are caused by limbic interference in the form of emotions like worry, anxiety, anger, depression, greed, and fear. When your mind dwells on or reacts to fear thoughts and feelings, awareness becomes constricted and you are unable to even perceive synchronicities and hunches, let alone process them. Anything that reduces fear clears the way for intuitive insights. I like to compare being in a fear-based state to trying to tune into a wireless signal from inside a steel bunker. The signal cannot get through. Unfortunately, in such a fearful state, you lose the benefit of intuition when you need it the most!

Sometimes we carry fearful beliefs that we were taught or otherwise came to accept when we were young. Perhaps well-intentioned caretakers wanted to scare us away from making mistakes or committing wrongful acts. The unfortunate side effect of security-oriented beliefs is that they teach us to avoid taking risks instead of trusting our intuition, blocking our ability to tune into our full potential. Such beliefs give rise to emotional reactions that may feel similar to an abdominal sensation of intuition (like when we literally have a "gut feeling"). It's common to mistake a strong feeling of anxiety as an indicator of what is the right or wrong way to go, when there may be a third option that we haven't considered yet – so be especially mindful of what is motivating your emotions.

In a world that glorifies rationality – and, on the other hand, can consecrate the irrationality of blind faith – being a person who trusts intuition and the grace of synchronicity is somewhat daring. Accordingly, every great discovery and bold move is accompanied by some amount of risk and fear – whether physical fear, or fear of ridicule, fear of loss, and fear of embarrassment. As entrepreneur Rick Beneteau put it, "Not a single person has ever accomplished anything of significance without first feeling scared to death."[41] Making visionary decisions is not for the faint of heart!

In her book *Feel the Fear and Do It Anyway*, Susan Jeffers – an author I had the pleasure to interview on my Pathways radio show (podcast on Divination.com) – shares a technique for peeling back one's fears. The process consists of posing the query, "What if [the feared event] did happen... then what? What is the worst thing that could happen?"[42] After you answer that question, you repeat the process – e.g., "If that worst thing happened, then what could happen? What is the worst thing?" – and so on. In taking this series of what-ifs as far as you can, you eventually get down to the core belief that is the bottom-line of all the fears we ever experience. And that is the fear that you won't be able to handle it, that you won't be able to manage or cope. Ultimately that you could fall apart and die is the ultimate fear behind all of our fears.

Once you acknowledge your primordial fear of death, the next step is to recall your personal history. Even though you've been afraid many, many times, the vast majority of us have always managed to resolve the predicament and come out of it intact, if not unscathed. Now it becomes easier to appreciate that if you consciously cultivate the self-confidence to believe that you can handle whatever comes up, *you will be able to handle it – because you always have!* Your life history is proof that you are more resourceful than you give yourself credit for. Peeling back your fears is an excellent way to keep your intuitive antenna from blockage by fearful thinking.

When we succeed at accepting and then letting go of fear – which was basically just focusing on *what we don't want* – we create an opening for intuitive receptivity. We download impressions and receive inspirations, accept them gratefully, play with them, and, when the timing is right, we act on them. Positive changes were ready to happen for us for a long time, but fear was shutting down the reception of intuitive signals that could help us realize creative opportunities. Anything we can do to let go of fear will enhance our creative and strategic intelligence, bringing us the freedom to choose and manifest what we desire.

The Heart Checks the Gut

Fear and other strong emotions are like thick concrete bunkers encasing our little intuitive antenna, effectively blocking out all reception. Add this to the din of sensory distractions and the constant chattering of the mind, and it's a minor miracle that our sensitive intuition antenna ever picks up anything! When it does, the transmission of the message can be so quiet and subtle that it is hard to tell that our intuition is operating. Intuitive reception can be a formidable challenge, but there is another center of bodily intelligence that can help.

The brain has long been considered the seat of intelligence, but science has recently discovered that there are millions of nerve cells located in the human gastrointestinal system – almost as many as in our brain.[43] What this means is that your gut has the ability to process information about what's going on and generates a response independent of the brain. This is exactly what happens in dangerous situations when survival requires immediate action.

The same gut-felt sense can be used proactively to support intuitive decision-making – if we pay attention. "Go with your gut," as the saying goes. Malcolm Gladwell pointed out in his book *Blink* that our initial intuitive instinct can be incredibly accurate.[44] It's the thinking mind that complicates things, causing us to dismiss what our feeling sense is trying to tell us. "I should have listened to my gut-feeling," we later lament.

Since intuition often arrives in the form of a bodily feeling, it is important to differentiate intuition from emotional reactions that can also produce physical sensations. One way to differentiate between an intuitive gut feeling and a visceral fear reaction is to check with your heart. Is the feeling connected to something or someone that you care about? Intuitive gut feelings will have a positive heartfelt component while an emotional reaction to fear will be more head-oriented (as in catastrophic thinking).

For millennia, indigenous cultures have believed that the mind and intuitive sense are located in the heart rather than the head. Love has also long been associated with the heart, which seems to be the center for the experience of inspiration and attractions that can evolve into passion. Authentic heartfelt passion provides the launching power to propel you through a visionary decision and creative breakthroughs. If a desire is not coming from or through the heart, you can be fairly sure that it is ego-inspired rather than destiny-driven.

The Role of Mindfulness for VDM

In order to access your intuitive sense, it is necessary to clear your mind and ground your energy. As noted, the intuitive side of the brain needs space and quiet to receive hunches and signals via the intuitive antenna. The practice of meditation is an excellent way to consistently create these conditions, because it is all about letting go of thinking, which frees the mind to download creative ideas and inspirations. One of the best ways to tune your intuitive sense is a deliberate exercise that facilitates a wider awareness known as *mindfulness.*

Mindfulness is the art of paying attention to what is on your mind and in your field of perception – including sensations, random thoughts, feelings, intuitive impressions, as well as, possibly, a greater awareness of synchronicities. It is the moment of pure awareness before the ego-mind steps in to make its interpretations and judgments. Mindfulness is one of the primary skills that my cousin Lennie the hunter relies on when he sits very still in his blind, opens his field of awareness, and pays wide attention to the forest. In daily life, mindfulness allows you to penetrate or absorb the truth of the moment so you have more freedom to make a conscious decision on how to respond before reactive, judgmental, or emotional responses completely take over. As a practice, it can serve as an internal intervention against knee-jerk emotional reactions, thus allowing a wider array of options.

Mindfulness of the body is a traditional approach to the practice of formal meditation. A person may experience intuition as either mental or emotional, but what happens in the mind and heart cannot be separated from how we experience our physical self. In this practice of mindfulness, we enhance our receptivity to intuition and synchronicity by focusing our attention on some aspect of the physical self – our breathing, body posture, sensation of muscles relaxing or tightening, and so on.

As an example, take a minute right now to pay close attention to the feelings in your body. The feeling of your weight against the chair (if you are sitting), the feeling of your skin against your clothing, the subtle sensation of your nostril hairs as you breathe. During the day, the practice of mindfulness can also be used to note subtle physical responses to information, people, and events that come your way. In order to feel the clues coming via physical sensations like a gut feeling, it's important to keep your body balanced and the mind healthy and relaxed – through nutrition, exercise, yoga, as well as meditation or prayer.

Progressive Relaxation Technique: Stress, whether emotional or physical, is always an obstacle to mindfulness. Relaxation is an important aid to achieving a receptive mindset. One of the most widely used relaxation techniques was developed more than fifty years ago by the physiologist Dr. Edmund Jacobson.[45] *Progressive Relaxation* can be done anytime and anywhere, even while sitting at your desk or in a cramped seat on an airplane. The technique works best when you're seated or lying down, but it can even be done standing. First, tighten the muscles in the calf of your right leg. Hold the tension for five to ten seconds, and then let the muscles relax. Repeat the process with the muscles in the lower part of your left leg, and do the same by isolating other muscle groups in different parts while moving up your body. As you release the tension in a particular muscle group, the muscle relaxes not only to its pre-tensed state, but actually relaxes well beyond that point. If you have time to tense and relax all your major muscle groups, you'll feel the stabilizing, grounding sensation throughout your whole body and clarity in your mind.

Because it is the systematic use and cultivation of mindfulness, the practice that benefits the opening of intuitive intelligence more than any other is a meditation practice. Traditionally known as *Raja Yoga,* or "royal yoga," meditation has been a part of every religious tradition. Traditionally delegated to monks and nuns, it has now gone mainstream, and its benefits are readily available for anyone who learns how to do it. By developing a regular meditation habit, you will become more open to life's signals and synchronicities, and increase intuitive sensitivity.

The current widespread interest in meditation arose out of the popularization of Eastern religious practices like yoga. It was once difficult for Westerners to learn meditation without going to exotic countries, or at least adopting their cultural trappings, rituals, and even religious dogma. These days, however, it is easy for anyone to learn to meditate without joining a religious group or adopting specific beliefs. The skill of intuitive mindfulness transcends all religions and no beliefs are necessary at all – just a willingness to try it and see what happens.

Whatever your beliefs, connecting with spirit through meditation will bring a stronger sense of meaning into your life. The systematic practice of mindfulness of the body or breathing (or focusing on an object) quiets the chattering mind, ignores distractions, and creates space for intuition to operate freely. It turns down the volume of the five physical senses so that you can fine-tune your inner "wireless connection," surmounting the challenge of finding a clear channel in a wild and wooly sea of noise. What your intuition is sensing does not originate inside your mind; insights are the natural result of becoming conscious of your connection with Infinite Intelligence.

The Go Master: The game of "Go" has long been the national game of Japan, though it originated in China alongside the I Ching, more than 2,500 years ago. An ancient Chinese emperor demanded that a sage develop a game to improve the intelligence of his son, the prince. Like chess, Go is a board game for two players, which uses black and white stones (yin and yang). Master champions of Go are revered in Japan as national heroes. One Go Master was famous for using meditation as part of his strategy. His specific meditation focus was letting go of caring about winning. Ironically, he usually won and made a fortune. However, he was not attached to any of it; despite his glory and fame, he remained a modest man whose example influenced a lot of people... and all because of his secret weapon: meditation.

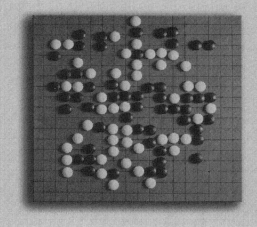

How I Discovered Meditation

Meditation retreats are the best way to develop a meditation practice, and I had my first experience of one near the end of my Stage One. When I was 29 years old, I took a sabbatical from my software career to embark on a worldwide pilgrimage. Among other places, one of my desired destinations was India, where I wished to delve into meditation and yoga and see if I could meet an "enlightened being." India was a vast overpopulated country where I didn't know a soul. In any case, I thought it would be a good idea to learn how to meditate before I took off, so I enrolled in a 10-day meditation retreat at Ananda Village in northern California. It was there that I heard a talk that changed my life, delivered by Mataji Indra Devi, a well-known 83-year-old yoga teacher who was visiting from India. I had never heard of her.

At the end of her talk to our retreat group (which was about the relationship between love and non-attachment – a talk I was destined to hear again many times), the elderly yoga pioneer demonstrated some yoga poses, including one that had her standing on her head – an impressive feat at any age. At the end of her talk and demonstration, Mataji made the sudden announcement that she was looking for a strong individual to help take her husband, who had suffered a stroke in California and was now paraplegic, back to India. She would pay all expenses and provide the caretaker with a place to live and be of service in India. Any volunteers?

There I was, passport in hand, having disposed of my worldly possessions and ready to take a year to cap off my Stage One period of self-discovery. Along with visiting my new friend Nigel in his home of New Zealand, going to India to study with masters of yoga and meditation was at the top of my list. It was perfect synchronicity to meet Mataji at exactly the right place at the right time. My hand flew up, but so did those of six or seven other yoga students. Impressed by the synchronicity of her announcement coupled with my total readiness to go, I had no doubt that of all my destinations, I was meant to go to India and work for Mataji.

And that is what happened. But rather than retaining me as her husband's caretaker, she came up with a new idea – to have me help her write her autobiography. When I called her and she surprised me with this change of plans, I noted that it was also quite an amazing coincidence. Unbeknownst to her, I was an aspiring writer and a fast typist, which I then told her. Ever comfortable with the workings of destiny, this wise woman replied, "Good!" as if she had known it all along.

After living in India studying yoga with Mataji and other masters for eleven months, and visiting the ashrams and monasteries of some of the prominent gurus that she knew, I was bounced out of India for overstaying my 6-month visa. I jumped over to Sri Lanka, an island nation nearby, with the intention of getting a new visa to return to India as soon as I could. Sri Lanka is more of Buddhist than India, and it was there that I took my first Buddhist meditation retreat, offered in English by a Buddhist nun named Ayya Khema at a beautiful hilltop meditation center. It was a silent retreat for 10 days (quite a challenge for an extravert like me), but each student had an interview with Ayya every day. When she learned what I had been doing in India, she came up with the idea of giving me an all-expenses paid volunteer position as her assistant on her upcoming world tour, with my primary job being to help *her* write a book of her talks in good English (she was originally from Germany). In the process of traveling throughout Australia, New Zealand, and Europe with Ayya while working on her book, she also trained me to teach meditation. (After I returned home from what turned out to be a 2-year worldwide sabbatical, I taught insight meditation classes for the City of Portland and became the meditation minister for a large New Thought church.)

One of the texts I used for my meditation classes was *The Three Minute Meditator* by author David Harp.[46] In this book, Harp explains how the essence of meditation is letting go of *thinking about* distracting thoughts and feelings that arise, while paying attention to and noting whatever arises in the field of your conscious awareness. Harp emphasizes that this technique can be done anytime and anywhere even when you're in line at a grocery store or bank. So, in addition to setting aside a period for daily meditation practice, you can also practice mindfulness throughout a busy day – if only for a few minutes at a time – by noticing thoughts or feelings as they arise and letting go of your attachments or reactions to them.

To anyone who says they don't have time to meditate, Donald Altman, a psychotherapist and author of *The Joy Compass* and *One-Minute Mindfulness*, points out that many people actually spend hours meditating while online.[47] Engaging in ego-stimulating tasks – like surfing social networks, internet shopping or following celebrities – are what he cites as examples of online "meditation." Taking responsibility for where you put your attention – and mindfully choosing activities that support clarity and relaxation instead of worry and anxiety – will make you less stressed, happier, and, incidentally, more in tune with intuition.

Meditation can provide a clear channel for impressions from the unconscious. Its practice involves two key elements – concentration and insight. Interestingly, these are analogous to the Hunter and Gatherer energies. The yang or Hunter element of meditation is the part that focuses on the "object of concentration" (the mantra, breath, picture, candle flame, music, and so forth), in order to pointedly focus the mind. The yin, or Gatherer, aspect is openness and receptivity to any insights that arise via meditation after the mind has calmed down.

Concentration: The Left Brain's Role in Meditation

The general technique for meditation is to induce stillness achieved via a period of focused concentration. This exercise of paying attention to just one thing settles the mind, allowing the emotional limbic brain to rest a bit and the intuitive channel to open. A single object of concentration helps the meditator focus, which in turns quiets down the internal dialogue. Objects of concentration that have proven beneficial for this purpose include the breath, the physical sensations of the body, an external object such as a candle or mandala, or an internal state of being, such as joy, love or compassion. Sometimes guided scripts, which can be read or listened to, do the job, helping us get our minds into a more receptive state. The breath is an excellent object of concentration because it is always with you, and it is also ideal for discreetly practicing mindfulness in public.

As a meditation teacher, I have heard students complain that they will never be able to meditate because they can't stop the thoughts. I point out that this belies a common misunderstanding about the aim of meditation, which is not to prevent thoughts from arising but to learn how to observe and let go of following or identifying with whatever comes up. By merely observing the thoughts and feelings and letting them pass us by, we can avoid getting caught up in the spiral of dwelling on a thought, seeing images of it in your mind's eye, having an emotional reaction to the image, and giving rise to more thoughts – in an endless cycle.

Letting go is the simplest thing in the world, but too easy to forget (which is why I arranged for vanity license plates on my car that read "Let Go"). Letting go may be mechanically easy, but it can become extremely difficult due to our attachments and aversions. As I once heard an Indian poet eloquently express the paradox on Delhi TV, "It's simple to be happy, but it's difficult to be simple."

Although the benefits are many, meditation is not about achieving anything. Rather than a striving for perfection, it is a practice of letting go, a process of elimination, a form of *mental fasting*. Like dietary fasting, it is a challenging practice. The mind has a habit of immediately "taking a bite" of whatever thoughts happen to show up. We even refer to them as "my thoughts," although we didn't welcome or desire them. The tendency to identify with thoughts – to invest one's attention in them – is a compulsive mental habit for human beings most of the time. The truth is the thoughts that *seem* like they belong to you only appear that way because you have identified with them in the past. You have made a nest for them. Each of us has thinking patterns we must be willing to break if we want to go beyond our comfort zone to do anything important or bold. We need to learn to pay attention and let mindfulness intervene in order to break up the way we reflexively identify with types of thinking that we are used to.

Try this short exercise. Close your eyes for a few moments and let go of whatever thoughts arise – noticing them but just letting them float by as if they were passing clouds. Do this for a minute or two and see what happens in your mind. I guarantee you that thoughts will keep popping up whether you want them to or not. Soon, if you sit still long enough without getting hooked into thinking about the thoughts that arise, you will start to experience a quieter, more spacious aspect of the mind that is like a clear sky. In the meantime thoughts just come and go, seemingly on their own. Since you didn't invite them or even want them, what could make the thoughts that arise *yours* any more than the clouds passing in the sky? Once you practice the natural mindfulness of our hunter-gatherer ancestors, you will gain the freedom to not be obliged to give attention to obsessive thoughts and worries that can do you no good.

One Indian meditation master used an interesting analogy to clarify the function of the concentration object in meditation practice. He said to imagine that you had stepped on a bed of thorns, symbolizing all the thoughts that stick in your mind. Pull one of the thorns out of your foot and use that one to dig all the others out. This is analogous to using a particular thought, feeling, or sensation as your object of concentration (like a mantra or the breath). You let go of thinking about all the other thoughts by focusing on that one. When you have let go of thinking about everything but the one single thorn, you can let go of it too and just notice whatever arises without attaching to any of it. This puts you into a blissful state of openness that the modern mystic Krishnamurti referred to as *choiceless awareness.*

A Beginning Meditation Session

Here's an easy way to begin a meditation practice: Find a spot where you can be alone and undisturbed for fifteen or twenty minutes. Sit comfortably in a chair or on a cushion on the floor, close your eyes, and begin to concentrate on your breath. Bring your attention to the bare sensation of inhaling and exhaling. The point is not to produce any special kind of breathing – deep or otherwise. Just quietly watch the rise and fall of the breath, noting the subtle physical sensation of air coming in and out of the nostrils. Or, if it is easier for you, note the rising and falling of the abdomen with each breath.

Sit still long enough to allow the chattering of the mind to simmer down, which can take up to fifteen minutes, especially in the beginning of practice development. Just use an object of concentration like the breath and continue until stillness of the mind is achieved. I compare this slow settling down of the mind to how water settles after you take a pan of boiling water off a burner. The flames represent the desires and attachments that stir up the mind. Even when you turn off the flames of desire, the boiling water will continue to churn before it simmers down to a tranquil state. It takes a little time. This process can be frustrating to a novice meditator, because he or she lacks confidence and wonders if the settling down of the mind will ever happen. But after just a little bit of patient practice, you will find that you will be able to slip into a meditative state more quickly and easily.

When first starting a meditation practice, I suggest using a timer and committing yourself to *sitting still* – and only committing to that – for twenty minutes. Forget about striving for any results other than just sitting and being still. The results you are looking for will come of their own accord as a result of letting go of thinking, but if you are attached to the achievement of results... well, that is just another clinging thought! Letting go of attachment to outcome reduces a tendency to put pressure on yourself to do it right or to wonder if you are being successful at meditating. If you commit to just sitting and stick to taking such a "time out" on a daily basis, you *will* start meditating – if only because as long as you are just sitting, there is nothing better to do! With enough practice, it will become second nature for you to meditate whenever you make time for it.

> The breath is an excellent object of concentration because it is always there for you – when you are standing in line, riding an elevator, or during other in-between times throughout the day – without it being obvious that you are meditating. While it is useful to also have a formal sitting practice, there is benefit from every possible instant of mindfulness that you can muster. Ayya Khema, the meditation master nun, used to say that every single moment of mindfulness is mentally purifying. The technique is simple: let go of identifying with rapidly changing thoughts and feelings by concentrating on your breath (or other object), while being open to and mindful of whatever arises in the field of consciousness.

My Letting Go Mantra

A mantra is an object that can be used for concentration. In the ancient yogic tradition, a teacher or guru would assign the student a phrase in Sanskrit – the ancient language of India – to repeat as a mantra. When the phrase is repeated over and over, the mind becomes "one-pointed" – concentrated on the mantra to the exclusion of other passing thoughts. The human brain can only focus on one thing at a time. For instance, you can't simultaneously write a poem and do a math problem. Nor can you remember your high school reunion and look forward to your son's college graduation in the same moment. Likewise, when you're focused on a mantra, the static in your mind has no choice but to simmer down because of your attentiveness to one object of attention.

When I taught meditation, I invented a mantra that I shared with my students. I found this phrase particularly useful for clearing the mind and increasing mindfulness throughout the day (which I later discovered made me better at noticing synchronicities). My little mantra consisted of only two words: *Letting Go.*

Try it right now. Just close your eyes and take a full breath, thinking the word *Letting* as you inhale and the word *Go* as you exhale. Repeat. When you reflect on the meaning of these two words, this mantra is reminding you (in English) to do what meditation is all about – the letting go of attachment to thoughts and feelings. You can use my "Letting Go" mantra anywhere and at any time. (I do this one often every day.) It helps instill inner peace and serves as a conscious reminder that letting go is the key to having a clear and open mind. In addition, letting go of "busy mind" creates an opening for intuitive insights to alight like butterflies settling onto a sunflower.

Harvesting Intuitive Insights During Meditation

Traditional meditation is aimed at letting go for the sake of cultivating transcendent consciousness. But, as we have seen, another major benefit is intuitive sensitivity. Considering the value of insights that might arise during a meditation session, it can be useful from a decision-making point of view to interrupt your concentration efforts long enough for the left brain to record valuable insights. Rather than placing all the emphasis on just letting go of thoughts that arise – especially if you are facing a major decision, make a point to note insights that come up during your sitting.

To do this, you will need a pen and paper or a recording device to capture insights as they arise. Once you've recorded an insight, go back to letting go of thinking – about it or anything, for that matter. Just return to focusing on your breath, mantra, or other object of concentration.

Although this approach to meditation is somewhat unconventional, there is creative value in adapting your meditation practice in this way if you are already on the lookout for signs and omens. It is a way that a practice of mindfulness can be used to develop an ability to hear the voice of intuition that has connected you with Creative Power.

Intuitive Intelligence Tilts the Odds in Your Favor

Developing intuitive mindfulness will improve your odds of manifesting anything that you can seriously envision. Every individual is unique; so feel free to customize a way of cultivating intuitive mindfulness that feels natural to you. And then make it a habit!

Great decision-making is the litmus test for intuitive intelligence. The more you exercise intuitive intelligence and learn to trust it, the more reliable your higher instincts will become. On the other hand, the less it is exercised, the less trustworthy your intuition will feel, and the more likely you'll end up letting others make your most important decisions for you. And by not trusting your intuition, you will miss opportunities to develop it.

Intuitive intelligence is a skill that needs to be cultivated, like learning to dance. At first you feel awkward and will occasionally trip over your own feet. But through practice, you'll find a natural sense of rhythm and will be in sync with a power much greater than anything you've ever known. Even though it is not an exact science, cultivating intuitive mindfulness will tilt the odds in your favor and give you an advantage on every playing field in your life.

Improve Intuitive Skill by Taking Risks!

Intuitive skill improves by trial and error. Actively test intuitive hunches by taking little risks. Make a game out of it – like gambling for insights. Follow up your hunches by asking tough questions, interviewing others, and testing your perceptions. Was it truly intuition in action? How well can you differentiate between a gut feeling or a wonderfully imaginative idea and ego-driven wishful thinking? You may be surprised at how many hunches the controlling ego routinely overlooks or discredits!

For instance, if your intuition tells you this is a good time to make an important phone call, you don't have to think twice, you can go with your hunch and just do it. By starting out with small risks, you can discover how good your sense of timing can be. You can learn how to let go of interference and blockage, and gain confidence in your ability to draw on intuitive intelligence when you need it most. Start with small bets, but do start taking risks!

The more you come to trust your intuition by awakening it through mindfulness practices, the more perceptive and aware you will become over time. You will start noticing all kinds of guideposts and signs – including unexpected synchronicities on a regular basis. Your intuitive antenna will start to hum. Synchronicities – which have been happening the whole time – will become apparent more easily and often. Awareness of synchronicity will inform you and improve your decision-making – almost like a guardian angel. You will handle obstacles more easily, make fewer mistakes, and bounce back more quickly from the slips you make. You will maintain a higher awareness of Infinite Intelligence and the creative powers available to you. Achieving goals will happen more easily and your confidence will progressively increase. It's gratifying how much more smoothly life becomes as you develop intuitive mindfulness, but this receptivity is just the first half of realizing intuitive intelligence.

The other half has to do with giving the left brain a way to make sense of intuitive impressions. In the next few chapters, we will explore archetypes, dreams, and divination systems. Each of these can help the left brain make sense of intuitive information received by the right brain and make it possible for our conscious mind to put them to good use.

CHAPTER 7

Invoking Archetypes

Archetypes resemble the beds of rivers: dried up because the water has deserted them, though it may return at any time. An archetype is something like an old watercourse along which the water of life flowed for a time, digging a deep channel for itself. The longer it flowed the deeper the channel, and the more likely it is that sooner or later the water will return. —CARL JUNG[48]

T he last chapter discussed how to develop intuitive mindfulness to enhance intuitive receptivity. In this chapter we investigate one way that intuitive impressions can be interpreted by the conscious mind using psychological structures called archetypes. An archetype is a pattern of thought or image that's collectively inherited, unconscious, and universally available to us via the unconscious. The archetype's role as a psychic structure emanating from our collective unconscious was another of Carl Jung's groundbreaking contributions to psychology. According to Jung, archetypes serve as a kind of psychic blueprint for how humans perceive, interpret, and respond to their experiences.

Archetypes are dynamic patterns that can provide psychological powers we can tap for strength and wisdom. Its pattern may take the form of a familiar character, an image, a story, or even a feeling-state. Often coming via dreams or fantasies, they are first picked up by the holistic and more instinctual right brain, as aspects of the unconscious seeking our attention. The intuitive antenna that connects the right brain with the collective unconscious helps us tune into these archetypal powers, themes, and patterns of behavior. These give form to the images and impressions that are taken in by the right brain, which allows our left brain conscious mind to be able to interpret and make some sense of them.

Jung referenced three kinds of archetypes: the five main aspects of the psyche, anthropomorphic or "personified" archetypes, and what he called "transformational archetypes." The five main archetypes of the human psyche include the *Self* (commonly known as ego); the *Shadow* (the "dark" side of that ego); the *Anima* (the feminine aspects of a man's psyche); the *Animus* (the masculine aspect of a woman's psyche); and the *Persona* (the appearance we present to the world – like a mask, our personality). Personified archetypes are the ones that take a human form such as the Damsel in Distress, the Child, the Martyr and so on. Transformational archetypes are life experiences and processes such as falling in love, growing old, having a religious experience, or losing a friend to betrayal.

One way that archetypes can be considered is as if they are our unconscious companions, on call to protect and inspire us on our path to psychological individuation and personal fulfillment. Since they reside within the collective unconscious mind but operate through us individually, becoming more mindful of archetypes will expand your self-knowledge and help guide your behaviors – including more skillful decision-making.

Even though archetypes may appear as mythological characters, it's important to remember that such projections are but colorful approximations. The cultural trappings that archetypes assume vary, but what Jung discovered was that the fundamental identities of archetypes remain intact throughout time and across cultures. Vividly featured in ancient myths, they are also on display in the popular culture of contemporary film and music. Marilyn Monroe can be thought of as the Siren or Goddess of Love and James Dean or Marlon Brando as the Rebel. The Wise Old Man is clearly embodied by Gandalf in *The Lord of The Rings*, as well as Obi-Wan Kenobi in the *Star Wars* films. As you watch film and television, pay attention to how significant the role of archetypal characters embodies nearly all of storytelling.

The Hero is a prime example of a universal archetype that has prominently appeared throughout human history. (Even at the age of 5, my grandson related to the hero archetype in the form of Spiderman!) The narrative patterns of the archetypal hero in ancient epic stories, religious writings, poems like Homer's Odyssey and the myth of King Arthur, as well as modern storytelling, informed renowned mythologist Joseph Campbell's concept of the Hero's Journey, which he explored in his book, *The Hero with a Thousand Faces*.[49] The Hero's Journey reveals a roadmap of sorts for our personal struggle to individuate, as well as the process of an entire culture developing a collective identity. It is a central archetype for the courageous activity of strategic decision-making. In a sense, it can be said that this book is about manifesting one's inner Hero through bold decisions.

Archetypes in Dreams

One place that archetypes show up is in our dreams. According to Jung, the symbols and images that appear in dreams represent aspects of our process of fully developing the Self. In order to become whole and able to fulfill our life's purpose, we can learn from archetypal symbols that arise into the field of our conscious awareness, including via dreams that we can remember and record. Dream interpretation can be a helpful guide in our development as visionary decision-makers.

Archetypal symbols and themes have appeared in the dreams of people of cultures around the world and throughout history. It is especially important to take note and analyze the occurrence of an archetypal dream – or "big dream," a term that Jung started using after visiting the Elongi tribe of East Africa. He learned that they distinguished between "little dreams" that carry personal meaning and "big dreams" that come from the collective memory and contain symbols that are common to all humans. Big dreams often occur during times of great change or crisis, and contain messages from archetypal figures. For example, the Wise Old Man may show up as a teacher, father, or other authority figure offering guidance and wisdom. The Great Mother could appear as your mother, an old woman, a queen, or goddess. An archetype can manifest in your dreams to provide nurturing support and positive reinforcement, but it could also appear as a dangerous and domineering figure, such as an ogre or dragon.

In modern times, many scientists have revealed that great discoveries came to them in dreams, so never dismiss dreams as a resource for information and inspiration. At the very least, paying attention to them will put you in touch with subtle currents flowing inside your psyche and help you to accelerate the healing of inner conflicts. Dreams can be understood in karmic terms, like the popular movie, *Groundhog Day*, where we keep having versions of the same dream (or life pattern) until we make changes represented somehow in the dream. If we ignore the offered guidance, there are consequences. In this sense, archetypal dream interpretation is a powerful decision-making aid once you learn how to make use of the wisdom that is available.

Jung was a master of dream interpretation, a skill he developed beyond his peers. Freud recognized the significance of dreams, but he viewed dreams primarily as expressing our repressed and disguised (naughty) desires. For Jung, dreams were more than a symptom of such neurotic struggles. Part of his genius was that he was the first to show how dreams, which indeed can reflect the personal unconscious of unresolved conflicts, can also be "big dreams" acting as messengers from the collective unconscious.

Jung felt that our dreams were meant to be understood, shared and lived. For him, the real purpose of dreams was to be a catalyst for change and a guidepost to one's personal evolution. He taught that we should learn and manifest the lessons of our dreams in how we approach our lives. He was clear about this in one of his letters to a friend: "You tell me you have had many dreams lately but have been too busy with your writing to pay attention to them. You have got it the wrong way round. Your writing can wait, but your dreams cannot, because they come unsolicited from within and point urgently to the way you must go."[50] Besides recording his own dreams, Jung taught his five children to keep dream books and to engage in a dialogue with the unconscious through them. He also made visual images of his dreams, now beautifully collected in the recently published book, *The Red Book*.

Nowadays there are numerous books and dictionaries to help with dream interpretation, but symbols that appear in dreams are subjective in that they reflect the dreamer's personal experiences and memories. Because of this highly personal aspect, Jung believed everyone had the power within them to unlock the meaning of their own unique dreams. He even advised activating your intuition before consulting an outside source. In another letter, he described his dream perception process: "Who or what has come alive [in a dream]? ... Who or what has entered my psychic life and created disturbances and wants to be heard? Switch off your noisy consciousness and listen quietly inwards and look at the images that appear before your inner eye, or hearken to the words that the muscles of your speech apparatus are trying to form. Write down what then comes without criticism. And images should be drawn or painted assiduously, no matter whether you can do it well or not Meditate on them afterwards and every day go on developing what is unsatisfactory about them. The important thing is to let the unconscious take the lead."[51]

There is more than one way to keep track of dreams. Jung kept a notebook at his bedside, as many people do. Immediately upon waking, he wrote down what he could remember of his dreams. If Jung could have recorded his dreams using a tape recorder – as I prefer to do – he probably would have embraced the newer technology (because it is so much easier, and you don't have to turn on the light, find the pen, etc.). Once you've recorded your dreams, you can start to interpret what they mean. The key here is to avoid self-censoring or second-guessing your impressions. Let your mind generate free associations based on images you recall from the dream and record them.

Even if you're looking for help with an important decision, don't narrow your dream interpretation to that specific issue – at least not at first. Be open-minded and receptive. Answers and insights may emerge in an order that is different from what you had been seeking. Record them as quickly as you can, without dwelling on what you put down. First impressions are most useful!

Since dreams are not to be taken literally, you may want to consult a dream dictionary to tease out the meaning, reconstructing what you remember of the dream into a narrative story or letter to yourself. By the way, the familiar people and objects that appear in your dream do not represent the same people or objects in your waking reality. Every person who appears in a dream represents *an archetype* that is reflecting back a part of you that is psychologically active. (Explore Jung's methodologies of dream interpretation, in *Dream Analysis: Notes of the Seminar Given in 1928-1930.*)[52]

Invoking an Archetype

Have you experienced how different you can feel by changing the way you dress? An archetype can be compared to a costume you put on to embody the energy of the sage or elder, the sovereign or warrior, the trickster, maiden, eternal child, gods, goddesses, demons, and angels. Many people find personalized projections easier to relate to and through them are more easily able to commune with the mystical and unknowable.

Archetypes are not always anthropomorphic, however; some are templates for situations and experiences such as growing and evolving, an epiphany or flash of enlightenment, loss of innocence, being stuck in an unresolvable conflict, or achieving ecstatic union with Divine Mystery. Dreams can be thought of as synchronistic occurrences in themselves – which are bringing "situational" archetypes to our attention.

Archetypes reside in the collective unconscious, that reservoir of Infinite Intelligence to which we all have access. These power resources are not off in the distance on a foggy mountaintop. When they are called upon, they can immediately come alive within you, in your heart and soul. These are energies that you can recognize and learn to channel, in order to use them to resolve dilemmas or make creative decisions.

When you call up an archetype, you are drawing from a realm of awesome power, so don't get carried away. Like the two wires that run power to an electrical appliance, the ability to safely channel this powerful current requires limiting or throttling it (I use the term "channeling"). It is *a current* that you are invoking to flow through you, rather than an energy that you generate from within yourself. The danger is that people get so caught up running archetypal energy that they forget who they are, start to think they are personally all-powerful and get into trouble.

Starting to think that you *are* a god or goddess is a grandiose delusion. Becoming possessed by an archetype to that extent is usually overwhelming and self-destructive and, in extreme cases, can feed a narcissistic personality disorder and the shadow self. The Goddess or Sovereign gets greedy and becomes the Tyrant. The Warrior becomes the Pillager. The Lover transforms into an Addict. The Magician becomes the evil Sorcerer, and so forth.

We certainly do not want to reenact the folly of young Icarus of Greek myth who, against the advice of his father not to go too high, soared too close to the sun melting his wax-glued wings and crashing into the sea. If you use archetypal power carefully, you can avoid being taken over by it. And once you learn how to channel archetypes, these powerful resources can help you make more effective and timely decisions and produce significant positive changes in your career and life.

The Archetypes that Support Visionary Decision Making

Many archetypes can play a role in decision-making, including the Mentor, the Trickster, and even the Lover (especially when someone is inspired to do what they love). Archetypes that are central to VDM are the Muse, the Sovereign, and the Magician. The Warrior is another crucial archetype that one must activate when it becomes necessary to defend boundaries.

Both the Hunter and the Gatherer are dynamic and active archetypes that are also relevant to Visionary Decision Making. To the Greeks and Romans, Ceres was the goddess of the harvest, the ultimate gatherer, and Artemis (or Diana) was the goddess of the hunt. The Hunter is more outgoing and the Gatherer more receiving, but they are two sides of the same harvesting coin. They both play an active and important role in the VDM process.

The Hunter archetype helps you connect with the energy of vigilance, exploration, and the perseverance of focused attention. It helps you set your sights on what you want the most. All forms of vigilance are associated with the Hunter because she (or he) is sensitively attuned to noticing clues and signals. In the VDM process, this especially includes being on the lookout for signals and synchronicities.

Invoking the Gatherer results in a greater receptivity to the bounty of Infinite Intelligence, which can manifest in the form of good ideas, inspirations, and intuitive sensations. It is a receptive dynamic, an active and deliberate openness. You are opening to the bounty of the universe – specifically what will nourish you and your group or tribe. The Hunter and Gatherer archetypes reinforce one another toward the attainment of their overarching objective, which is the realization of abundance for personal and collective well-being.

To understand the dynamic of Hunter and Gatherer energies, I return to my cousin Lennie who embodies them both. Even though he never kills for sport, Lennie often wins the annual award for most successful deer hunter in the county; he is also an exceptional fisherman and gardener. Operating from the solar-assisted house he built for himself in the woods, Lennie has carved out a highly self-sufficient life through a combination of hunting and gathering, of initiated action and receptivity to opportunity.

The Hunter and Gatherer archetypes correspond to the Taoist principles of yin and yang – two complementary energies that mix in physical reality, but also in thought, emotion, and consciousness. Yang is what we typically regard as left-brained functions. Exploration and analysis are the yang elements of the Hunter archetype. The active probing and scanning function of the intuitive antenna is a yang function – as in probing the creative aspect of Infinite Intelligence, collecting information, and analyzing what it means. Yin, on the other hand, is open and receptive. Yin reflects what we sometimes refer to as right brain energy. Yin creates the inner conditions that attract and pick up on insights. The Law of Attraction, which we looked at earlier, is about leveraging one's receptive yin power.

The Muse archetype is a psychological agent of fascination that can help us channel the power of attraction and magnetize a creative direction. In Greek mythology, the Muses were minor goddesses who personified knowledge and inspiration. Invoking the Muses stimulates intuition and creativity, but writers, artists and musicians aren't the only ones who can benefit from the Muse's help. Channeling her can help anyone tap into Infinite Intelligence to activate the expression of his or her talents.

Visionary Decision Making leverages the four foundational archetypes highlighted in the book *King, Warrior, Magician, Lover.*[53] Each of these plays a central role in the VDM process.

The archetype of the Lover increases passion for your highest vocational or personal priority, facilitating a fulfilling outcome for any inspiration, dream, or aspiration. The Lover archetype inspired the meme, "Do what you love and the money will follow." Focused love becomes passion, which affixes your attention and energy to your goal. Devotion – whether to a cause or creative invention or path in life – is the booster rocket that gets you into orbit where you can navigate life almost effortlessly through one adjustment at a time. The shadow side of the Lover archetype is the addict.

Invoking the Magician energizes creativity and inventiveness. The Magician archetype enhances your ability to see new combinations and connections, and it helps you come up with innovative new solutions. The Magician views all problems as learning adventures, sees through appearances, and gets right to the heart of things. This archetype ultimately creates a more abundant playing field. In my experience, the Magician energy supported me in the invention of multimedia versions of divination systems to aid intuitive decision-making. It served me so well that I made a giant replica of The Magus tarot card, which I keep in my office to remind me of my connection to it. The shadow side of the Magician is black magic – the use of creative power to manipulate or cast a spell in order to control, take advantage, or even harm others.

Invoking the Warrior archetype is necessarily about being aggressive, although assertiveness may be called for under certain circumstances. The Warrior's primary job, however, is to *defend the boundaries* as well as to protect the tender unfolding of new directions and what we value most (including children, as in the "mama grizzly bear" syndrome). Internally, the Warrior might guard against distractions and temptations that diminish the ability to pay attention to what's truly important to us. Addictive temptations or "shiny objects" that distract our attention are deliberately ignored until they fade out of our mind. The shadow side of the Warrior archetype is a violent or abusive personality.

The Sovereign (King or Queen or CEO) makes decisions and sees that they are carried out for the welfare of the realm – the common good of a community or enterprise. The realm may be a corporate body with employees and customers, or it may be an extended family. The Sovereign's role is to exercise authority and allocate resources to take care of his or her people – not to be served by them (although that reciprocally happens). This executive function is at the very center of Visionary Decision Making. The shadow side of the Sovereign is a self-serving tyrant or power-monger.

The mature Sovereign is present in the histories and mythology of the world's religions. The Buddha was a prince and heir to a kingdom, which he abdicated to dedicate himself to solving the problem of human suffering (leaving a beautiful wife and a harem behind). According to biblical myth, King Solomon was invited by God to choose any power he wanted. He could have become an embodiment of the Magician, Warrior, Lover (but, according to the Bible, he already had 700 wives and 300 concubines), or some other archetype with magical powers. Instead, he chose the Wise Ruler (or "Elder"), and became renowned for his decision-making.

Consciously connecting with the Sovereign archetype helped me better run my company – a small "kingdom" that included thirty employees and millions of subscribed members. I made a conscious effort daily to identify with the Sovereign and the Magician archetypes. Every morning I would recite an invocation similar to this: "Today I call upon the Powers that be to help me do a good job taking care of my people." Among others, I was invoking the Sovereign archetype to support, direct, and empower my job of taking care of business and people throughout the coming busy day.

Prayer as Invocation

Praying to an all-knowing, all-powerful God is the most common form of invoking an archetype in the West. If prayer was something you were taught as a child, you were being taught to invoke an archetype. You can envision infinite power as a single unitary deity – e.g., God – or you can see it in terms of an impersonal universal law like the Buddhists do. It may be a matter of belief for you, but in terms of your creativity and decision-making process, it doesn't matter either way. You can petition an almighty King who grants favors, a forgiving Father, Mother Earth, a font of wisdom who knows everything, or simply Nature itself. In the Catholic church's system of archetypes, there are different saints to pray to: St. Anthony, who knows how to find things that are lost; St. Jude, who helps you find your way when *you* are lost; and St. Lawrence, the patron saint of cooking (who was designated so by the Church because he had been martyred by himself being roasted on a spit).

The shortcoming of the prayer technique most of us were taught as children is that it takes the form of petition – a more or less passive plea for rescue. It is good to be humble, but petitioning prayer can blur the line between humility and low self-esteem.

There are other forms of prayer, however, that engage and co-create with Creative Power (an impersonal way to conceive of God), which is psychologically different than begging a Creator to do something for you. In this more empowering form of prayer, you are channeling archetypal energies to help you, not do for you. You invoke divine energy to bolster your confidence – your faith in yourself – to rise to an occasion, for blessings upon your endeavors, and to inspire you to do your best.

Throughout history, significant rites like births, weddings, and funerals always began with an invocative prayer. In the ancient world, aid was requested from the god or goddess whose help was considered most relevant and beneficial. Thus, *The Iliad*, the Greek epic composed three thousand years ago, begins, "Sing, O goddess, of the anger of Achilles..." The poet is calling upon the goddess of poetry to aid in the recitation of the poem, but psychologically speaking, he is asking the goddess to sing *through* him. The poet essentially views himself as a channel for the divine archetype of poetry. In ancient times, events like wars, sporting events, marriages and banquets all began with an invocative prayer to a god or goddess, and called forth an infusion of empowering archetypal energies.

Like the word "God," prayer is a word that can be compelling or off-putting depending on your orientation to traditional religion. As noted, there is a major difference between the praying we were probably taught and invocative prayer that is part of the Visionary Decision Making approach. The primary function of invocative prayer is invoking creative and supportive archetypes that you invite to flow through you. It is an expression of your intention and a feeling gratitude-in-advance as you welcome good results that you and the creative powers are co-creating.

Invocative prayer is the conscious summoning of archetypal energies. Unlike traditional religious prayers, invocative prayer is not a matter of asking for something from the higher power. And it is not bargaining. ("I'll be good if you help me one more time.") It's simply calling upon the kind of energy needed for a specific purpose or a decision. Courage, wisdom, creativity, resilience, and intuition are various energies that may be invoked for the purpose of making visionary decisions.

When you go through major transitions, it is helpful to practice an invocative prayer ritual on a daily basis – not so different from the habit of morning and evening prayers. Returning to a ritual that frames every day will help you to stay more connected to Infinite Intelligence during the day and through dreams at night. After you wake up in the morning, you welcome a greater awareness of synchronicities throughout the coming day. Depending upon what you intend to create or build or preserve that day, you also summon and activate other powers. At night, your affirmative prayer calls forth the healing and enlightening power of dreams.

One invocation to go through your day more open to insights is the Synchronicity Prayer: "May I notice synchronicities that arise during this day and pay attention to them. If I don't understand their meaning, I trust that will be revealed in due course. In the meantime, I am grateful to notice the signals."

No matter how you word your prayers (I recommend composing them in your own words in a file that you can edit on a computer, tablet, or smartphone), it helps to create a routine like this:

- *Sit and breathe* with your back fairly straight. If you need to lean against a cushion, wall, or back of a chair, that is fine. The mind tends to be sharper when we sit or stand in a balanced position rather than slumping or reclining. Take three deep breaths to let go of tension in your body. If I am not going to disturb anybody by doing so, I find it satisfying to make an audible "ah" or "om" sound with each exhale.

• *Read* your invocation – preferably out loud to yourself – taking the time to understand each word as you recite it.

• *Breathe slowly,* as you let yourself project into it, and feel the archetypal power of state of mind that you are invoking.

• *Feel the bliss* of being mentally magnetic through the clarity of your intention – and emotionally magnetic through the infectious power of your desire. Sit still and stay in the emotionally magnetic state for as long as you can.

• *Make a resolution* to notice this attraction consciousness sticking with you throughout your day.

Here are a few suggestions for how invocative prayers might be phrased (feel free to borrow from these examples and customize your own as well):

Sample Morning Invocations

May I notice all the magical moments today, as life unfolds synchronistically and perfectly, according to Destiny's plan.

As I face an important decision, I invoke the power of Courage, so that my choices will not be distracted by fear.

May Wisdom guide my decisions today; may the wisest choices become clear to me.

I am creating the mental and emotional space to tune in my intuitive sensitivity in order to make the best choices today. I am guided to the best paths of action.

Sample Evening Invocations

May the Dreamer bestow upon me symbolic dreams that I will remember and record, which will shed light upon my life and true self.

Let my dreams flow tonight, and may their symbolic meaning bring me a greater awareness of who I am, my best direction going forward, and the most enlightened choices I can make.

The Creative Manifestation Treatment

This powerful invocative prayer designed to help you manifest a dream or goal draws on the supreme archetype of Creative Power in the form of a guided meditation, based on the work of Ernest Holmes, founder of the Church of Religious Science. I revised Holmes' treatment, adding a couple of powerful steps. Anyone of any religion can use my *Creative Manifestation Treatment* [54] to attract and attain whatever his or her heart's desires.

Find a comfortable but alert sitting position. Take a few deep breaths, making an "ah" or "om" sound with each exhale. When you are relaxed but alert and ready, read aloud a Creative Manifestation Treatment like this one:

> • *Step 1: Recognition.* I acknowledge Creative Power, the universal magnetic energy that unites and makes things whole. Divine power expresses itself as love, wisdom, and courage. It is reflected in the vastness of space, the sun around which Earth revolves, the beauty of nature, the joy of love and miracles. This unlimited resource operates according to the law of cause-and-effect that begins with attraction. First the image, then the declaration, and then manifestation. There is no limit to Creative Power.

> • *Step 2: Identification.* I identify with Creative Power, which not only surrounds me but flows through me. My breathing reminds me of my interconnectedness with all of nature, and I can feel the connection any time I close my eyes. Divine love and wisdom surround me, and go before me, making my way easy and successful. I AM capable of facilitating any results I visualize and feel. I don't need to know what exact form the results will take, but solutions appear quickly and easily. I deserve what is good for me.

> • *Step 3: Declaration.* I declare that I am *now* enjoying the realization of [my desire]. This feels [liberating, joyous and pleasurable, etc.].

• *Step 4: Thanksgiving.* I give thanks for the fulfillment of [my desire], the joyful anticipation of which I am feeling already. I feel strong on my path. I AM confident, full of faith, and my heart is filled with gratitude.

• *Step 5: Release.* I let go of tendencies to worry or interfere by trying to make results take shape in any particular way. I know that the law of cause-and-effect is operating on this treatment right now, even if my senses have no proof of it as yet. I am attracting [my desire], and [my desire] is attracting me. The manifestation of this, or something better, is in process. Creative Power is synchronistically producing the right results for me in a way and according to a schedule that is perfect. I am letting go of trying to control things and surrender to the good that is my destiny. My "faith" is my intuitive sense of the manifesting process that is happening behind the scenes right now.

• *Step 6: Emotional magnetization.* I am letting myself *feel* the presence of what I have declared, which is in the process of manifesting. As I let this feeling radiate throughout my entire being, I become magnetic.

• *Step 7: Action steps.* I make the right moves at the right time, starting with better decision-making that taps my intuition, intellect, and receptivity to good advice. I make and follow up on commitments to myself. In the two-steps-forward, one-step-back dance of life, I am taking good steps in a timely manner. As long as I am in connection with Creative Power, I know I can't go wrong!

After you are finished reading the Creative Manifestation Treatment, stay in place and breathe. Feel the bliss of being spiritually magnetic, via the clarity and power of your now expressed intention, and emotionally magnetic, through the infectious power of the feeling you get when you project your imagination into your vision. Make a resolution to take your attractive attitude with you throughout your day.

If this Creative Manifestation Treatment resonates with you, find it online at divination.com/resources/manifestation/ and edit it to develop a personalized guided meditation script. Once you have the wording formulated in a way that feels powerful when you speak it aloud, print it out, and read it every morning before you start your daily routines. The use of the Creative Manifestation Treatment draws on creative powers to help you stay focused on the fulfillment of your highest priorities, empowered by an optimistic and creative attitude.

Archetypes provide a powerful source of inspiration, guidance, and power for the visionary decision-maker. Interpreting their appearance in dreams and learning to deliberately invoke archetypes adds power and momentum to your Hero's Journey.

CHAPTER 8

Divination and the Book of Changes

The oracle of Apollo at Delphi was closed in Christian times. It had fallen into misuse and had lost its numinous power. People were asking ego questions - how to have more - rather than how to go beyond desire to destiny. There was no room left for miraculous wisdom, and so it passed away without protest when the emperor discontinued it. Oracular wisdom may be demolished in us once ego ambition crushes the spirit of a transcendent intent.

—DAVID RICHO, *The Power of Coincidence: How Life Shows Us What We Need to Know*[55]

Perceiving meaningful coincidences is a function of intuitive sensitivity. When we maintain an awareness of what's most important to us, synchronistic events seem to occur more frequently. But we can't just order up signs and omens at the precise time we may need their guidance most. Fortunately, however, there are special tools that can actually *generate* meaningful coincidences for you and help the conscious mind decipher the meaning in them. These tools are the classical divination systems.

In this chapter, we explore the phenomenon of divination using the I Ching, one of the oldest and most revered divination systems. The I Ching supports intuitive decision-making by operating on its set of 64 archetypes with the help of a synchronistic pattern that is created by the tossing of coins at the same time as we are thinking about something of importance.

Divination systems are not dark arts or fortune-telling gimmicks, as skeptics are inclined to assume. Divination has gotten a bad rap because of the erroneous assumption that its purpose has been to predict the future, which has led to its appropriation by – and association with – hucksters, gypsies, and fortune-tellers. As a result, Western religions eventually got around to condemning divination – in spite of the fact that there are several Biblical verses where Jahweh is favorable toward divination and sometimes mandates its use. (You can view all the verses at Divination.com.)[56]

The exact composition of the Urim and Thummim is not known, but scholars believe they were sacred dice, perhaps made of precious gems. They were stored in a pouch that was kept behind the high priest's "breastplate of judgment," which he wore whenever he was seeking divine guidance with regard to legal judgments or strategic decisions of state. There is no way to confirm the exact details of how the Urim and Thummim were cast or read. However it worked, the Bible makes it clear that divination was sacred and that God was behind the answers it produced.

An earlier book, *Divination: Sacred Tools for Reading the Mind of God,* lists all the biblical verses regarding divination, positive and negative.[57] In my research for that book, I discovered there are more passages that look favorably upon divination than those that condemn diviners and astrologers. Since there are occasions where Jahweh actually chooses to provide answers or direction via the Urim and Thummim, it is interesting how the fundamentalist dogma keepers of the Church have condemned divination so vehemently.

In the first century, as he was defining what later became Christian dogma when bible and church were set up in the 4th century, Paul described an ability to decipher God's plan as the "gift of prophecy" – a form of channeling available only to faithful believers. Nowadays, thanks to universal access to the classical systems of divination, anyone who approaches the effort with sincerity can connect directly with Infinite Intelligence.

Historically, the Israelites of the Bible, as well as their Christian and Muslim monotheistic offshoots, viewed God as the agent of destiny, and used divination techniques to stay in tune with divine will. In addition to sacrifices and other rituals, at least two divinatory practices are mentioned in positive terms in the Bible. The primary one appears in a number of Old Testament stories where Jahweh tells the Israelites to perform a decision-making ritual using the sacred runes of the High Priest, called the "Urim and Thummim."

Since I had been a software executive, after the idea of divination software came to me, colleagues would ask, "Do you really believe in this stuff?" I knew where they were coming from, which was a culturally biased viewpoint influenced by fundamentalist interpretations of sin, fear of the devil archetype, and so on. I would carefully try to explain to them that belief is not required – because the real purpose of divination is only to activate and support the intuitive sense. It works well for this, but it is not a crystal ball.

Activating intuition for problems that logic can't handle is a valid reason to use the I Ching or any other authentic divination system. Anyone with a sincere interest and an open mind can use a divination system that offers a balanced set of archetypes (like the I Ching or Tarot) to support creativity and decision-making – without having to believe in anything. All it takes is an open mind that is free from fear and a willingness to experiment. No worries... either it stimulates your intuition or it doesn't... simple as that!

Because Tarot – another authentic divination system – offers so many more possible configurations, interpreting the intersecting archetypes that turn up requires some training. The greater complexity of astrology means that delivering an astrological reading requires even more instruction. Unlike Tarot or astrology, however, the I Ching is simple enough that, with the help of a good interpretive text, individuals can quickly learn to consult it for themselves.

The *Visionary I Ching* app is a great tool if you would like a compact and easy-to-use way to cast an authentic I Ching reading (available in iTunes and Android App stores).

Through his friendship with Richard Wilhelm (the most famous translator of the *I Ching* from the Chinese), Carl Jung became intimately familiar with this Taoist divination system. He used and studied the I Ching for decades. In his forward to Wilhelm's translation published in 1951, Jung explained that the I Ching works on a synchronicity principle that operates on the set of sixty-four archetypes.[58] He saw the I Ching as a way for individuals to leverage the archetypal dynamics of the collective unconscious.

How the I Ching Works

According to legend, King Wen of Zhou formulated the I Ching 3,000 years ago. Nowadays most people consult the I Ching by tossing three coins six times (sorting yarrow stalks was the older method) and recording the way they land in a 6-line pattern called a "hexagram." Based on the pattern that the user casts, the I Ching points to one of the 64 archetypes, each of which has multiple possible permutations, or "changing lines." Jung wrote that the I Ching interprets an "inner unconscious knowledge that corresponds to the state of consciousness at the moment."[59]

Jung saw the I Ching as a reliable way to gain psychological and spiritual insights into changing conditions – not by taking a problem apart and analyzing its components, but by viewing a situation in the context of a seamless whole. "There is no need," Jung wrote, "of any criteria which imposes conditions and restricts the wholeness of the natural process. In the I Ching, the coins fall as happens to suit them."[60]

When you write down your situation, problem, or dilemma and then focus your mind on it, you enter a state of receptivity to whatever pattern the casting of the coins reveals. As Jungian psychotherapist David Richo writes, "Oracular, ego-transcending wisdom of the archetypal Self emerges from deep in the psyche. The Delphic priestess has always been sitting here inside us, but we may never have traveled far enough within ourselves to consult her."[61]

By tossing the coins for a pattern that the conscious mind can't control, you inject a seemingly random element. But since you are the one who is tossing the coins – in a focused, expectant state – the ritual takes on a personal aspect. The way the coins land is coincident with whatever you are concentrating on. By casting the coins, you are creating a coincidence that can be interpreted and plumbed for its meaning. Since all the archetypes reside within the unconscious, the casting of the coins is just calling out one aspect of our humanity for your particular attention.

Given the intuitive stimulation that comes of this synchronistic experience, a new idea, thought, or solution to your issue or dilemma is able to pop into your conscious mind. As the Synchronicity Principle explains, events suffused with connective portent may have no apparent causal relationship, but they are not just random. An intersection of events that triggers a sense of inner knowing is meaningful, and the two entities coming together stimulate yet a new reality – a new idea or sense of direction – within the conscious mind. (An analogy would be how two people who come together intimately form a third entity of the relationship.) By the ritualistic casting of coins around a focus, you are deliberately producing a meaningful coincidence, making the I Ching a method of "applied synchronicity" that can stimulate your intuition around a dilemma or matter of concern.

Activating the intuition is the true purpose of divination, which can provide great support for creative thinking and timing. Beyond such practical usage, the I Ching is a philosophically elegant representation of a sophisticated, holistic point of view that credits a cosmic order that is beyond human understanding.

The Creative and the Receptive

Taoist sages compiled the I Ching to gain better access to Infinite Intelligence through a system and ritual that produces a meaningful coincidence. They perceived that the divine resource we are calling Infinite Intelligence generously provided for human creativity, nurturance, and balance between yin and yang energies. The first hexagram of the I Ching – entitled "Heaven" or "Creative Power" – is the one hexagram where all six lines are yang, with no yin lines at all. Yang is that outgoing "make-it-happen" quality of energy. If you receive the first hexagram in a reading, the message would be about outwardly expressing your creativity.

The second hexagram, entitled "Earth" or "The Receptive," is the one that consists of all yin lines. The Receptive was considered equally as important as the take-initiative energy of Creative Power. In its balanced structure, the I Ching system shows how the Taoist originators of yin and yang equally valued the feminine, "attract and let-it-happen," side of the manifestation. The Receptive represents the power of coming into form and relationship, the power of containing or holding energy and of supportive nourishment.

In the Taoist view of the universe, humanity is a bridge between Heaven and Earth – between inspiration and insemination on the one side and reception or fertility on the other. This dance between the yang and the yin – the outgoing, creative yang force and the receptive, supportive yin – is central to the VDM approach. Like an artist or a juggler, the human being mediates between heaven and earth. The executive skill of creative decision-making is a wonderful example of this balancing act, and this exercise of leadership and power largely determines whether greater harmony or greater chaos prevails in human affairs.

As noted in so many ways, the Visionary Decision Making process involves the interaction of the creative and the receptive. Receptivity to dreams and synchronicities for inspiration and guidance stimulates creative thinking and movement. If our intuitive sense is unblocked and sensitively tuned to receive signals of meaning, it is acting as the mature feminine principle, which is not only receptive but also discriminating.

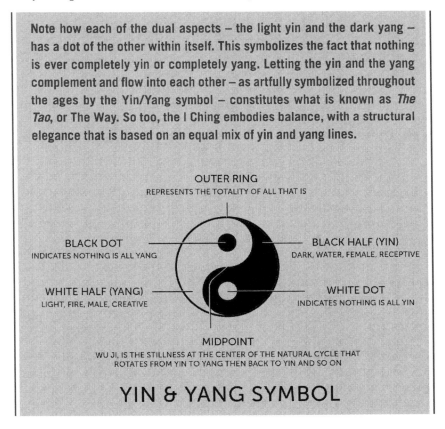

Note how each of the dual aspects – the light yin and the dark yang – has a dot of the other within itself. This symbolizes the fact that nothing is ever completely yin or completely yang. Letting the yin and the yang complement and flow into each other – as artfully symbolized throughout the ages by the Yin/Yang symbol – constitutes what is known as *The Tao*, or The Way. So too, the I Ching embodies balance, with a structural elegance that is based on an equal mix of yin and yang lines.

OUTER RING
REPRESENTS THE TOTALITY OF ALL THAT IS

BLACK DOT
INDICATES NOTHING IS ALL YANG

BLACK HALF (YIN)
DARK, WATER, FEMALE, RECEPTIVE

WHITE HALF (YANG)
LIGHT, FIRE, MALE, CREATIVE

WHITE DOT
INDICATES NOTHING IS ALL YIN

MIDPOINT
WU JI, IS THE STILLNESS AT THE CENTER OF THE NATURAL CYCLE THAT
ROTATES FROM YIN TO YANG THEN BACK TO YIN AND SO ON

YIN & YANG SYMBOL

Our hyper-yang patriarchal culture – so biased in favor of action over contemplation, honors Creative Power and sometimes gives short shrift to Receptivity, which is equally important. Taoist philosophy, as expressed in the *Tao Te Ching* and the *I Ching*, is more balanced because it actually predates the egocentric attitude and cultural biases of patriarchy. It is philosophically sophisticated but also in alignment with Nature.

How to Approach the I Ching

The frame of mind with which you approach the I Ching is a crucial factor in its effectiveness. Sometimes people turn to the I Ching when they feel anxiety, doubt, and frustration. If you are feeling confused or emotionally upset by changes in your life, it's easy to be blinded by fear. Unfortunately, fear thoughts easily dominate consciousness and block intuition when you need it most. When your hands are involved in the act of casting the coins, make sure your mind and heart are focused on your issue of highest concern. And be receptive to the truth, no matter what it may be.

Create a ritual that begins with centering yourself. This sets the tone for a fruitful I Ching experience. Enter a meditative mindset (as discussed in Chapter 7) that supports your sincere desire for truth and wisdom. Perform whatever centering technique or ritual works best for you prior to any I Ching consultation. Do your best to enter a state of focused relaxation.

It's also vital to be clear about what you hope to learn or achieve. Possible goals could be making an important decision or reducing stress around changes in your life that are currently beyond your understanding. These are not the goals of the ego, which always wants to make things happen. A centering practice is an intentional process that will help move your ego out of the way so your mind can be receptive to deep guidance. This is valuable in and of itself.

For some people, taking a soothing bath with candles is a good way to calm down and relax before you begin. After you relax, consciously let go of any attachment to receiving a specific answer or outcome. Commit yourself to caring only about truth. By giving the ego a "vacation" from its usual preoccupations, you increase receptivity to archetypes that can inform your conscious mind and support your decisions and actions.

Some people prefer a more elaborate ritual at a certain time of day, special garments, an amulet, or even some form of chanting. You don't need to go that far, but it can be a good idea to set aside a special space. This doesn't need to be an indoor fountain with palm ferns and Buddha statues, but if that feels right and you have the resources, inspiring art can be supportive. An inspirational photo – perhaps of an ancient temple, natural landscape, or divine image – is a portable device that you can take with you to support serenity. Simply lighting a candle, burning incense, or taking a few deep breaths with your eyes closed can facilitate focused relaxation. Choose what feels the most comfortable for you. The information you receive from a reading comes from within you, not from the external environment. Once you've entered into the proper frame of mind, you can begin consulting the I Ching.

Before you cast a reading, take a few moments to affirm your allegiance to what is real and true. Confidently adopt the attitude that everything will work out the way it is supposed to – for some reason or another. This will be the case whether or not you understand the reason now. Only consult the I Ching when you feel balanced and clear enough to listen to the wisdom it provides and to tap into your intuition.

Formulating Your Query

Approach an I Ching reading with the kind of question or issue you might present to a wise counselor or mentor. No matter how good the advice you receive, you will be the author of your own decisions. The way things turn out is still up to you. In my case the advice I received from an I Ching reading inspired me to create a multimedia version of the I Ching itself. The I Ching acted as a muse, but I was responsible for the decision. Even though I had never before considered the idea of designing a software program – or starting my own business, for that matter – inspiration coupled with intuition led me to venture forth and invent something that seemed worthy of my time and energy, even if that meant taking what felt like huge risks. I had consulted the I Ching regarding my life's mission at a time when I needed extra motivation to make a bold leap of faith.

It's important to ask the appropriate kind of question to get the information you need and can trust. You wouldn't ask an electrician how to change the transmission fluid in your car? You wouldn't ask a mechanic for stock tips. Likewise, divination systems like the I Ching are designed for certain kinds of questions. The process works best if you are looking for insight, wise advice, or a sense of which way the wind is blowing with regard to changes happening in your life. The I Ching is not designed to deliver data, yes/no answers, or predictions (although a reading often can present trends or probabilities).

The wording of your query is important because it influences your mental state as you perform the ritual. Ask for guidance in the form of, "What is the best approach to take in relation to this situation?" It is not necessary to formulate your issue of concern in the form of a question. You can hold a specific subject in mind at the beginning of the divination process, or just write down one or more keywords to represent the situation, person, or decision that is on your mind. The extra clarity of writing down the subject of focus will produce a clearer reading.

After you have had a chance to glean the primary gems of insight from a reading – thoughts that stimulate new ideas and a broader perspective – you will be able to make a better decision. And you will have taken a humble step toward a future that is in alignment with who you are meant to be – that is, your destiny.

There are two classes of divination queries: the big picture and the snapshot. Big picture questions work well when you are not in a specific crisis, but are interested in personality traits or trends in your life. My vocationally-oriented query mentioned above is an example; another might center on compatibility with a person with whom you are having strong feelings. Beware of overly broad questions such as, "What is the meaning of life?" Although it is philosophical and can be used to inspire meditations, the I Ching was not designed to explain too much.

A snapshot type of query works best when you need to make a decision for a specific dilemma, need a new approach, or just a bit of good advice in the moment. When dealing with an immediate problem, it is skillful to ask the I Ching about the attitude, method, or approach to take, rather than for details about what is going to happen. Avoid asking for data like, "Where will I get a job?" or "Who is the partner of my dreams?" Notice the difference when these issues are rephrased: "What is the best course of action for finding a satisfying job?" and "What should I look for in a suitable partner?" If you present appropriate kinds of queries, you are likely to have a beneficial and satisfying reading.

As much as humans fantasize about being able to foretell the future, divination systems don't really work for queries looking for predictions. What they can do, however, is provide insights that give you a better sense of direction, along with pointed advice based on archetypal patterns and timeless wisdom.

Important areas of life present problems that are beyond the ability of logic to resolve, which is where divination can be most helpful. Questions about relationships, timing, and dynamic negotiations fall in this category. Career and work-related questions are popular topics for I Ching consultations. For instance, people who are wondering what is next after transitioning from a job might be looking for ways to improve their career or seeking wisdom about their true calling. Such questions focus on the individual's connection to the outside world, passion, purpose, or vocation.

Self-improvement and introspection are also legitimate reasons to cast a reading. Such readings reflect on individuals' connection with themselves, their goals and dreams and their destiny. Sometimes people naively ask an oracle about how other people feel or will act. This is a common example of an inappropriate query. Even when you would like to inquire for or about someone else, the oracle can only respond to your energy and your issues – such as fear of confrontation, insecurity, or lack of trust – instead of being able to reflect anything about another person. Remember, you are the one tossing the coins and generating the hexagram that synchronistically turns up!

Perhaps you wish to inquire about another's intentions because you're feeling jealous, afraid, hopeful, or shy? Or maybe you just want to help them. In any case, the I Ching will only reflect what is going on for or inside of *you*. You can find meaning in a reading by examining your own feelings. If a friend or loved one is asking you to do a reading *for* them, point them to the instructions on Divination.com or some other resource that shows how to easily consult the I Ching for themselves.

Remember that the goal of a reading is not to predict the future. Your destiny is yours to create through decisions and actions. The primary purpose of a divination reading is to help you understand situations better in order to make more skillful decisions with better timing. Sometimes, if all you get is one creative new thought, the I Ching has done its job!

The Real Meaning Lies Between the Lines

The text of an I Ching reading is not designed to give a literal answer to any question. No matter which version of the I Ching you use, the system depends upon intuition to read between the lines (with your query in mind). Rather than being a limitation of the I Ching, this is its real purpose. This is how it activates the intuition using archetypes that represent powers within you. The I Ching stimulates and empowers creative decision-making from the inside out.

Although the I Ching sometimes does provide rather specific advice, a reading more often points to a new direction or expanded perspective for you to consider and contemplate. Sometimes all a first reading does is stimulate a new idea that helps you to better sharpen your query, which can then lead to a more refined experience of a subsequent reading. The idea is not to control anything but to gently nudge intuitive intelligence's ability to "think outside the box," giving rise to new ideas and inspirations.

Often what first pops into your head captures the core message or central truth. However, if the meaning of a reading isn't immediately clear, take a break and come back to make another effort to read between the lines, still without jumping to conclusions. Sometimes an oracle's response is simply about another issue on your mind that's more important than the question you posed.

One I Ching user I know described the perplexing results of a reading he received when he asked about his failing marriage. When the meaning of the hexagrams escaped him, he sought deeper levels of meaning. Every succeeding layer of depth only seemed more confusing. Later, looking back on the results, he found that the titles of the hexagrams he had gotten had provided an answer to his question – one he had refused to hear because of his attachment to receiving a certain answer in a certain way. Only with time and reflection was he able to see the true meaning of the hexagrams he received.

It is helpful to take notes when consulting the I Ching, so have a pen and paper at hand or your electronic device of choice. (The *Visionary I Ching* app conveniently allows you to cast a hexagram using a smartphone or tablet, read about your hexagram, and save it for later review.) Saving your readings in a journal of some kind lets you evaluate and compare them in the future. Take note of your full *experience* – including the details of your divination ritual and approach, your *interpretation* (a sentence or two that summarizes what the I Ching is reflecting), and the *result* (the after-effect of the decision you made following your reading). Over time, an I Ching journal will give you a broader perspective on the patterns in your life. The overview will help you to get clear about situations that routinely bring up certain hexagrams, reflect on how your readings have impacted your decision-making, and improve your ability to use the I Ching itself.

As you become more experienced with the I Ching, you'll find the future hexagram feature to be useful. The future hexagram is derived when whatever "changing lines" (in the coins method, this is when you get three of a kind) you may have cast are flipped from yang to yin, or vice versa, producing a new hexagram (the simple procedure of deriving the future hexagram is fully described at Divination.com). While the I Ching provides insight and advice based on timeless wisdom, the future hexagram offers a glimpse of how the present situation will evolve if you follow the counsel of your reading. In this way, the I Ching also supports predictive intelligence. Some readings do not include any changing lines at all, which indicates that the situation you inquired about is relatively stable for the time being.

It is not always easy to discern the quiet voice of intuition – or to give it credit – but we need intuitive intelligence in order to make the best decisions. Sometimes we need to go back to the well more than once to get the clarity we need. But getting in touch with intuition in order to achieve clarity of purpose is central to the achievement of success and happiness. The skillful use of an authentic divination system like the I Ching can help you avoid major missteps. I encourage everyone who is willing to give it a try to approach divination sincerely with an open mind, heart, and soul.

How the I Ching Encouraged Me to Become an Entrepreneur

In my last regular job, I was VP of Marketing for a high-tech software company. I worked long hours, but I was paid well and had a good livelihood, supporting a lively social life and a beautiful home.

I was a single father raising an intelligent, beautiful son, and I was in a loving relationship. All in all, it was a good place to be, and as far as jobs went, I was relatively fortunate. The only thing missing was *meaning* – a sense of personal mission or compelling purpose.

Even though I had carved out a career in a growing industry, I had not been drawn to high-tech as much as I was to my early visions of the potential of multimedia. Approaching the age of 40, I was at a crossroads with no clear sense of direction. I could see that many of my peers were also zooming through busy lives on auto-pilot, making a good income, but without the passion, excitement, and drive that comes from an inspired vision and an aroused heart.

To make matters worse, after notable success marketing its first product, my company's R&D department developed additional products that were doomed from the start. As the one in charge of marketing and sales, which had become lackluster in an effort to sell products that the market didn't really want, I became the corporate scapegoat for the flagging sales revenues. I found myself suffering "slings and arrows" of office politics largely instigated by the CEO, who was the chief engineer as well as founder of the company and who would never admit to poor design decisions. I was at a loss as to how to respond to the backbiting and passive-aggressive hostilities coming at me from all sides. I was losing respect for the CEO and felt pessimistic about the company's culture – or product line – ever improving.

Because of all the stress, I started lugging my heavy *I Ching* book into the office for emergency use to keep my head about me – a support I had never resorted to at work in the twenty previous years of using the I Ching. Although it was a hassle, it did provide some moral support and guidance that I badly needed to stay balanced in the turbulent and confusing situation at the office. As was my habit, I would meditate for a few minutes to let go of attachment to any particular outcome before I turned to the I Ching for wise counsel.

The message I received from multiple I Ching readings at this time was to make a break and move on. Now, at that time, Portland, Oregon, had few software marketing positions, and I had no opportunities lined up. Leaving my job to find another one, just as good, in Portland would require an enormous leap of faith, especially since I didn't want to move. On the other hand, I was "stuck," the I Ching counseled, and I needed a "breakthrough." So one fine day, when a senior director of the company, whose place it was to advise the CEO, came to town for a company meeting, I made my decision and executed it by turning in a letter of resignation.

Destiny can work in strange ways and what happened next took me by surprise. The director, an older, mature, and accomplished high-tech guy whom I respected, called me in and asked what it would take to keep me from leaving the company. By then, I was so stressed out that, despite all uncertainties, I had almost dismissed any possibility of things working out. I asked him if I could sleep on it, and when I got home that night, I turned to the I Ching again. This time I got hexagram No. 60 "Limits and Connections." This recommended biding my time while reasoning through issues and making plans. Not a signal for immediate bold action.

So, the next day I submitted my conditions for my continued employment – which included more than I thought I could get – expecting that they would reject my stipulations and I would have to move on. But the director agreed to everything and even offered me a 10 percent higher raise than I had requested! When I asked him why, he said they wanted me to stay and be happy. Impressed by this vote of confidence, I accepted the offer with a smile saying, "I can't be bought, but I can be rented." We all laughed and the tension was broken (for a while).

I thought that this was the "breakthrough" referred to by the I Ching. I felt that I was resolving the issues and moving forward productively, instead of just bolting when the going got rough. Ironically, however, the most significant aspect of me having used the I Ching at work was a seed that the experience had planted in my mind, which would soon stimulate a real breakthrough that was life-changing.

Lugging the large book to work and finding a private space to toss three coins had been cumbersome. As a result, it occurred to me that it might be possible to create an interactive I Ching experience via multimedia running on the Macintosh – the first graphical computer to go mainstream. Pursuing this line of active imagining, I began to visualize how a Mac might be programmed so that a mouse could perform the work of casting a hexagram in an "energetically authentic" way compared to a person tossing three coins six times. I also could see how the computer would take care of the busy work of recording the results, looking up and displaying the text of a specific reading, and so forth. Building on this new product vision, I also imagined producing a new version of an I Ching experience with new text that would be more relevant to modern life.

The more I visualized it, the more I liked the idea of using a multimedia-capable computer with a mouse (like Macintosh) to deliver easier access to the intuitive stimulation of the I Ching in an engaging way. After all, I mused, casting an I Ching reading has a lot in common with a computer game. Certainly, both are interactive. I searched for existing I Ching software, but I could not find it anywhere. Rudimentary versions had been programmed onto huge computers at MIT and other places, but there was still no such software available for personal computers, or anything like it. The thought occurred to me that perhaps there wasn't a market yet. On the other hand, I knew that there was at least an enthusiastic market of one – me! Developing anything that would work might require the investment of my savings, but I thought there must be others like me who would appreciate a modern I Ching program. The creativity of it was so compelling, I felt strongly moved to take the risk.

It was obvious that a computer could easily handle the mathematics of casting the six-line figure called an I Ching hexagram. The bigger challenge would be how to use a mouse to replicate the tossing of three coins six times in a way that allowed the user's energy to determine the outcome. A random number generator routine that spit out an entire hexagram would be simple and fast to program, but it would not be, to my way of thinking, *energetically authentic*. (Note: Almost all of the other I Ching software or web developers who copied our work took the easier programming route, which was not energetically authentic.) I felt strongly that the user had to be the one doing the casting, not the computer. I was also intrigued by the possibility of combining a user's query with beautiful graphics and peaceful sounds. A bit of soothing multimedia could help the user stay focused and set the mood of a calm, meditative state of mind while they are casting their reading.

An overall vision of using a computer to provide "ritual space" for consulting the I Ching began to gel in my mind. I was having that "Eureka!" moment that happens when an idea taking shape is so cool it creates a sense of excitement. My natural curiosity was getting revved up and so were my creative juices. In that moment, I wasn't thinking in grand terms of destiny, or even a business plan with an exit strategy. Hell, I was overlooking considerations of my material well-being! I was going to spend my life savings on what most people would have considered a hare-brained scheme... but I was mightily inspired!

After all, the project was an intersection of my two major fascinations – the I Ching and multimedia. Even at the time, the urge to invest all of my resources on such a far-flung idea seemed illogical and foolhardy to the extent I analyzed it. And yet, I was too excited not to think about trying to pull it off and finding out. It would be a creative adventure at the very least, and there was no way to do market research. Even then, I instinctively knew what Steve Jobs later explained – when it comes to new kinds of products, people don't know what they want until they see it. So it came down to how willing I was to take the biggest financial and career risk of my life just because I was fascinated with an idea for an esoteric invention.

I took some time to meditate on this big question. I mentally prepared myself to consult the I Ching about whether to risk time and money and career to try to produce an authentic I Ching program that I couldn't even be sure would work. Closing my eyes and invoking both love and non-attachment, I tossed the coins for a reading on this. The hexagram I got back was "Enthusiasm," with changing lines that flipped into a future hexagram entitled "Abundance." I felt clear that the I Ching was encouraging me to create a software version of *itself!*

Following your fascinations is the same thing that Joseph Campbell was referring to in his famous advice, "Follow your bliss." The I Ching had directed me to do just that!

Having used and studied the I Ching for more than 40 years now – including authoring a new and modern version – I have experienced time and again the power of an I Ching reading. Readings help me rise above the black-and-white, all-or-nothing thinking that the ego so easily gets caught up in. If nothing else, learning to use the I Ching has trained me as to the importance of open-mindedness and attitude. Authentic divination reflects and clarifies one's intention as much as it dishes out advice or wisdom. Although I am not dependent on the I Ching for every decision I make, I still can consult it if I need to expand my perspective beyond the capacity of human logic. It's like traveling to a foreign land, feeling an empathic resonance with people of a different culture, and coming back with what my favorite travel guide, Rick Steves, calls "The best souvenir – a wider perspective."[62]

This profound Taoist divination system has helped me learn to more skillfully navigate the changing conditions of mind and body through timely decision-making. Emperors and sages used the I Ching for thousands of years in essentially the same way that I do – as a strategic decision-making tool to help them see the bigger picture, make better choices, and execute strategic plans with better timing. It is not necessary to embrace a divination system in order to benefit from Visionary Decision Making, but if you were open to the possibility, it would give you one more way to tap Infinite Intelligence.

CHAPTER 9

Execution and Timing

Vision without execution is hallucination.
—WALTER ISAACSON (using a quote often attributed to Thomas Edison)[63]

The ordinary man is involved in action, the hero acts.
An immense difference. —HENRY MILLER

The skills this book has thus far presented will help you answer the question, "What is the best next move to make?" – with regard to any situation, dilemma, or important decision. But getting an answer to the "what" question is only half of the decision-making process. You still need to commit to a course of action (or non-action, in some cases) and *execute* your plan. Execution is the setting of things in motion when the time is right. Without well-timed execution, much if not all of the potential of even the most excellent decision will go unrealized.

The four steps to implementing a visionary decision are: determining *what* is the best next action you can take; committing to that action; deciding *when* to make your move; and, lastly, executing your decision by moving forward confidently, without looking back or second-guessing yourself.

Take Your Time Getting to the "What"

Modern society great suffers from "hurry sickness" – the chronic feeling that we have too much to do in too little time. But when it comes to making the decisions that will affect the long-term future, it's important to take as much time as is needed. Remember, intuition cannot be rushed. And be careful not to confuse strong impulsive urges with genuinely intuitive hunches. In addition to checking for synchronicities and messages in dreams that may come your way, use logical techniques like the ones in Chapter 5 to winnow your best options down to two or three. Remember my counselor's admonition that there are always more than two solutions to any problem. Reality is never just black and white, so stay open to a small range of inspiring but plausible possibilities.

Even when you think you already know the best solution, sleep on it before you finally decide your best next move. Let the fruits of your brainstorming steep in a subconscious dialogue with Infinite Intelligence while you sleep. If the decision is important but not urgent, give it as much time as you can. In the meantime, record any dreams that you can and list all the synchronicities that you notice.

Never let anyone (especially someone trying to sell you something) hustle you into making a decision prematurely when it is not urgent for you. Ironically – if only because it gives you that much more time for intuitive processing – one could argue that all big decisions that are not made by committee should be made at the last minute before the window of opportunity closes. Always consider when a decision has to be made and give yourself maximum "pondering time." This will usually lead to a more creative solution. Whether your decision is of a personal nature or on behalf of a wider community, it is often best to wait a little while and decide not to decide... just yet.

Learn to invoke the power of impulse control and delayed gratification, even when it comes to decision-making. Get comfortable with saying, "Not right now" or "Probably not, but I'll think about it" or "Let me sleep on it." Or tell the other party that you need to confer with a supposedly higher authority – your spouse, an advisor (even if the advisor is an inner archetype, like the Sovereign), or some vague "board" of advisors. When important values are at stake, take as much time as you need to make the best decision in a way that feels right to you. When it comes to decisions that affect you more than anyone, other people's priorities take second place, even if they are "experts"... or your investment bankers. Sometimes it is necessary to assert yourself and defend your boundaries to secure the time you need, but you have a right to it. You are the CEO of your life, and you owe it to yourself to never be rushed into a strategic or important decision.

If you feel that you are inside a cauldron of change wherein a breakthrough decision absolutely needs to be made, create as much mental and emotional space as possible to support your intuitive receptivity. Adopt an optimistic point of view. Studies have proven that a positive mood is associated with more efficacious decision-making. If you are feeling rushed or overwhelmed, it can help to find a relaxing way to turn your attention away from the matter. Give your intuition a better chance to kick in around an important decision by taking a nap, watching a movie, going out for a walk, or running an errand.

The VDM Meeting Technique

Sometimes the ramifications of a pending decision are so complex, the situation feels overwhelming, or there is the extra pressure of a hard and fast deadline. Making an important or strategic decision requires an ability to concentrate. Fear of making a big mistake can keep you up at night, making it difficult to concentrate during the daytime. If you feel stuck or virtually paralyzed, schedule a *VDM Meeting* with yourself every morning for as many days in a row as necessary. Consider your options around the important matter every single day – until you are ready to make a decision and commit to a course of action.

Always schedule a VDM Meeting as early as possible during the day. Try to make it your *first* item of business in the morning until you have had enough of them to get to clarity. There doesn't need to be a set length of time for your VDM Meeting, but 45 minutes to an hour gives you enough time to review and reconsider your options.

Here are some ideas for a VDM Meeting:

• Review your viable options, as winnowed down by the Weighted Pros logic technique.

• Read a guided meditation script aloud to yourself. This will put you into a state of mind that is positive and receptive to Infinite Intelligence. If you are not able to do this because of interruptions or emotional interference, stop the process and reschedule a VDM Meeting with yourself early the next day.

• Invoke the Sovereign archetype to support yourself as the chief executive decision-maker of your life.

• Invoke the archetype of *The Sage* and summon forth a "letting-go" state of egoless mind. You may feel empty and vast, as you open yourself up to creative potential. (I am reminded of the fertile Void of Creation that existed before the Big Bang, when all things were possible.)

• Do a short I Ching reading for one last reflection, asking for perspective on your decision. Use three coins and the hexagram lookup feature on Divination.com, *The Visionary I Ching* ebook, or run the *Visionary I Ching* app on smartphone or tablet.

• Optional: Meet with one or two of your most trusted and objective advisors, and share your latest thoughts about the strategic idea with them. Keep the focus on your decision-making.

• Be the CEO and make a final decision on your best next move. Move forward, or step back, or do nothing and be patient as matters undergo changes on their own. It is quite possible that, unless you're procrastinating, doing nothing for now might still be the best move!

As you become more experienced with the process, you will rarely need more than one or two VDM Meetings to make a decision, except when there are too many complex factors for one person to sort out by themselves.

The Power of a Signed Agreement with Yourself

If you have paid close attention to synchronistic signs and omens, have consulted your dreams, met with advisor(s), or consulted the I Ching, your best option has probably become clear by now. (If not, keep repeating these steps until the option that best balances inspiration and plausibility blossoms within you.) You will have answered the "what" question and made up your mind about the best next move to make. Now that you have made that decision, you need to *commit* to a course of action. A tremendously supportive ritual for doing this is to write an agreement with yourself... and sign it.

Since this agreement is entirely between you and yourself, your statement of resolution can be short and to the point. No need for fine print. In addition, announce your decision to any key advisors, which further solidifies your commitment. At this point, set fears and considerations aside, and boldly take a stand. You have deliberated long enough, have analyzed the options, and created enough peace and quiet for your intuitive antenna to be operative. Now is the time to summon forth your inner chief executive and declare your decision.

Even with all this preparation, making meaningful commitments when the time comes is not easy. In the case of strategic or lifestyle-changing decisions, there can be substantial risks. For example, major investment decisions are often based on recommendations from financial professionals. However, studies show that few financial advisors beat the market average after taking fees. So these decisions informed by an "expert" still feel anxiety-inducing to the loss-averse emotional brain of the average investor. (You probably know this feeling: when you are on the verge of buying or investing in something, excitement can turn into buyer's remorse.) Nevertheless, in order to seize an opportunity, you have to commit yourself and make a move, in spite of trepidation and the temptation to obsess on all the things that could go wrong. (It's a safe bet that Mr. Murphy of Murphy's Law was not a great investor!)

A common misunderstanding about commitment is that it should precede and motivate one's efforts. But this is backwards. A commitment is the outcome or by-product of inspiration or passion, not its goal. A desire to conform to some ideal of commitment for its own sake should never drive a decision. When we are drawn upwards by a "higher affection," we are inclined to make whatever level of commitment is necessary to realize the goal. A solid stance – based on understanding your situation and accepting yourself unconditionally – is always the best position from which to make the right move at the right time.

If a commitment is too difficult for you to make right now, either the time is not right or you are not ready for that agreement. Never force a commitment. Avoid making a commitment because you think you *should* or try to force a vision to manifest because you believe it is "the right thing to do." Your current self may not be the idealized self your ego wants to claim, but it is your real self right now. Sheer desire plus willpower is not going to improve circumstances if you are not totally honest and real with yourself.

Make a commitment to action when you feel motivated by an authentic and passionate desire. This will not just be an impulse, but a drive that gains strength inside you that is not the result of pressure from an outside influence or internal "should." It is crucial to know the difference between what *you* truly want and what someone else wants, even if that person is close to you. (This is especially true if that "someone else" happens to be the internal voice of parental figures.)

Focus on What You Want, Not on What You Don't Want

Commitment expresses itself through declaration and following through with focused attention. What we pay attention to in life is a choice that is an important aspect of the decision-making process. The game of golf nicely illustrates the power of what we turn our attention toward. According to the best instructors, the process of hitting good golf shots requires making a commitment to the result you are aiming for, rather than focusing on any of the possible bad things that could happen. For instance, if you are worried about hazards like a pond or sand trap and are focused on avoiding one of those, your shot will invariably seek out the hazard, because, even though you didn't want it, that is what you were focusing on! It is a clear demonstration that whatever we focus on is what we will subconsciously expect... and what we expect is what we will get. The best way, therefore, to actually avoid hazards is to single-mindedly focus on the target, commit to the shot you have in mind, and then trust your swing (your decision-making). In golf as well as life, a steady target-oriented approach produces confidence and efficacy.

The power of commitment grows with a focus on your target. Your vision is energized by your passion (in golf, to complete our example, this could be a strong desire to play better or score well). Make the commitment and become the change you want. Hold on to your vision. Hold on to yourself. Derive strength of purpose by channeling archetypal Sovereign energy as the CEO, King, or Queen of your own life.

For any major decision, the very last stage is making a firm commitment to accept the consequences of your decision whatever they may be. Formalizing the commitment in the form of a written agreement can be a powerful and positive way to do this. To help, I recommend writing an Agreement with your Self (e.g., the Self archetype) that goes something like this:

Dear Self, I hereby make the following commitment to you:

[write a short description of your decision]

I am letting go of fear and doubt and resolve to do my best to implement my decision with power and grace.

Signed: _____

Once you have signed an Agreement with Self, don't second-guess it. You've taken your best shot at formulating the best decision; that part of the work is done. Don't keep replaying options in your mind. A visionary is someone who has developed enough confidence to start making his or her own strategic decisions. The primary cause of the worst financial decisions I made in my life was a lack of confidence in myself, and deferring to the judgment of others with credentials.

With the energy you've invested in the VDM process, you have done as well as you could under the circumstances. Second-guessing or climbing a wall of worry will only unbalance you and possibly cause you to sabotage a brave decision by making a more fearful one. The past is one of the things in life that we can never change. The strategic route is to focus on creating the future, mustering our confidence, and being receptive to support wherever it is available to us.

Getting to "When" - The Timing Part of Your Decision

Once you have decided on and have committed to *what* your next move should be, you still need to answer one last, important question: *"When* should I make my move?" Making your best next move at the right time is the secret of becoming great at games like Chess and Go – as well strategic decision-making over a lifetime. An excellent sense of timing will naturally arise from the steady practice of more conscious decision-making that thinks ahead.

As said before, when it comes to the most important decisions, it's never advisable to rush. On the other hand, if you don't implement a strategic decision in a timely manner, the window of opportunity will pass. So *how* can you know when the time is right to execute a decision and start taking action?

There is no purely logical way to answer the timing question. Logic can help address the question of when to make your move, perhaps through a review of the past to discern trend lines that might repeat in the future. But such a projection is not enough to negotiate big shifts or life-changing decisions that represent creative departures from the patterns of your past. There is no pat formula for perfect timing.

Deciding when to make the next move is almost entirely intuitive. When it's time to effect dynamic action, a feeling in your gut (or however intuitive signaling works for you) can provide the signal you need. Rather than impulsively plunging toward the instant gratification of an appetite or desire, we need to invite intuition into the process and give it the space it needs. If your mind is quiet enough to perceive it, an intuitive signal will arise.

When you follow your intuitive instinct, you get a visceral sense of being in the flow, in sync with life. This is similar to the blissful feeling of being in *the zone* during athletics or dancing, negotiating a win-win deal, or co-creating a relationship. Of course, because intuitive signals can be subtle, making a move may still feel risky to the ego. And, sure, you will make some errors – especially when you mistake an emotional reaction for an intuitive feeling.

Learning to activate intuition is a trial-by-error process. Progress may be three steps forward then one step back for a while, but as you make fewer emotional decisions and more conscious ones, you will create a life of greater abundance and joy. Because timing is an intuitive decision, it will improve the more you tune your conscious mind into intuitive sensitivity.

That's right – become more intuitive regarding the "what" questions, and you will automatically develop better timing around the *when*!

Using the I Ching to Improve Your Timing

As we saw in Chapter 8, the ancient Taoist divination system known as the I Ching was designed to help us see how things go together in time in order to synchronize decisions and actions accordingly.

For the ancient Chinese, using the I Ching was a sacred practice, carrying a feeling much like the Greeks had when they visited the oracle at Delphi. The I Ching, when consulted with sincerity and openness, generates synchronicities that are relevant to the seeker's state of mind at the time. Sometimes its reflections are crystal clear; on occasion, it speaks in riddles like Delphi. Using it helps us transcend our linear conception of time and invokes a sense of enchantment as well as new possibilities.

In the case of a timing question, it works best to frame your I Ching query in the present tense. Try asking something like, "What is the best approach to take to [the situation or relationship] now?" Then look at the response you receive to see which one of three directions that it might be pointing to. Just like it is taught in the martial arts – the philosophy of which is based on Taoist classics like the *I Ching* – there are three options: When it's skillful to assert oneself; when it is advisable to do nothing; and when it is best to retreat (or run like hell).

Bide Your Time

Good timing doesn't mean that something must happen immediately. Sometimes just waiting for the right moment and doing nothing is good timing in action. This point is beautifully illustrated in the Hermann Hesse classic *Siddhartha*, where the main character becomes enlightened and finds inner peace by mastering three skills: meditation, fasting and *waiting*.[64] For decision-makers, waiting is an important ability, always remembering that we have the option to take our time when implementing any important decision.

An experienced intuition produces well-timed decisions – knowing when to say yes, when to say no, when to sleep on it, when to go for it, and when to delay gratification and wait it out for a while. Daniel Goleman's groundbreaking research on "emotional intelligence" sheds light on how we can balance the right and left sides of the brain. Emotional intelligence shows up when we are receptive to good advice from trusted sources, and it provides a rationale for delaying gratification as a marker of personal maturity and good timing. The antithesis of emotional intelligence is compulsive or addictive behavior. You can be sure that when addictive impulses kick in, good timing becomes virtually impossible.

Perfect timing is the ideal, but who is to determine perfection? Philosophically, we realize that synchronicity is taking place all the time, even if we don't perceive it yet. From a cosmic point of view, things unfold perfectly according to some grand pattern that we cannot fully understand. Sometimes this includes the moves we make and when to make them. Even if we make an imperfect decision – some kind of relative "mistake" that produces an educational lesson, that might be exactly what we need right now. When it comes right down to it, the only way to perceive perfect timing is by *feeling* it. The modern expression, "I'm not feeling it," captures the essence of perceiving good or not-so-good timing. Unless you are feeling your intuitive sense, you should avoid executing major decisions.

Pull the Trigger, Then Let Go

When you realize that you are feeling it, it is time to execute. Call forth your inner Hero's fierce resolve, which good decisions naturally build up to. Call the shot and give yourself (and any delegates) the command to make it happen. At this point, you have set things up so that you can put one foot in front of the other, take one step at a time, and let the Universe (or your staff) take care of the details. The situation will change before your eyes, whether you try to control the way it takes shape or not. Let go of managing details and let the chips land where they may. Breathe a sigh of relief that you have risen to the occasion and don't look back.

Making significant decisions causes extra stress to the extent that we put pressure on ourselves by becoming attached to results, including *the way* that we think results should occur. After making and executing a decision, it is time to let go, relax, and let the chips fall where they may. Letting go of worry or of "sweating the small stuff" allows you to feel an ecstatic sense of freedom. You accept that you made the best decision under the circumstances.

Now you are in position to make more, smaller moves – intelligent tactical moves that support your strategic decision. These don't require an abundance of intuition to figure out. You can usually take one logical step at a time. Things will change in front of your eyes, whether you try to control every little thing or not. So don't try too damn hard! Do your tasks, delegate to others if you can, and let go of attachment to its exact form as change occurs. Exercise unconditional acceptance and go bravely with the synchronistic flow.

CHAPTER 10

Perseverance and Mastery

Perseverance furthers. —BOOK OF CHANGES

Executing a bold strategic decision is not a one-time action or a single signature move in a new direction. The execution of long-term decisions must be renewed day after day in order to give the strategy a chance to thrive. That is why perseverance is a character trait that I emphasize when speaking to students and entrepreneurs.

"Perseverance furthers" is the most common sentence in the I Ching, serving as a necessary reminder that reaching a destination can sometimes require a gritty determination. Even then, in spite of our best efforts to be creative and quick, destiny plays out in its own good time. The timing of providence is usually not fast enough to suit the eager imagination or anxious ego, which is why it is important that we make it a point to renew our commitment to heartfelt strategies on a daily basis.

When people commit to a plan of action on the basis of inspiration or love, a fierce determination can arise inside of them, despite all the risks and challenges. After I launched my first enterprise, I remember gritting my teeth and bravely repeating to myself, "I will never give up!" – especially when the going got rough. When faced with daunting circumstances or the threat of bankruptcy, I would repeat my determination mantra, put my head down, and focus on taking care of business as best I could. Fortunately, I had learned and developed valuable business skills I could always put to good use.

In his best-selling book *Outliers*, author Malcolm Gladwell shows how the life stories of innovators like Steve Jobs and Bill Gates demonstrate that mastery of skills is a key indicator of success. True mastery, reports Gladwell, takes 10,000 hours of practice.[65] During the first 15 years of my own software career when I worked for others, I had put in over 10,000 hours at direct marketing. This gave me a core competency that would be invaluable for a startup. Mastery is a combination of this kind of preparation plus a gritty perseverance. A famous saying of Abraham Lincoln conveys the idea: "I will prepare and someday my chance will come."

Nevertheless, even with strong competencies, a healthy intuition, and a passion for your calling, business survival for a bootstrap enterprise is bound to be a struggle. It's extraordinarily difficult for a startup to survive even a few years, especially if it lacks financial backers. The challenge of keeping things afloat can test every ounce of resourcefulness, determination, and perseverance, not to mention the ability to sleep at night. Visionary Software, my first company, came close to bankruptcy more than once, (before it finally succumbed years later under new management). The strength of my desire to develop the intersection between two fascinations was so strong that I couldn't bring myself to give it up early. I managed to hold things together long enough to learn some great lessons, and even thought that first company didn't survive, eventually the applying those lessons more than paid off.

In spite of the hardships, there is nothing more rewarding than following your muse and doing something meaningful to you, perhaps something you love. The power of an inspired calling – coupled with intuitive decision-making and good timing – is the true source of "good luck." People who have mastered a skill and develop a knack for good timing may seem to be merely lucky to a casual observer, but if you scratch the surface, you will probably find that their success may have much more to do with the mastery of skills and great decisions. In addition to a positive and expectant attitude, these factors take years to develop but at least they are under your control. Part of life's learning is to understand the synchronistic aspect of timing. When you master how to recognize and use synchronicity to improve your own timing, you will be that much further ahead in the game.

Defying good business logic and the advice of my peers, I clung to my belief that the world could come to appreciate computer-assisted divination systems. In the beginning the only thing I knew for sure was that at least one reasonably sane person wanted it – myself! The *Visionary I Ching* app is fairly popular these days, but in 1989 I was one person on a short list who appreciated the idea of I Ching software, the likes of which had never existed. I supported my resolve with an invocation like this: "Oh, Spirit of Divine Providence, if I am the only one who likes what I am creating, and if I am the only one who benefits from using it, let that be enough for me." This was my perseverance prayer.

As daunting as the expensive and exhausting project of developing a new kind of software was, the very idea of bringing the I Ching to life in a modern way energized my passion, and I accepted the challenge. It also occurred to me that if a computer could be used to cast an authentic I Ching reading, there would be other possibly elegant applications to be discovered. My sense of risk was offset by the realization that, at the very least, this was an exciting adventure that would grow me. I was inspired about the challenge of using technology to make psychologically sophisticated spiritual technologies more accessible in an engaging way.

Armed with encouragement from the I Ching itself, I created my own luck by taking the risk of allowing Infinite Intelligence to work through me in support of an offbeat inspiration. Sometimes a period of great difficulty or dissatisfaction holds a hidden blessing, and that had been my situation. My job, as prestigious and well-paid as it was, had become a source of great unhappiness. This aroused my innate desire for creative freedom. If you are willing to be open and pay attention to what's going on inside and around you, you never know what the future has in store!

My difficulties at work forced me to turn inward at a time when I was ready in terms of skills – but also psychologically and emotionally – to discover my calling and build something. I perceived that there would be a synchronous elegance for me in producing an accessible, interactive I Ching experience that had been prompted by the feeling of gratitude I personally had for the I Ching, which I had been using for 20 years.

A major self-discovery aspect of this was to see if I could make a living doing something I cared about. Because it was inspired by a desire to invent products and services that support a broader vision, I called the company "Visionary Software" and gave myself the title "Chief Visionary." Our original company slogan was "Creative Freedom through Vision and Humor," which was printed on the first *Synchronicity* packages that appeared on the shelves of software stores back then. When I sold the second version of the business after 18 years of ups and downs, my original vision had evolved to produce much greater levels of creative freedom than I ever had imagined. In the process, I learned that being inspired by a vision and maintaining a sense of humor are two elements of successful risk-taking that keep you from going crazy.

For me – perhaps more than most – becoming an entrepreneur was all about trusting my intuition, because there was no way to rationalize a decision to develop I Ching software in 1989. In truth, my peers were dumfounded that I left an executive position in a growing industry for such a wild project. They didn't understand my passion for the I Ching or my visions of multimedia, and could not relate to my determination to invest everything I had to create and market such a program. But I was determined to give it a try. In the process, I would learn that, even when supported by enthusiasm as fervent as mine, the day-to-day work of manifestation requires exceptional levels of determination and perseverance. Grit is at least as crucial for successful outcomes as inspiration and talent.

A Tale of True Grit

Even before the *Synchronicity* program was finished, getting my unique software product onto store shelves was a critical goal. In 1989, there actually was such a thing as software stores, and Egghead Software was the largest chain in the world with over 200 stores. It was one of the only retail outlets that carried programs for the Macintosh computer, which had about a 5 percent share of the personal computer market at the time. Survival as a software developer of a consumer product for the Mac depended tremendously upon getting onto Egghead's shelves for the holiday buying season. Egghead's deadline for placing a large purchase order was the end of September.

In March of 1989, as we were nearing the completion of the *Synchronicity* program and product, I was also trying to make contact with a fellow named DJ, who was the Merchandising Manager of Egghead's Macintosh division and its only buyer. As with any bootstrap entrepreneur, it is critical to get profitable sooner rather than later, and convincing DJ to place an order was critical to the survival of our fledgling enterprise. Having spent all of my savings and just keeping it all together on my consulting income, I knew I didn't have the resources to stick it out another year unless we ramped up sales. DJ was the only Mac software buyer in the country.

It was not easy getting on the phone with DJ. In fact, it was virtually impossible. His schedule was incredibly hectic, because his unit had to spend $60 million per year in marketing funds from Microsoft, who controlled 80 percent of the software business at that time (including Mac office software). This made him a busy man in a high pressure situation – and I could feel it – but empathy for DJ was not going to save my company. Only a large purchase order for my strange little product could do that!

DJ was young, arrogant, and extremely overloaded. But I persisted. Since he literally never called me back, I began ringing his extension throughout the day, every day, only leaving a message once a week or so. (There was no caller ID in those days, so he didn't know that I was pursuing him.) My hope was that one of these times he would pick up the phone. One evening in May around 6 pm – after the end of normal office hours – I had the impulse to try his extension one last time that day. Lo and behold, he answered the phone, probably thinking it was his wife. From that point on, I called him every couple of days at 6 pm, hoping he would pick up. In this way, I succeeded in getting a conversation with DJ about once every two or three weeks for the next several months.

Somehow, he clearly found our unique new product interesting. Like most Mac aficionados at the time, he thought of himself as a pioneer and he wanted to stay abreast of the latest software tech-nologies. He liked the idea of putting his stamp on something. He agreed to let me send him a beta review copy of the *Synchronicity* program. Thus began a long, laborious, and sometimes tortuous back-and-forth. When I was fortunate enough to get him on the phone, he would invariably create new hoops for us to jump through.

Some of his demands were outrageous. For instance, he insisted that we include a little rubber frog in every box, as a nod to our multimedia effect of randomly croaking frogs in a Japanese garden. (Just for fun, I trademarked *Random Frogs*, so that we were the only software that could ever offer this special feature.) Increasingly desperate to win his approval in order to get that large initial order, I was in no position to argue. I did everything he asked (including procuring a couple thousand expensive little rubber frogs) without audible grumbling. The seasonal ordering deadline was drawing near and I was running out of money. It was a stressful period of uncertainty, made all the worse by DJ's attitude of casual arbitrariness. As the deadline got closer, I was having nightmares of going bankrupt and losing everything.

One day when I got a hold of him, DJ sardonically asked, "How is it that I seem to talk to you more often than I talk to Microsoft?" With a wry smile on the other end of the line, I replied, "I don't know... must be the luck of the Irish!" The good news was that he kept talking to me when I would catch him at the end of the day. He was beginning to soften. But the clock was ticking and time was running out for our little company. I knew that if I could not get DJ to place an order soon, Visionary Software would go bank-rupt. Our survival depended on one person – the fickle Mr. DJ.

September arrived, but still no order, not even an indication from DJ that he was leaning in that direction. And it was on my mother's birthday – September 17 – that I received dreadful news when I called for DJ. "He is no longer with the company," I was simply told. I was devastated. This was a dark night. Perseverance furthers, eh?

One week later in the mail, I received a purchase order for 1000 units of the *Synchronicity* program for placement in all 200 Egghead stores. Placing that order had been DJ's last offi-cial act. Perseverance *had* furthered! An order from Egghead was the only thing that kept us from going bankrupt that first year. (Interestingly, DJ came to work for me a couple of years later as a consultant, and we became friends. I officiated at his wedding – and I'm pleased to report that he is still very happily married. Let's hear it for synchronicity!)

Thanks to a gritty determination, I had not given up, and the business had survived a major hurdle. After investing so much blood, sweat, tears, and fears, if my little business venture had not survived that first year, I may have never pursued a big creative dream ever again. Certainly my life would have been hugely different – and probably much more limited – as a result. Was this a "miracle"? Depending upon your definition, I suppose so, but I also know what a huge part perseverance played.

The Role of Sacrifice

The concept of personal sacrifice is not a popular one, because it brings up the fear of losing out on something. Nevertheless, sometimes we face choices that are mutually exclusive. One of the costs of manifesting what you want is that you may have to make some room for it by letting go of something else. For instance, I had let go of the security of a well-paying executive position and all of its perks to dedicate myself to manifesting creative freedom.

The kind of persistence it takes to launch a new enterprise from scratch involves a tremendous amount of sacrifice – much larger than most people are willing to make. I know that I paid a high price – and not only in terms of long hours, frustration and recurring fears of catastrophe. I also swallowed my pride when dealing with the ridicule of people who thought I was crazy. And, as noted, I dealt with the whims of at least one person who had the power to waste a tremendous amount of my time and energy and to possibly devastate my hopes and dreams.

No matter what it is you want to manifest, life will offer many distractions. It is often essential to give up some comfort or pleasure to focus on an important decision or task. This sacrifice is made easier when your heart is involved as you are attending to a "higher affection." Inflamed by a passion for my creative vision,

I was motivated to sacrifice time, energy, a social life, and practically my first-born son for the cause. In love with my venture, I committed myself to it and took it all the way. In the process, I effectively sacrificed being available for much of a romantic commitment, which was also something that I wanted. But I was already "married" to my dream.

Energetically, I was not available for a deep, intimate relationship at that time. It would have been helpful to have a parenting partner, but like an artist obsessed, my heart was absorbed with my creative passion. It may be possible, but I think it must be quite difficult to develop and maintain an intimate partnership and family while also devoting oneself to making a go of it as a bootstrap entrepreneur. Unless relationship partners share the same vision and have complementary skills, it would require a mate willing to sacrifice a substantial portion of her or his own needs in support of the person who feels compelled to risk everything to get a startup off the ground. That would be noble, but it is a lot to ask of anybody!

This brings up the question of the types of sacrifices that are made by people who set aside their own dreams to support or take care of others, even when providing such services may not be the optimal livelihood for them. They might make the sacrifice for love – or lots of other reasons – and if they are driven more by love than duty, their efforts will create some happiness for themselves as well as those they help. To support others in times of need is a noble accomplishment even when (perhaps *especially* when) it competes with the development of a broader personal expression.

We never know for sure, but it's possible that selfless service is a part of a person's destiny or karma. At the very least, being of service is a "day job" that cultivates acceptance, humility and unconditional love – qualities that support a deeper sense of meaning and fulfillment. In this way, selfless service embodies an interpersonal or social definition of success. No matter whether a sacrifice involves a creative enterprise or taking on a caretaking responsibility, anything that expands and deepens your heart is *a risk that grows you* and ultimately a movement toward happiness.

We make choices in life according to our strongest values at the time. We may need to let go of something that we like or enjoy very much, but has become a lesser desire. In order to devote ourselves to a lofty purpose or goal and be able to summon forth the required determination and perseverance, our mission must be our priority and primary focus. Staying aware of the fact that there may be a need to make tradeoffs that will involve pruning some of your desires will help you make more conscious decisions and feel less conflicted when you are called upon to do so. Letting go of a desire or attachment, for the sake of a stronger goal or greater good is a sacrifice that enhances self-esteem and is an important aspect of the Hero's Journey.

Patience and Delayed Gratification

The practice of patience is a form of sacrifice in itself – the letting go of an immediate desire in favor of a higher affection that may take time and effort to develop. Patience is a major challenge in our hectic world, plagued as we are by an epidemic of "hurry-sickness." People are so used to feeling rushed all the time that it diminishes their ability to pay attention, while increasing their stress levels. In order to escape the pressure of making important decisions, our fragmented attention is easily diverted to omnipresent novelties like entertainment or gossip. The unfortunate result of scattering our attention is an inability to wait much for anything without experiencing anxiety. Furthermore, our ability to fully enjoy an activity may be compromised by the hurrying habit of thinking about what's coming next and getting ahead of ourselves rather than living in the moment. We find it impossible to fully enjoy the present when we are preoccupied with multitasking or anticipating the future.

Delaying gratification is a conscious practice of patience, which is making a sacrifice in the dimension of time. The ability to control one's impulses is a foundational trait of emotional intelligence and wise decision-making. Otherwise, a world of constant distraction will toss you about and have its way with you. Delayed gratification is a sacrifice worth making, if you believe that your eventual fulfillment will not only happen, but will happen in a more satisfying way because of your investment in letting it happen in its own good time.

Grandma's Law

As a single parent, I tried to pass the lesson of delayed gratification on to my son. I called it "Grandma's Law" and it went like this: "Sure, you can have some ice cream... but only *after* you finish your green beans." It was a lesson I had learned from my mother at a young age: do your chores first, before going out to play. Specifically, I invoked Grandma's Law with my son to persuade him to make a habit of doing chores and homework on Saturday, reserving Sunday as his full day set aside for play, rather than the other way around.

Learning Grandma's Law early in my own life helped me experience the efficacy of delaying gratification. I was less stressed, felt good about staying ahead of the game, supported myself, and ultimately I was able to thrive as an entrepreneur. A nice benefit of putting work before play is that when the time for leisure comes, you can enjoy it more with less anxiety. After all, you are ahead of the game, without tasks hanging over your head until the last stressful minute.

A Little Help from Advisors

Perseverance is easier when you have an able support system. Some people prefer to go it alone and try to do without help as much as possible, but they are only making life more difficult than necessary. Perhaps they think that they shouldn't need anyone's help, that they should be able to do it all on their own. Or perhaps they don't feel they deserve the time and caring of others.

A refusal to seek and receive guidance from mentors or advisors invariably stems from an ego-based need to prove oneself, which could be the outgrowth of a history of sibling rivalry or domineering parents or something like that. Sometimes people fear that they won't get enough credit for results if their decisions and actions are informed or improved by the input or advice of others. This is just a form of all-or-nothing thinking that can arise out of stubborn rebelliousness, an inaccurate self-assessment, or a prideful need to prove one's specialness. In one way or another, it's the immature ego trying to prove itself as worthy of special esteem.

Independence becomes self-defeating when it gets to that point where the need to assert one's autonomy is so great that you are not receptive to help from willing and qualified sources. Failing to accept support due to insecurity only leads to worse decision-making, which leads to more insecurity and so on – a perverse downward spiral. Persevering is never easy, but being receptive to the advice of mentors and wise elders can help tremendously. We all need support.

Support Groups

While I was pursuing the aloof and elusive Mr. DJ at Egghead, it was a day-to-day challenge to sustain my faith in my vision. I needed moral support and operational advice, but I didn't exactly know where to turn. Operating from a vision that was ahead of its time, I couldn't expect the average person to understand multimedia software, the I Ching, or how I envisioned the one enhancing the other. Nevertheless, feeling the need for support, I joined a *Mastermind* group at a church where I volunteered as meditation minister.

Mastermind groups are over a hundred years old and had something of a resurgence in New Thought circles during the 1980s. The purpose of such groups was to help its members clarify their visions and support each other. Of course, part of this was helping to dissolve doubts that people hold about what they deserve and whether they are up to the challenge.

The five other people in my Mastermind group were the only people at that time who were aware of my efforts to get a purchase order from DJ and how important it was to my company's survival. This weekly meeting was my only source of support or encouragement. Even though the other group members didn't really understand what I was trying to do, they helped me keep faith in myself... and my right to have a vision of my own. These supporters could not provide practical business advice for a startup software company, but I benefitted greatly from their moral and emotional support. Having the ability to be receptive to support – whether intellectually or emotionally or financially – is a central requirement of VDM. And backing yourself up with a support group will help you persevere.

Receptivity to Good Advice

Everyone has opinions, and people enjoy giving advice to friends and colleagues. Unfortunately, as much as we may resonate with friends emotionally, they rarely make objective advisors. This is especially true when it comes to strategic decisions that involve big changes or staying on track through the ups and downs of a calling that they don't understand or can't relate to. After all, your friends like you the way you are – that's why they are your friends! They are naturally resistant to seeing you change much because it threatens the relationship as they know it. Look to friends for moral and emotional support, but seek elsewhere for objective feedback and strategic advice when it comes to manifesting a bold new vision.

A primary function of a board of directors is to advise the CEO or Executive Director. Directors of large companies are paid handsomely to attend meetings and perform advisory roles. In a startup company, however, there is often a small, unpaid group of otherwise busy people on the board, if only to fulfill the state's legal requirements for having a board. I had learned from previous ventures that it is difficult to get high quality, experienced advisors to sit on the board of a startup company lest legal liabilities arise, especially when there is no insurance or compensation involved.

When I started Visionary Networks, my second venture, I decided to do without a Board of Directors and filled both required seats as President and Secretary, which is allowed in the state of Oregon. Instead of trying to assemble a larger board of experienced directors, I chose to assemble a small advisory board with two advisors. I asked two successful entrepreneur friends – both of whom had already succeeded at software development and publishing – if they would help me in a "low risk" advisory arrangement. It would involve neither legal liability nor a lot of time on their parts. I offered to give each of them one percent of the company's stock, to be issued immediately, and all they had to agree to was to meet with me once a week to discuss my decision-making agenda. On top of that, Visionary would buy them lunch! These two guys were already successful software entrepreneurs, had served on a board with me before, and were inclined to help, so they agreed to my unusual proposition. Thereafter, I bought each of them lunch and discussed strategic decisions with each of them separately every week for the next ten years.

The agenda of both weekly meetings was always the same: to go over the most important decisions that I faced as CEO. On occasion, I would show an advisor a list of "weighted pros" formulated for the options that I saw before me. Both of these fellows were analytical types whose perspectives complemented and balanced my inspiration-driven approach to strategic decisions. I called them "No Men," because they were the furthest thing from "Yes Men." They were constantly shooting down my too many creative ideas. (I like variety and want to do everything!)

Under an agreement I made with myself, I decided that I would not make a strategic decision without getting at least one of my No Men to agree that it was worth trying. I did not have to abide by their advice, but this was a discipline I used to govern my rambunctious right brain.

During that ten-year period, I only made one major decision that both of them had advised against. That financially risky decision was to acquire the domain name, Tarot.com. Ironically, buying that five-letter domain turned out to be one of our better business decisions, later becoming worth a fortune in itself – which shows how the exception can indeed sometimes prove the rule.

Over the years, my advisors were generous and patient – two qualities that eventually paid off handsomely when I sold the company and wrote them each a check for $200,000. And that was in addition to 10 years of weekly free lunches!

You can recruit your own Advisory Board without giving stock away, although options linked to successful results could make sense if your venture is a corporation with stock. Or if you use your advisors judiciously, you could pay them for meetings (plus lunch) or find another way to reward them beyond the satisfaction they might derive from mentoring you (which is enough in some cases, depending upon their motivation and needs). In any case, make sure you select people who are willing to tell you what you *need* to hear, not what you *want* to hear. Being confronted rarely feels comfortable, but what you are looking for is sound advice, not fuzzy feelings. That can come later – in fact, over the years both of my advisors became close friends.

A challenge is to find advisors who balance your personality and skills, and have a record of success in a comparable field. Former executives are often interested in mentoring. Another option is to retain an executive coach, especially if you can find one with experience related to your field. A coach will help make sure that you are making conscious decisions and following through on the commitments you've made. However you set it up, it's good to have advisors who can focus on helping you make strategic and tactical decisions, as well as providing moral support to help you persevere through the challenges that will arise.

Knowing When to Pull the Plug

Perseverance involves adapting to conditions that are beyond our control, but even this has its limits. Your vision could be off in terms of scope or timing. No matter how strong your determination, an idea that is too big or too far ahead of its time is not going to be able to take off. Examples of this abound. Take the world of alternative energy. Nobody disputes the fact that cold fusion is a wondrous concept. Unfortunately, we are nowhere near being able to produce it. And, even if one had the scientific aptitude and skills to make it work, the scope of the project would require hundreds of millions of dollars, which is far beyond what a lone scientist or creative genius could raise.

When I developed the first divination software, it was 10 years ahead of the marketplace and, after a few years, my first startup went bankrupt. Fortunately, I was in a position to develop the same idea ten years later when the World Wide Web was taking off as a platform for marketing and ecommerce. After I sold the company in 2007, people remarked how perfect my timing was! That may have been true with regard to the selling of the company, but the timing didn't feel great during the ten prior years, when I was struggling to hold things together. I never really pulled the plug – the new managers drove it into the ground – but considering how far off my timing had been, it would not have been shameful for me to do so. There is a time to call it quits, or at least take a long break. As the lyrics of the song *The Gambler* put it, "You've got to know when to hold 'em, know when to fold 'em, know when to walk away, know when to run."

Regrets Be Damned

Perseverance is a forward-looking quality grounded in the faith of our vision. When we are too focused on the past, perseverance will suffer. One form this can take is through holding onto feelings of regret, perhaps over unfortunate decisions we have made. Regret can be thought of as holding on to negative judgments of the past. A feeling of regret is a signal that there is some mistake for which you need to forgive yourself. It is a residual emotion that inhibits personal growth.

We need to let go of regret, perhaps by taking refuge in the belief that that everything happens for a reason. Who are we to say that our mistaken timing or some unforeseen obstacle was not necessary to lead us toward a critical piece of learning or a new opportunity? What if you missed a train but met your lifetime partner as a result? Would you classify that as a regrettable mistake? Or was that destiny working itself in inscrutable ways? We need to maintain respect for mystery.

It's impossible to notice new opportunities or make great decisions when we indulge in regret or self-recrimination or harbor doubts about our worthiness. Feelings of embarrassment or shame disempower us and make us more desperate. Despair leads to more self-defeating decisions, and so on in a downward spiral. Let's improve our ability to forgive ourselves for the learning-curve decisions of the past – starting now. It becomes easier to stop judging yourself when you remember and appreciate the wonderfully mysterious way that the universe tends to bring everything back into balance again and again.

To the surprise of some people I know, I say that I have no regrets. Of course I know I have made plenty of mistakes. But when a feeling of regret begins to arise, I take it as a signal that I need to forgive myself, let go, and move on as soon as possible. Not only does this habit of self-forgiveness free up my mind, it is a prerequisite to fully learning from whatever comes next. Once you have forgiven yourself (and have made amends to others, if necessary), there is no reason to hold on to negative memories of past mistakes. Just forgive yourself and move on – knowing that even though you may have made mistakes, you did the best you could have done under the circumstances. Accept yourself with all your imperfections. Focus on feeling grateful for learning something and resolve to make brighter decisions going forward. Letting go is a freeing process, liberating your soul's creative imagination to soar again.

So, don't fret too much when you make a mistake! It's going to happen. If a decision does not play out the way you intended, restart your brainstorming and decision-making processes, beginning with a fresh review of options you have now. Things change, sometimes rapidly. Give thought and energy to the practice of conscious decision-making, like an Olympic athlete who is steadily perfecting her or his form. Perseverance and resilience play huge roles in the manifestation process.

The Challenge of Unconditional Acceptance

A prerequisite for perseverance is unconditional acceptance – of ourselves, others, and whatever is happening – whether we fully understand all of what's happening or not (we never do). Our peace of mind can be disrupted by a pressing desire to know *why* something has taken place, especially something that we didn't want or can't expect. Caught up in resistance to the way a situation has turned out, we demand an explanation. Unfortunately, questions like "Why did this happen to me?" are a waste of time and our attention. Sometimes we just need to accept the fact that the way things are working out may not be comprehensible for the time being. Coming to a full understanding of why something happened cannot be forced, no matter how urgently you might want to know.

If we get stuck on the "why me" question, we are only keeping ourselves off balance. We need to develop unconditional acceptance – of ourselves and the way things are. The higher challenge is not to figure everything out, but to accept life and our role in it unconditionally whether our limited brains can make sense of it or not. This is humility – to roll with the punches, get back in rhythm, and regain our balance by accepting everything, including the limitations of our own capacity to know all the answers.

Paradoxically, acceptance is the most powerful catalyst for change. Now, this is not the same as resignation. When we accept people and situations just the way they are, we allow them the space to evolve according to their own temperament or nature. Joyful acceptance is a simple and beautiful form of love. Resistance or lack of acceptance, on the other hand, stimulates conflict and polarization. (Just ask the parent of a teenager!)

As Lao Tzu, the most famous of the Taoist sages and author of the *Tao Te Ching,* is reputed to have observed, "Life is a series of natural and spontaneous changes. Don't resist them; that only creates sorrow. Let reality be reality. Let things flow naturally forward in whatever way they like."[66] Trying to get the universe to give you answers on demand is like going out in the backyard and pulling on a bush to make it grow faster. The effort to force things will only harm the plant. Instead of always trying to force changes to happen the way you want or your ego thinks they should, try thinking of yourself as a *fledgling warrior of acceptance* and let it develop however it will.

Calling up the Warrior archetype helps me connect with the strength to accept the things I don't understand or don't like, because unconditional acceptance is not easy. I include the adjective "fledgling" to remind myself that I'm a beginner at this – I am not very good at it and may never be. Although we love to learn, demanding to know all the answers is not only unrealistic, it is arrogant. As we develop in wisdom, Aristotle's adage, "The more you know, the more you know you don't know," is a truth that becomes more obvious to us and supports a capacity for unconditional acceptance.

We would all like to change things, including other people – if only to help them adapt to and share our favored ways of seeing and doing, our schedule, our lifestyle. And sometimes we are anxious to change things fast. But perseverance is about learning to flow in time – bobbing up and down like a surfer waiting the right wave, the right time. In order to persevere with alertness intact, we need to be comfortable with some degree of ambiguity. Mastery at life requires that we be nimble and improve our ability to change speed or direction, which will help us respond intelligently to the waves of change as they rise and fall.

From Perseverance Comes Resilience

Although I eventually achieved business success, I experienced financial failure twice – once as a young investor and again in my first foray as an entrepreneur. Both times I lost my entire net worth and even slid into debt with nothing to show for it other than hard lessons learned. With hindsight it became clear that I made the same fundamental mistake both times – poor decision-making. Specifically, as the result of a lack of experience and confidence, I delegated the authority for my most important financial decisions to others whose hierarchy of values was different from mine. Starting over was painful, but I had to do it twice, before I learned the importance of trusting myself and being true to my own values.

Both times that I failed financially, I had taken a huge risk for the sake of possibly realizing an ambitious monetary return. Taking risks is important, and it is something our inner Hero is wired to try. But it was only after I pursued a vision that was more about heart than money that I came out ahead, including financially. Unfortunately, it's not easy to take one's focus off money when debt collectors are circling. Perseverance in extreme circumstances requires strong resilience.

When you realize that everything, including mistakes and failures, happens for a reason, it gets easier to delay gratification, make sacrifices and rebound from missteps. The development of resilience is like a muscle-memory of the mind – remembering that you can handle setbacks and bounce back. Resilience comes from a sense of growing mastery coupled with perseverance.

Summary of VDM Process

In Part II we have focused on Visionary Decision Making skills. Just as carpenters and mechanics develop a liking for certain tools, I encourage you to try them all to discover which work best for you. It is not essential that you adopt every technique or practice covered in Part II. Before we move on to some philosophical conclusions in Part III, let us just pause a moment to summarize the sequence of making a visionary decision.

1. Train yourself to be on the lookout and notice synchronicities, dream symbols, hunches, and random ideas that pop out of the collective unconscious. Some of these may seem miraculous. That's fine. Carefully take note of them as they come within the range of your hunter's perch, and record them for reflection and analysis as needed.

2. Call upon your intuitive sense to decode the *meaning* that synchronicities, hunches, and archetypal dream symbols hold for you. Meditation and mindfulness practices of any type are excellent ways to filter the mental and emotional static that can block intuitive receptivity. In addition, once your mind has settled down, you can also generate and interpret a synchronicity using the I Ching.

3. Consider meanings picked up by your intuition relative to your hierarchy of values and your personal priorities. Evaluate what is the best choice for you right now from a short list of feasible options that become apparent. Ask yourself "What is the best next move for me to take in this situation when the timing is right?" Make as many VDM meetings as you need to contemplate this until you receive a clear answer. Persevere in this process by recombining logic and intuitive gut feelings about your values. Sort (and re-sort) your options until you know you are clear about the best next move for you to make. Sign a written commitment agreement with yourself.

4. Focus on receiving a clear answer to the "when" question, the timing part of executing your decision. Fiercely act on your best next move as soon as your intuitive mind feels the timing is right. Feel it with excitement and pull the trigger. Send out necessary communications. Delegate what you can. Set the wheels in motion. Let the inner CEO execute!

5. Be prepared to accept the outcome of your decision without regrets or second-guessing yourself. Once you have executed the

decision, don't look back. Do not invite comparisons or indulge in buyer's remorse. You did the best you could to make the most skillful decision possible. Then you bravely executed your decision by moving forward in the face of uncertainty. By making a bold move in an intuitively informed way, you have done as well as anyone could have done in your position.

6. Perseverance furthers. Maintain awareness of your highest priorities and execute the visionary decision and renew your commitment over and over again, day by day. Be patient. You can't make a plant grow faster by tugging on it. Let the sapling of your vision grow with confidence knowing that if you don't let yourself get too distracted, your daily nurturance will ensure that it flowers and bears good fruit.

PART III

The VDM Philosophy and Lifestyle

CHAPTER 11

Belief Engineering

Man is a credulous animal and must believe something... In the absence of good grounds for belief, he will be satisfied with bad ones.
—BERTRAND RUSSELL

Cease to cherish opinions. —ZEN SAYING

From an Eastern point of view, all beliefs are opinions based on the best perceptions we can make right now, given our upbringing and conditioning. Understanding this helps us be more open and flexible and able to allow our beliefs to naturally evolve based on new learning experiences.

Self-help author Catherine Pulsifer declares, "What we believe becomes who we are."[67] And, who we are changes as we grow. Since beliefs have such a major impact on everything we say and do – including every decision we make – we need to be aware of what we believe. This is not so easy, but it's important to be careful about the beliefs that we identify with and rely on to make decisions. Every belief is a choice itself – one that we are making now or had made long ago.

Many of our beliefs are such deeply ingrained assumptions that we take them for granted as being reality and are hardly aware of them. Ironically, their very invisibility has the effect of making these beliefs even more influential on a subconscious level.

We seldom take time to reconsider our most basic assumptions. Nevertheless, for the sake of making better decisions, we need to take conscious ownership of the beliefs, because they determine the kinds of choices we will make.

Carol Dweck, a psychologist researching workplace dynamics at Stanford University, writes: "We usually assume that skills, motivation, and drive are the most important determinants of success. Now we know that belief and mindset are often at the heart of that drive."[68] We leverage our beliefs – especially self-confidence, which is a belief in our own resourcefulness – whenever we make a visionary decision. Such personal empowerment, however, often runs counter to heavy cultural conditioning, including by dogmatic religions that have imposed forms of magical thinking and fearful biases onto human consciousness for 2,500 years. Even if you are not religiously trained, this has had an influence on cultures across the world, affecting the governance of every man, woman, and child.

In the normal course of events, we operate on the basis of assumptions that make sense and will work for us. To use a simple example, if I don't believe I can walk across the street, my body will act out the mind's belief: it will stiffen and I will not be able to move my legs freely. If I unknowingly take a placebo believing that it is going to make me feel better, it is likely to work. Not just our bodies, but also our character is affected by what we believe about who we are and what we are supposed to be doing. As Dr. Dweck put it, "Beliefs matter, beliefs can be changed, and when they are, so too is personality."[69] And beyond the personal level, human beliefs have a profound impact on our species and planet.

Believing Your Intuition

Nobody has explained the conflict between blind acceptance of beliefs and trusting one's intuition better than the Buddha, which I learned during my first Buddhist meditation retreat. The Buddhist nun, Ayya Khema, told us a revealing story. During the period of his life when he was a wandering teacher, the Buddha arrived at the village of the Kalama tribe to give a talk to the villagers who had assembled. At one point, an elder politely asked him, "Excuse me, sir, but we are confused. Every few weeks, another teacher passes through our village. And all too often tells us something that contradicts what a previous teacher said. Then we truly don't know what to believe. Do you have any advice for us about how to resolve the confusion?"

The Buddha replied, "Your confusion is understandable and my advice is this: Don't put your faith in teachers. Don't put your faith in scriptures or tradition. Don't put your faith in authorities. Don't even believe what I'm telling you right now – unless it rings true for you in your heart."

There are many brilliant Buddha stories, just as there are marvelous stories about Jesus. (The Buddha's teaching period lasted 35 years, so even though he lived about 600 years earlier than Jesus, there are many more stories.) Hearing this one struck me like a ton of bricks. At the age of 30, this was the first time I had ever been taught that my spiritual life had anything to do with trusting my own judgment rather than obedience, the adoption of creeds, and a self-denying humility.

In my strict Catholic upbringing, I had always been told what to think and believe, as well as how to behave and what *not* to do. I had even learned that God, who was watching every move I made, even counted some *feelings* as sinful (like anger toward one's parents, for instance). To top it off, we were taught – as fundamentalists of all religions are – that to doubt the teachings given by our church or temple is to be tempted by the devil, and all such traitorous thoughts needed to be summarily dismissed.

The lesson of the Kalamas contradicted everything I had ever been taught on this score. The Buddha's injunction to trust my intuition was not only unique, but it had that powerful ring of truth. It was a startling new teaching for me, but it seemed like mature advice compared to blindly holding onto whatever I had been taught as a child. This lesson inspired me to learn as much as I could about intuition and how to better to trust my own. It also gave rise to a process of examining and reevaluating old beliefs that influence my ability to clearly perceive reality.

Trusting one's subjective judgment brings up the general question of truth and whether it is possible to be objective. Physicist Werner Heisenberg's Uncertainty Principle, a ground-breaking discovery in the realm of quantum physics, provides some pro-found insight. It proved how the subatomic activity of particles and waves is altered by the act of observing them. Because of the *observer effect,* nothing can be perceived or accurately measured in a fixed or absolute way.

Extrapolating from this scientific proof of a lack of fixedness in the physical world, we can conclude that nothing – including what we believe – can ever ultimately be proven. This radical idea may seem absurd or even frightening at first (even though he could not refute it, even Einstein had a lot of trouble accepting it), but it's also liberating if looked at from the point of view of intuitive intelligence and creativity.

Now, let's not misunderstand – beliefs are important. Even if they exist within the context of one's limited capacity for knowing, useful *operating assumptions* are necessary to get anything done. Rather than depending upon unchanging articles of faith, however, we can rely upon intuition and *choose* what we believe according to what makes sense to us. In the context of VDM, this is a synergy between what passes the test of logic plausible and what feels right in our gut. In the creative process, intuition is more powerful than convictions – quite the opposite of what we are taught as children by moralistic authorities. In this respect, the VDM paradigm is an exciting call for personal freedom. As biologist Bruce Lipton put it, "I was exhilarated by the new realization that I could change the character of my life by changing my beliefs. I was instantly energized because I realized that there was a science-based path that would take me from my job as a perennial 'victim' to my new position as 'co-creator' of my destiny."[70]

How We Adopt Beliefs

Making observations and forming beliefs is a human being's adaptive response to living in a complex world. A child's mind starts forming opinions about everything that happens almost from birth. This world would be overwhelming if beliefs were not form to help us make sense of what to expect, how to feel safe, etc. When we are totally dependent, we instinctively trust that our parents know everything and will take care of us. And we automatically adopt the beliefs and traits of primary caretakers and teachers.

This is the social price of belonging to a family or tribe. As we age, it's easiest to hold onto the beliefs that we were taught when we were too young to know any better. However, if we want to make better decisions for ourselves, we need to be willing to reconsider what we think is true and grow beyond the limitations imposed on us by beliefs that we adopted when we were infants.

Our legal system stipulates that ignorance of the law is no excuse. In a parallel way, ignorance of what you believe is no excuse for the way your life turns out. Therefore, it is incumbent upon mature, self-determining adults to become conscious of and reevaluate the beliefs that were formed in childhood and how we continue to adopt them even now. Of course, it is your right to retain beliefs that were adopted by you at any age, especially if you consciously make the choice to do so. But adults cannot get away with blaming bad decisions on what they were told by parents, teachers, ministers, or bosses just because it is more convenient to do so.

It is imperative to get to know yourself and take full ownership of what you believe as soon as possible. The meaning of your life depends on it.

The Value of Beliefs

Beliefs are important from a practical point of view, even if they are not sacred like dogma-centric religions make them. A debate has raged since St. Paul, in the earliest days of the Christian movement, extolled "faith" as the key to salvation rather than "good works." Paul was referring to "faith" in the belief that Jesus rose from the dead and trusting that he would redeem his followers. What he originally meant by "works" was the strict observance of Jewish law and the traditional rituals. In fact, St. Paul advocated letting go of the requirement for several Jewish rites (like circumcision) to facilitate his zealous efforts to convert Gentiles.

After the Council of Nicaea (325 CE), "faith" came to mean believing in and adhering to the newly assembled Bible and the Nicene Creed – a codification of beliefs that formed the dogmatic basis of an organized Christian Church. The process of choosing which books to include in the Bible and the Nicene Creed – the first required "credo" for "believers" – was organized and sponsored by Constantine, the first Roman emperor to endorse Christianity. "Works" eventually came to mean charity and helping others, but in terms of winning the heavenly reward, faith has continued to reign supreme according to Church teachings.

The idea that we are saved on the basis of what we believe and profess to believe – rather than on how we behave or whether we do good things for other people (which even pagans do) – was central to Christianity when it was formed 1,700 years ago, and this position has maintained currency in belief-centric Western religions ever since. According to this point of view, in order to be "saved" from eternal torture, you need to pledge allegiance to stone-age scriptures and orthodox beliefs that are derived from them. Trusting oneself is a sin of pride and must not be allowed lest it lead to "heresy." Such independence was vigorously discouraged throughout the ages – under the penalty of ostracism or "excommunication," if not torture and gruesome execution.

Believing something with all your might – and even converting others to accept your articles of faith – does not make what you believe any truer. Taking refuge in orthodox beliefs might make one feel better or more secure, but those beliefs will not contribute to personal fulfillment. Faith is not a magical shortcut.

It is my studied opinion that we are not "saved" by believing. In terms of fulfilling your destiny – your purpose in living – useful beliefs are important in order to make the right moves at the right time, but the believing itself is not what does the trick. Despite promises of eternal life, rigid convictions that can't stand to be doubted – and a meek acceptance of the suffering they may entail – are not pathways to freedom.

The word "confidence" in Latin means believing in oneself. This is the faith that really helps you to evolve. It encourages you to experiment and take risks that grow you. A belief worth maintaining is one that both makes sense for *you* and actually works for *you*, by supporting your freely chosen value system.

You will become a far better decision-maker if you trust yourself enough to review and upgrade your beliefs throughout your lifetime. Committing yourself to learning what presumptions are most effective for you, voluntarily putting your faith in them until proven otherwise, and owning your own beliefs is a heroic and self-empowering act of personal responsibility.

A Special Category: Core Beliefs

You may think that you are aware of what you believe, but that is undoubtedly not the case. Some of your operating assumptions have very deep roots. From the day we are born, we do our best to make sense of the world by interpreting things and forming conclusions (i.e., beliefs) that are in alignment with needs for safety and nourishment. Because deep impressions were formed at a pre-conscious age, there is a category of beliefs below your awareness that resist becoming conscious and which can control you for a lifetime. These are referred to in some personal development circles as "core beliefs."

The tendency to identify with core beliefs is strong because they are unconscious. They feel like a part of you, rather than just one way to look at the world. Our core beliefs are reconfirmed by selective evidence as we focus on events and feedback that seem to support them. We simultaneously ignore evidence that contradicts them. Eventually, the core beliefs are simply accepted as the way things are. As a result, they play a huge role in determining what is possible for us. Because they are invisible to the conscious mind, core beliefs have a negative impact on intuitive receptivity and decision-making without us even knowing it.

Here's an example of a core belief from my own life. A conclusion that I formed at a very young age was that I needed to be perfect in order to be loveable. This was based on coming to the false conclusion – based on my experience – that love is something that must be earned. This situation created pressure and anxiety, and made me work hard to win a few crumbs of intimacy. I carried this self-limiting assumption and expectation into all my relationships – always trying to be as "perfect" as I could be in hopes of achieving a little bit of love. I only became aware of the pattern and realized how it was holding me back around the age of 29.

Make the effort to become conscious of your core beliefs as soon as you can. It doesn't matter what experience or teachings gave rise to them. Becoming aware of unconsciously held core beliefs liberates us from being at the mercy of blind spots. The good news is that, whatever your old beliefs are, they can be upgraded to a level of usefulness that will truly help you get what your heart desires.

Upgrading Your Operating Assumptions

It behooves us to make it a habit to question and test *everything* we believe and ascertain whether our beliefs are helping or hindering us. Doubt is not evil, except from a self-righteous, fundamentalist point of view. Doubt has a necessary role to play. We need to delete or upgrade beliefs (like apps on a smartphone) that are no longer up-to-date, realistic, or helpful. We can even try out new beliefs. Consciously trying on new operating assumptions, like a new set of clothes, is what I refer to as "belief engineering."

One of the considerations of belief engineering is practical: How well will a particular belief support a proactive mindset and better decision-making? Use both intuition and logic to figure this out. Even though it may involve some work, consciously reevaluating what makes sense to you and what needs more study is the philosophical requirement for self-actualization, maturity, and wisdom.

Your beliefs control your feelings and choices, so you need to consciously *choose* your own beliefs if you want to direct your own life. No matter what anyone else says – including powerful religious or political establishments that scare people into conforming to their orthodoxy (and their mind control) – you can summon the Warrior archetype to defend your personal boundaries by helping you let go of beliefs that hinder your success and happiness – no matter what anyone else might think. This *especially* includes the belief that we will be damned if we question or dare to doubt our indoctrination. I am reminded of a wonderful saying common to twelve-step support groups: "What you think of me is none of my business."

How to Upgrade Beliefs

Let's take an example of an entrenched belief: "I never follow through on anything, and I am unable to finish what I start!" Carrying such a belief almost guarantees that you will never finish anything in a timely manner. *The subconscious mind is always working to prove itself right, no matter what beliefs it consciously or unconsciously holds.* Thankfully, there is a simple technique for "flipping" a self-defeating belief. First, restate it and convert it to something like this: "I am a capable person, and if I keep working at this step-by-step, I *will* finish this project!" Now, this is a realistic idea that your brain can accept. If you repeat this revised assumption to yourself when the self-defeating belief kicks in, you will begin to approach tasks and projects with more confidence and less stress.

People holding a belief that they are incapable of finishing things were not born with such a thought in their mind. At some point, without realizing it, they formed an explanation in their mind – perhaps according to a relatively innocent but critical remark that a parent made – and accepted it as being true. Then, of course, the powerful subconscious is going to make them live up to it!

Fortunately, recent brain science has disproved the notion that "you can't teach an old dog new tricks." Early neuroscientists believed that the brain was the body's one organ that could not regenerate itself. After a certain age, it was thought, brain cells could only be destroyed. But, with the help of new brain scanning technologies, scientists have now established that the brain has an amazing "plasticity" and remains adaptable for our entire lives. So, no matter how old you are, you can grow new neurons and train your brain for the rest of your life. Discovery and learning need never end. You are not stuck with what you know now.

Belief engineering entails becoming more consciously aware of what you tell yourself, and changing that internal dialog for the sake of better decisions and better results. Once you realize and fully accept that your beliefs and actions are your responsibility, you know that it is okay to change your beliefs. You are an adult. Take responsibility now. *After all, either way – actively or passively – you choose your own beliefs!*

List your Core Beliefs. Here's an exercise you can try right now, or any-time. Take a moment and write down one or more beliefs you ascribe to, including one you think you might hold subconsciously and which could benefit from reframing. Across from each one, write out what a revised, more productive or supportive assumption might be. It is helpful to keep a small copy of this list on your fridge, in your wallet, or on your computer's desktop. Let it grow. The way to upgrade old beliefs is like training a puppy to go outside – by consistently reminding your brain on a regular basis.

Having a hard time coming up with ideas? The following list of areas of life where you may have a self-limiting core belief may help you in your brainstorming:

- Your talents and capabilities: "I'm no good at that stuff anyway, so why would anyone hire me?" Possible antidote: I am capable of mastering anything I am interested in learning.

- Your worthiness to be loved: "I'm only lovable if I... am perfect... look beautiful... make lots of money." Antidote: I accept and love myself unconditionally... I appreciate my kindness and resilience.

- Your luck: "Nothing turns out right. Everything bad always happens to me, so it's useless to even try." Antidote: I am far luckier than I know. I can improve my luck bit by bit starting now.

- Your world: "Most people will only take advantage of me; it's foolish to trust anyone you don't know well." Antidote: By allowing myself to give others a chance to be good to me, I gradually expand my circle of friends and supporters.

The Pitfalls of Magical Thinking

The fact that we ultimately choose our beliefs does not mean that we should make them up, believe whatever is most convenient, or whatever makes us feel good, even though people do these things all the time. Strategic decision-making is not powered by starry-eyed and impractical magical thinking, even though the ego thrives on assumptions that support the narcissistic fantasy that the world should provide you with what you want because you want it so badly. Magical thinking can take different forms: believing what you want to believe, imagining that you can get something for nothing, or expecting to get lucky because you think you are special and deserve it.

A popular form of magical thinking is believing that all you have to do is visualize an object of desire in order to attract it and somehow it will pop into your life. The now-famous Law of Attraction teaches that you pave the way for getting what you want by believing that it is possible and becoming energetically receptive to its appearance. In effect, you will what you desire to come to you.

There is some truth in the power of attraction – via a subtle magnetizing effect of held thoughts and feelings – but one needs to be wary of how a craving ego will create arguments and find "evidence" to support the effortless fulfillment of desires. The inevitability that things are not going to unfold according to any plan or schedule of ours is not given much consideration. Unfortunately for those who demand an easy solution, the process of manifesting what we want requires discipline and some measure of delayed gratification.

Magical thinking is not just the domain of the counter-culture. It permeates decision-making at all levels. Consider the words of Eileen Shapiro, the author of *Make Your Own Luck*: "Magic thinking in business (and life) decisions may reduce anxiety – and maybe that's why it appears in so many business plans – but it's a poor way to bet. If the odds are slim that your current set of bets will get you where you want to go unless a major miracle intervenes, you might want to reconsider whether more bets in the same vein are just bringing totally atrocious odds down to new odds that are merely horrendous. Magic thinking is widespread in all kinds of bets – corporate bets, career bets, and life bets. Once you spot it in your bets, you have the power to change your destiny by either changing your bets to ones with better odds of achieving your goals – or changing your goals to fit your actual bets."[71]

Magical thinking is a form of all-or-nothing thinking that does not factor in the unpredictable nature of change, which makes it costly. On more than one occasion, I learned this lesson the hard way. As I mentioned in Chapter 10, I took a sabbatical to go to spiritual centers around the world when I was 29. In order to free up my assets for the trip, I sold my house, my cars, and most of my property. An investor friend convinced me that I should let him convert everything I had into gold and silver (his specialization), which was at sky high valuations at that time. Due to what was later termed "irrational exuberance" – a sure symptom of magical thinking – it looked like the upward trend in precious metals was never going to end because of inflation, etc. This is a smart invest-ment, a "sure thing," my new financial advisor assured me – and in my naiveté, I put my faith in him.

With no experience as an investor and not feeling qualified to trust my own judgment in that arena, I delegated vitally import-ant decision-making to someone else. Another big factor was that I felt no personal connection to what we were investing in – it was entirely based on my desire to somehow make money while I took a sabbatical of self-discovery. Unfortunately, as it turned out, the precious metals market had reached its apex with nowhere to go but down (way down). The market value of gold and silver pro-ceeded to crash precipitously, wiping out my entire investment. I lost my entire financial net worth, but gained an expensive lesson on the negative potentials of magical thinking.

Betting and losing all my money revealed how wishful think-ing can be motivated by the desire for a quick fix. I could clearly see how trying to get something for nothing has a security-ori-ented, fear-based motivation lurking in the shadows, a sort of "Please rescue me, God" fantasy. Creative decisions may have a dream-like quality, but they are driven by heartfelt passion, rather than a desire to score a magical win or escape an uncom-fortable situation.

There is a huge difference between impulsive decisions that depend upon miraculous solutions and bold decisions that derive from a visionary approach rooted in who you are. In order to be able to feel a heartfelt passion, it is necessary to trust life and trust yourself. Trust is always a risk that requires courage, which itself requires adopting an optimistic point of view. (Pessimists don't take risks, if they can avoid it.) Optimism depends on beliefs that make sense to you and support the creative possibility that you are betting on. The Visionary Decision Making process reinforces useful and effective operating assumptions that favor the kinds of risks that will grow you.

The following are visionary beliefs I personally have found to be effective and true. You might consider trying them to manifest better results going forward.

Visionary Belief: Change is Your Friend

We are living through a period of accelerating change that can so easily feel chaotic. It is the instinctive tendency of animals (including humans) to automatically react to sudden changes as if they are threats. Indeed, throughout most of human existence, there *were* life-threatening dangers in our environment. A hair-trigger reactivity served to keep us safe in a world that included saber-toothed tigers, our nervous systems programmed to fight, flee, or freeze at a moment's notice. We are still wired that way, since we have not changed much biologically in the last hundred thousand years. When we are triggered by fear, we still can barely think, only react. But once we learn how, we can intervene with the beam of conscious awareness known as mindfulness and a sophisticated intuition that is tuned to the challenges of modern times.

Fortunately for us, the risks we take nowadays rarely, if ever, involve life-or-death, split-second decisions. In the absence of constant danger from predators, we are free to become more creative and develop potentials that go beyond ensuring survival. Rather than feeling threatened by it, the most creative individuals have come to regard change as a friendly force, and these people effectively act as evolutionary change agents. Alert to synchronistic signals and new opportunities, they are psychologically prepared to make intuitive decisions and take risks. Learning how to navigate and manage change – the overall goal of the VDM process – empowers them to blossom as creative risk-takers and develop superior timing.

In a time of rapid and accelerating change, change management skill is more vital than ever. In the process of learning to navigate change (and sometimes to help facilitate it), we come into alignment with the rhythm of life. When that happens, we can feel the universe as a supportive realm that wants to help us – at least to the extent that we are willing to cooperate and synchronize with nature. Everything we need shall be provided and available. All we have to do is tap into Infinite Intelligence with the abundance of resources that are there for us – in the form of creative ideas, signals to guide our way, archetypes of wisdom and power and much more.

People who see change as friendly are more optimistic and more likely to enjoy the up-and-down flux of life. In order to embrace change, most of us need to develop a more fluid relationship to time. People who fear change essentially want time to stand still. Their frustrated wish is for a fixed and stable universe.

The mechanical division of time into hours, minutes, and seconds – brought about by the recent invention of clocks – has clogged the spontaneous flow of life energy. In order to be able to fully relax, visionaries find ways to free their minds from the domination of linear time. They understand the high value of "time-outs" to intentionally loosen the domination by modern society's over-controlling mechanical approach. This is good, but in actuality, there is nothing to escape, because if we take our eyes off the clock, our experience of time has a natural plasticity to it.

When we enjoy life, time seems to go too fast. When we are in resistance to circumstances, it seems to crawl. As so many great teachers have shown, the secret of joyful living is to become more aware of what is happening in the one time that is real – the present moment – and forget about the future and past. In addition to strategic thinking and decision-making – in fact, to improve them – we need to let go of trying to control things long enough to give our intuition a chance to be receptive.

Visionary decision-makers stay aware of how life is always in flux. The ultimate solution to "time management" is to develop a lifestyle where we can transcend the measuring and parceling of time, and strengthen our intuitive sense of *timing*. (Don't worry; this becomes much easier in Stage Three.) Good timing, a fundamental component of every decision, is the secret of surfing unpredictable waves of change. When we have come to regard change as a friendly force, the success brought about by our improving sense of timing will provide encouragement to cultivate intuitive intelligence.

Visionary Belief: Infinite Intelligence
is a Resource That's Always Available

When I was a bootstrap entrepreneur and asked if I had investors, I would reply, "Oh yes... my backer has infinite resources." Of course, I was referring to divine providence, or *Infinite Intelligence*. In Chapter 4, we saw how the divine realm of gods and heroic archetypes that Jung called the "collective unconscious" can be approached as a *resource* rather than as a God-King who judges behavior and controls our fate.

Psychologically or spiritually – however one chooses to characterize it – the Jungian concept that there is an unlimited creative and supportive resource that is always available to us is a reassuring belief. As recovering addicts come to accept, we need the help of a higher power to achieve the level of freedom we want. Individual will power, no matter how strong, is not enough all by itself. In order to evolve and grow in creative power, we humbly accept that we need the help of Infinite Intelligence, the archetype of creative power. Bottom line: Once we learn how to tune in via our intuitive sense, Infinite Intelligence provides us everything we need to be creative, productive, successful, and happy.

Visionary Belief: I Deserve to Have What
I Want (and What I Want is Good for Me)

Achieving success and a meaningful life requires believing in yourself, that what you want is possible and that you deserve it. Some of us – especially children from large families – came to believe at an early age that our wants and needs were a burden on our primary caretakers and that it was "selfish" to even express them. (This was my experience, and that of my parents as children too.) Believing that you deserve to have what you want lets you be more open and forthright and able to ask for what you want. If you believe you *don't* deserve to live out a heroic personal destiny, your subconscious mind will never allow you to manifest it. This could be in response to core beliefs based on unconscious guilt and shame cultivated during childrearing in a religious subculture. Whatever the cause, you will need to upgrade such beliefs in order to receive what your heart desires and what is good for you.

Taking charge of one's beliefs requires self-confidence, which produces positive changes in attitude. Learning to trust yourself, your intuition, and your interpretation of the meaning of things builds self-confidence. As your decision-making gets better, you will enjoy better results by making the right moves at the right time, which only increases confidence.

Self-confidence arises from discovering your natural talents and then practicing them until you achieve a level of mastery. As we saw in Chapter 2, skills that grow from your personal fascinations are the ones that you will be inspired to develop. During Stage One of life when self-discovery is the top priority, we follow and learn everything we can about whatever fascinates us the most. In the process, we develop skills and eventually, if we persevere and put in 10,000 hours, a level of mastery. Then we are in a position to create our own luck. As Louis Pasteur put it, "Chance favors the prepared mind."

When it comes to the power of attraction, nothing is more attractive than self-confidence. It attracts other people, because powerful and positive energy is magnetic. When I invoke the Sovereign archetype – that aspect of character that likes to "take care of my people" – I become more attractive. Why? Well, for one thing, everyone likes to be taken care of! A paradoxical result of generosity is that when people realize they are being cared for and looked after, they are happy to oblige their sponsor. They appreciate him or her, and want to reciprocate. Essentially, proactive generosity is what makes the best relationships work. The most effective way to get what you want is to use your intuition to understand what others want and help them get it.

The Synchronicity Belief: There Are No Accidents

One can hardly state this belief better than Jungian author, Robert H. Hopcke, in his book, *There Are No Accidents*. "If we bring a symbolic attitude to our lives, searching out the meaning of what happens to us and thereby allowing our own capacity to make wholeness out of the random and disparate events of our lives, then, no matter happens in the plot, wherever the setting, whoever the characters, major or minor, we will see that indeed, there are no accidents in the stories of our lives."[72]

The one belief that is at the heart of VDM is the belief in the Universe's perfect timing – even if our half-asleep mind cannot perceive the perfection of it or, conversely, just takes what happens for granted. For the sake of better decision-making, we experiment with the belief that there are no accidents... and start paying more attention. We choose to believe that there is a reason for what happens, even if we don't know the reason yet. We choose to believe that the universe is imbued with an intelligent way of doing things that is just beyond our current ability to comprehend. We trust in Infinite Intelligence.

Our decisions will no longer depend on – or wait for – deciphering the reasons why something happened. Perhaps we will look back at some future date and understand why an event occurred, but it is not our assignment – or ability – to know everything on demand. That's too much for human consciousness to expect. We only need to make enough sense out of things to make a slightly better decision as to the best next step. That's it! Making better decisions step-by-step in the absence of perfect knowledge – with the help of an activated intuition – is the crux of personal development and the achievement of success (however you define success for yourself).

Living a synchronistic life involves cultivating acceptance and wonder while letting go of judgment and resistance to the way things appear. This includes accepting your karma (substitute your particular concept of cosmic justice here) by taking refuge in the belief "what goes around comes around."

A synchronistic point of view renders difficulties easier to accept and surmount. It sheds the wholly unnecessary suffering that results from resisting the way things happen. When this operating assumption is working, you will feel grateful for the little miracles taking place. You will also benefit from remembering that *there are no accidents – only occasional failures to discern aspects of a larger unfolding pattern.*

As my story attests, a belief in the meaningfulness of coincidences is useful for expanding one's vision and can be helpful for one's timing. Noting and appreciating synchronicities that happen highlights the expansive scope of what is possible, as well as the grandeur of Infinite Intelligence. Respect for synchronicity serves as a bedrock for more creative thinking and superior decision-making. If we pay attention and look for it like a hunter, synchronicity will prove itself. The more we become aware of it, the more we can count on it. We unblock our intuitive antenna and open our eyes to what's happening on a level beyond the ego's control.

Synchronicities can mystically guide us to the people and situations we need so that we can wake up to new opportunities and better choices. David Richo touches on how synchronicity is perfect timing when he writes, "Everything that happens to us is synchronicity because everything fits perfectly into our step-by-step advance toward a fulfillment of our potential."[73]

As we take advantage of the synchronicities that we notice, we will realize with joy how perfectly everything unfolds in our lives according to some higher logic. Awareness of synchronicity eases the bumps and transforms our experience of life – with all its inevitable ups and downs – into a more rhythmic and meaningful journey.

Visionary Beliefs Create a Virtuous Cycle

Some of the visionary beliefs presented above may be new for you. Even more ways of looking at things will occur as you apply conscious decision-making techniques. Once again, there are no prescriptions for what you should or should not believe. The only essential criterion is that your beliefs make intuitive sense to you. Accepting the fact that humans are not equipped to understand everything, you adopt beliefs that make sense and reliably work for you when you try them out.

Upgrading your beliefs gives rise to a "virtuous cycle." Useful beliefs that make sense to you support your ability to make better decisions and enjoy perfect timing. When good things result from such improved decision-making, the upward spiral completes and reinforces the beliefs that have improved the more skillful way you approach people and situations. Our beliefs not only impact our decisions, but they constitute a way of looking at things that conditions our attitude and – given healthy blood sugar levels – our moods. This, in turn, increases both the pleasure and effectiveness of all our thinking, feeling, and actions.

The overarching result of the synchronistic philosophy is a freer and more joyful life that attracts other people, as well as whatever you desire. This virtuous cycle culminates in a fresh philosophy, a better personality, and a more satisfying and creative lifestyle – with lots of benefits.

Serenity

One of the most soothing benefits of trustworthy beliefs is serenity. This is a state of relaxation born of equanimity – maintaining a balanced and even-keeled point of view – via acceptance rather than resignation. The famous Serenity Prayer sums up the essence of synchronistic living: "May I change the things I can (by making and executing good decisions), accept the things that I cannot change, and develop the wisdom to know the difference."

Having arrived at a belief in synchronicity that is reinforced by your experience of better decisions, serenity will help you relax mentally and physically. It will have a soothing effect like swaying in a hammock under the shade of two palm trees on a beautiful beach, or a baby being cradled by a loving mother. Devotional types might want to visualize Divine Mother sprinkling life with nurturing sparks of synchronicity during the day and full-color dreams during sleep. Things that happen will become more interesting, as we open to the possible meanings contained in dark clouds and silver linings – sometimes in events that might have previously been dismissed as random. As serenity rules our minds, we stop sweating the small stuff, choosing to humbly accept the belief that there is a reason for everything. To the extent that we can leverage and take refuge in more evolved beliefs, everything will change for the better.

CHAPTER 12

The Synchronistic Lifestyle

There are two ways to live your life. One is as though nothing is a miracle. The other is as though everything is a miracle.
—ALBERT EINSTEIN

The Synchronicity Principle is central to the Visionary Decision Making paradigm. It enhances our understanding of how intuitive intelligence operates. Awareness of synchronicity is the marker of a higher awareness of good timing and a sense of being in the flow of life. The happy result of this approach to living is the development of what I call the "synchronistic lifestyle."

Visionary beliefs supported by an empowered imagination that is in alignment with your aptitudes, fascinations, and values provide a foundation for an expansive approach to problem solving and a playful approach to fulfilling your calling and ultimately co-creating your destiny.

Intuitive intelligence benefits from paying attention to the little miracles that arise in the form of synchronicities, dream symbols, and hunches, and, as noted, these start to become apparent to you more often. Once you trust your intuition with healthy self-confidence, life becomes – to use Einstein's word – more miraculous.

Miracle-Mindedness

As you allow yourself to adopt and be supported by more accurate and useful beliefs, your mind will download creative power more easily, receiving inspiration and guidance from Infinite Intelligence. This makes a new way of seeing the world possible, which I call "miracle-mindedness." Few people have better exemplified a radically creative open-mindedness than Einstein, one of the greatest geniuses of the modern era. But he didn't come by it easily.

A mechanistic worldview had ruled science and dominated thinking since Isaac Newton kicked off the scientific revolution with the laws of motion and gravity in the 17th century – that is, until Einstein applied his intuitive intelligence and mathematical genius to venture into uncharted territories. Einstein had a mystical, playful way of perceiving how the world works. He was gifted at math, but his rare genius derived even more from his imagination and visualization skills. Even though he had a specialty as a physicist, his mind was capable of opening to the broadest planes of consciousness. He was a brave individual who adopted a fresh perspective free of the limitations of the imposing scientific paradigm he grew up with. His thought experiments tested novel viewpoints. He possessed the mental flexibility to entertain revolutionary exceptions to the conventional ways of seeing, thinking, and believing.

Einstein's multi-dimensional imagination afforded him an extraordinary level of creative freedom. Few can hope to match his level of genius, but anyone can achieve higher levels of inner freedom by adopting a miracle-minded approach. This attitude and perspective practically defines the Visionary Decision Making paradigm and supports the cultivation of what I call the synchronistic lifestyle.

After sufficient practice, a miracle-minded approach becomes the way one goes through life. An attitude of open-minded wonder begins to permeate perceptions and support background feelings of awe, humility, and contentment. You don't have to be perfect at this way of looking at things. It's not all-or-nothing. But to the extent that your conscious attention is allowed periods of miracle-minded openness, amazing benefits and favorable outcomes will become more likely.

An ability to more adroitly navigate life with the help of visionary beliefs brings with it an improved sense of timing. With a better sense of rhythm, you will be able to accept the mysterious aspect of life's unfolding patterns and ride the waves of change without as much inner resistance or fear. Such a courageous orientation – which you can consciously adopt if you are not held back by old core beliefs – produces a feeling of excitement or adventure. This feeling state can trump our natural fear response to what's unfamiliar.

As you allow yourself to upgrade your beliefs, you will differentiate between working assumptions that serve your best prospects and the unconsciously held beliefs that hold you back. Creative, visionary beliefs will give rise to a virtuous cycle featuring a broader awareness that evolves into a miracle-minded mindset and intuitive sensitivity.

Embracing synchronicity requires that you trust your intuitive intelligence and give it the freedom to probe synchronistic opportunities and intersections that arise and which hold creative potentials and new opportunities. There is something to learn from *everything* that happens – even happenings you don't like or hadn't expected – and especially those seemingly miraculous events that occur.

Make Life a Game You Win More Often

Sometimes we can be our own worst enemy. Pain is a normal part of life, but the extent of our suffering is governed by our attitude – and, specifically, where we fall on the spectrum between acceptance and resistance. Resistance to realities – especially painful ones – is what causes mental and emotional suffering, not the pain itself (hypnosis' ability to relieve pain sensation proves this). But we don't have to accept a position as helpless victims who are defending ourselves against possible dangers. We have the option to follow the example of the gods and turn life's challenges into playful sport – even if this sometimes means taking five steps forward followed by three steps back.

From the point of view of personal development and evolution, it helps to look at life as a game of strategy and execution like chess or Go. Fortunately, your life is a game that you can't ultimately lose

– as long as you keep getting better at it. As with any game, winning depends on maintaining a positive attitude and exercising skills you have developed. With visionary beliefs supporting an active intuition, a virtuous cycle kicks in, reinforcing the positive attitude, etc. A miracle-minded stance of positive expectancy will help you make more intuitive decisions. And, as in the workings of compound interest, you will become exponentially more intuitive going forward.

When negative or catastrophic images tilt your mind toward a downward spiral of emotional depression, the synchronistic point of view can act as a counterbalance. The open-mindedness of an optimistic perspective allows images and magnetic feelings of healing, harmony and happiness a much better chance to arise. As Charles Dickens wrote in the famous first line of *A Tale of Two Cities*: "It was the best of times, it was the worst of times." Like the glass half-full or half-empty, the one we choose depends on attitude.

Navigating life more intuitively makes everything more fun. You may even come to enjoy making big decisions (like a high-stakes gambler who can read the cards)! You will not only enjoy the superior results you get when you operate from beliefs that support what's meaningful for you, but you will enjoy the unfolding process itself. The high pleasure of participating in strategic decision-making and bold action reminds me of the Hindu concept of *leela*, a Sanskrit word that defines the playful way their deities operate in and on the world. Like Greek gods at sport, these archetypal examples of divine playfulness encourage us to maintain a childlike and good-humored attitude about life to the extent we can.

With a sense of rhythm like a graceful dancer or athlete, you will feel increasingly more confident about the moves you make as you become more intuitively tuned in to the cosmic music. Being in the flow of good timing is exciting and fun – whether you are dancing, discovering new friends or transacting business. Perfect timing is making the right moves at the right time. An ecstatic and energizing sense of rhythm develops the more you get in sync with the flow of change. Even a slightly improved sense of timing will greatly improve your odds of taking your best next moves with better timing than ever before. (This progressive evolution reminds me of that wonderful movie about life's learning processes, *Groundhog Day*.)

Benefits of the Synchronistic Lifestyle

The benefits of a synchronistic lifestyle are multi-dimensional, interrelated and huge, because they lead to greater joy and abundance in all the important areas of your life. Here are some of the major benefits of living with a visionary level of awareness:

Creative Inspiration
Coming up with new ideas is always fun and exciting, but it requires unleashing the imagination. This is too much to ask if you are too stressed or preoccupied. To become more creative, we need to schedule ways to break out of our routines to create enough space to be able to take note of hunches and creative impulses. Then we can cultivate fertile creative ground by tuning the intuitive antenna to the imaginative realm of Infinite Intelligence – perhaps with the help of meditation, divination or other VDM skills.

As author Marney Makridakis eloquently put it in her book *Creating Time,* "Creativity, meaning and time dance together in an unavoidable, and rather effective, cycle: the more meaningful your projects are to you, the more likely you are to engage in them. Then, the more meaning you are experiencing, the more creative ideas you'll have for more meaningful projects. Meaning creates more meaning, and creativity begets creativity!"[74]

Consider a broader array of choices in a situation by asking "What if?" in order to bring up outside-the-box possibilities or alternative patterns. Once you get the hang of it, cultivating and maintaining a higher awareness of creative possibilities will add a highly pleasurable dimension to your life.

Confidence
Confidence is faith in yourself and your right to your own Hero's Journey and unique contributions to make in the world. Confidence arises from believing that you have a destiny that inspires and empowers you to exercise your will in risk-taking ways. Once you discover what fascinates you and what you love, as well as what you are naturally good at, you will also develop a greater awareness of synchronicities related to those things. Your viewpoint can evolve

from fear and scarcity-consciousness (e.g., the fear that there won't be enough) toward abundant learning opportunities.

Whenever meaningful coincidences arise, let yourself enjoy a delightful "aha moment" as you feel a sense of fulfilled expectancy and the encouragement to believe in yourself and your destiny even more. Confidence grows with the experience of good fortune, which attracts even more good luck. This is especially the case when we are operating from a heartfelt place. For instance, even though nobody else believed in my vision of divination software, I was inspired by a kind of love for what I was trying to create, which conferred just enough confidence for me to go for it.

Contentment

Contentment is a ripened state of happiness that comes with wisdom. It is a harmonious feeling state that is almost entirely neglected in modern society's frantic grasping for consumption and stimulation. The attainment of contentment requires wisdom derived from experience, which is helped enormously by paying attention to archetypal patterns, fascinations, synchronicities, and dreams. Contentment arises from a deep feeling of gratitude supported by a combination of unconditional acceptance and compassion for yourself and all beings. As a state of mind, contentment is the sweetest, highest pleasure of abundance.

Wisdom

As you practice fine-tuning your intuitive antenna to discern and digest insights, everything will take on a greater sense of meaning, which leads to the mature quality known as wisdom. Wisdom is a culmination of learning from experience. It takes time, but once cultivated, it helps us to balance taking care of our individual self with attending to the greater good of all. Things get out of balance when our point of view becomes too narrow or self-obsessed – a constriction of consciousness that can happen due either to lack of self-esteem or an inflated sense of self-importance.

It is important to be able to call upon a strong ego that is ready to defend boundaries but the ego should never be left completely in charge. The ego is properly a lieutenant who needs to take direction from the higher level of consciousness, sometimes referred to as the spiritual self. The ego does not make a good general. Forming an appropriate relationship between your ego and your higher consciousness is a beautiful fruition of self-knowledge. As Aristotle put it long ago, "Knowing yourself is the beginning of all wisdom."

Grace

Grace is the happy coincidence of receiving what your heart desires (often even before you think you deserve it). The gift of grace often comes in unexpected ways to a mind that is receptive. When grace is present, it inspires gratitude for Infinite Intelligence and creative power. When grace descends in the form of synchronicities, intuitive hunches, and good karma, the process of receiving it reminds you that the universe is a friendly place. The universe will provide everything you need as long as you cooperate by being true to your heart, pay attention, and remain receptive.

The grace of synchronicity highlights the fact that your efforts alone are not enough to achieve your heart's desires. We are connected to all that is and interdependent with all of it. If we define heaven as the state of freedom and joy to be experienced during this lifetime, the blessing of grace is at its core. The grace of Spirit or Heaven is available to us to the extent we stay tuned. In a state of gratitude, we learn to trust the universe. Jungian therapist and teacher David Richo puts it so well: "Grace is the higher power than ego at work in synchronicity. This power seems to have heart, that is, to want what is best for our growth."[75]

Share Your Synchronicities: Feel free to anonymously share your stories of amazing synchronicities and be inspired by reports of synchronicities experienced by others in a forum where people can help each other discover meaning. To be part of the Synchronistic Living Community, visit: www.GreatDecisionsPerfectTiming.com.

Grace is a part of life when you are in sync with your destiny. For instance, in the early days of running our website offering I Ching and Tarot readings, I got a call out of the blue from a man who said he owned the domain name, Tarot.com, suggesting he might want to sell it to me. When I asked how he had found me, he said he had purchased a copy of the original *Synchronicity* I Ching software some ten years earlier and had followed my efforts ever since. He contacted me because he liked the authenticity I brought to my divination software and websites. He had a personal interest in divination, he said, but his Tarot.com and I-Ching.com websites were little more than a hobby for him. Despite other offers, he thought that I might be in a position to buy and put these domain names to better use. He told me that he had a solid offer of $42,000 cash for Tarot.com, which made me gulp because, as valuable as the name might prove to be, such a figure seemed beyond reach for our little company. At the time we were barely keeping it together and didn't even have a line of credit with a bank.

Since he admired the way we produced authentic divination experiences, I asked if he would sell it to me for a lower price. Without hesitating, he replied, "I'd rather not." Not knowing how I would get the money, I did not hesitate, "Okay, we definitely want it, but one last question – and please don't let my asking this be a deal-killer – would you be willing to let me pay it off in twelve monthly payments?" I took a deep breath and started thinking my "Letting Go" mantra while waiting for his answer. It seemed like an eternity before he finally replied, "I guess so." Believe me, this seemed like a miracle, but now I know that there are no accidents. (As it turned out, we paid it off within five months and the Tarot.com domain name, with help from our marketing, was eventually worth millions.)

You attract grace when you are in alignment with what fascinates you or what you love; when you are in sync with your authentic self; and when you use your intuition to take risks in alignment with the flow of change. It is a wonderful feeling to realize that when you commit yourself to what you love, you are more likely to receive the support you need.

The Role of Destiny

Destiny can be thought of as an intersection between your passion and your vocation. Ideally, your destiny is reflected in your current vision and goals, because it is your Hero's Journey – the life that you are here to co-create with the help of Infinite Intelligence. Your destiny is the fulfillment of your highest potential as a human being, featuring your unique mix of aptitudes and talents, and your personal expression of productivity and contribution.

Your destiny is yours alone. It is *your* evolutionary path that unfolds with a vital assist from *your* decision-making and your mastery of skills. William Jennings Bryant had it right when he wrote, "Destiny is not a matter of chance; it is a matter of choice. It is not a thing to be waited for; it is a thing to be achieved."

The word "fate" is often used interchangeably with "destiny," but a useful distinction can be made. I like to think that fate is predetermined by the past, while destiny is future-oriented, creative, and full of potential. Unlike fate, destiny is not passive and you are not its victim. Basically, it is your choice whether to orient yourself toward creatively cooperating with your destiny or bemoaning and resisting fate. This is one of the central guiding decisions we all make for ourselves, over and over again.

The Roman goddess of destiny was called "Fortuna." She was the archetype that helps seekers steer the ship of their lives toward greater good fortune. In ancient statues and paintings, she is depicted holding a nautical rudder or steering wheel and a cornucopia of abundance. With Fortuna as your partner, you envision your destiny as a creative adventure. Under her influence, you will be guided toward great decisions and better timing.

In contrast to Fortuna, the Fates were deities who were responsible for all the troubles that befell human beings. This included whatever "karma" people might have coming as a result of some inherited character flaw or their past transgressions. The Fates were depicted as weaving, measuring, and cutting the fabric of a mortal's life. According to a "fatalistic" point of view, your future is predetermined, and you are a helpless victim in the cosmic casino of random luck. Resisting your fate – as if you have no control or influence – is never a basis for skillful decision-making. Victim-consciousness provides excuses to avoid responsibility and risk-taking. Ironically, it is negligence to your own best interests that will turn you into a bona fide victim – a victim of your own victim mentality and resulting passivity!

Moving away from victim-consciousness toward becoming the co-creator of our destiny is something we grow into. A big part of it is developing decision-making skills to get what you want in a timely manner with the least amount of suffering. Life will offer you myriad opportunities to realize the expression of your Hero's Journey. No matter how modest or grand your destiny in this lifetime may be, you are called to play the hand you were dealt and fulfill your potential, whatever it is. You can't control everything that happens, but you can greatly tilt the odds in your favor.

Dancing with Destiny

Making the right move at the right time is valuable for everyone, but it practically defines performing artists like musicians and dancers. Visionary Decision Making is a lot like dancing, and thinking of it in those terms will help you stay more flexible and nimble. Here's how VDM is like dancing:

- Intuition requires a light touch.
- When dancing with Destiny, you use your intuitive sensitivity to follow her lead, instead of trying to call the shots and lead with your ego. Picking up the "dance signals" via intuition is more like responding to a soft touch on the shoulder than forcefully imposing your will. In the

synchronistic lifestyle, you trust your instincts and feel the rhythms of the cosmic music.

• Timing improves with practice.

• As you learn to trust intuitive insights and hunches, you become more balanced and prepared to move in a new direction when you are guided to do so. How does Destiny guide you? Via synchronicities, dreams, and creative inspiration, of course!

• A graceful sense of rhythm develops.

• As you navigate changes in your career, family, and relationships, you are tuned to the flow of energy. When you stay conscious of and connected to your priorities, you are less likely to bounce around from one crisis to the next. When you navigate life with an imperfect but improving sense of balance, you start dancing with a graceful sense of rhythm.

Dancing is a perfect example of timing in action. All of us, clumsy or not, are dancers poised in a physical, mental, and emotional duet with our calling, or destiny. Even good dancers will miss a step now and then, but with practice their dancing achieves a balance between a vision of what they want to do and the improvisation of "feeling it." They're clear about their desires and intentions, and they are comfortable with their ability to respond with agility in a world where they know anything can happen.

Learning how to move gracefully through life is a defining spiritual accomplishment, a milestone on the path. When we are in the zone, as they call it, we become like the proverbial man of the Tao – bridging the gap between the heaven of Infinite Intelligence and the world. This is just like the balance of yin and yang energies flowing into each other, as depicted by the symbol of *The Tao*.

When you dance with Destiny, more profound experiences of meaningful coincidence arise, leading to seemingly miraculous results. This is what happens when profound desire and concerted action are in alignment with what ancient sages called the *Anima Mundi*, the soul of the world. When you know who you are, and you have discovered what you are meant to do based on your own natural fascinations, you are in sync. It doesn't matter that the manifestation of your dreams is challenging. You are too delighted in receiving all the support that helps you turn challenges into opportunities to let that bother you.

Destiny in Action

For one last anecdotal story, a wonderful example of synchronicity supporting destiny occurred shortly after we published the first I Ching software. My 15-year-old son and I needed to find a new house that would be large enough to house us and accommodate a startup business with a couple of employees. I located a nice, large house that was ideally located in the right neighborhood for my son's school, but I was concerned that my application might be turned down. For one thing, leaving secure employment to become an entrepreneur had affected my credit rating, making it difficult to compete in a tight housing market. Nonetheless, I was hopeful when I went over to the place to apply in person, unaware of the fact that almost one hundred people had already submitted applications before me.

When I met the owner of the house, she asked what I did for a living, and I told her I had just started a little Macintosh software business. I didn't expect her to understand about software (it was 1990, after all), but as it turned out she had just gotten one of those early Macintosh computers that were shaped like an ice cube and was curious about what I might have for it. Tentatively, I explained that my product was a bit quirky – an interactive version of the Chinese I Ching called *Synchronicity*. She was shocked. It turned out that she was one of the earliest buyers of *Synchronicity*. In fact, it was the only software she had ever purchased and, best of all, she loved it!

She and I both realized what a remarkable synchronicity this was. Happily for my son and I (and the business), she took it as a sign and leased the house to us on the spot. A year later, she sold me that house. Thirteen years after that, the profits from the business (which had outgrown the house and moved out years earlier) paid off the mortgage. I had raised my son, as well as started and restarted the business, in that house over the next 19 years. Once I took out a second mortgage on the house to be able to make payroll. Later, the house supported the company as collateral for a line of credit with the bank. In my mind, that house is the house that synchronicity built. It was destined to support my work – and ultimately was paid for by it. How perfect!

Synchronicities like this – and having the tarot.com domain name come to me – arise to support you when you are following your calling and dancing with destiny. You still have to make good decisions and execute them, but it is so much easier when the universe is helping out. As David Richo put it, "Synchronicity is one of the forces of grace. It is the spur of the moment in that it spurs us on and it happens just in time for us to learn or make a move or grow in some new way."[76]

Living From the Inside Out

The Visionary Decision Making approach was not invented overnight. It represents decades of study and thought experiments, trial and error, risk-taking in the real world and learning from mistakes. It is the fruit of the long practice of insight meditation and authentic divination systems to awaken, stimulate, or support my intuition. It is a proven way to navigate the journey of life by staying open to your sense of direction in changing tides. It is a way to let creative power flow through you and support passionate action.

Over time, the practice of VDM skills will change your perspective and produce the confidence you need to fulfill your own destiny. It starts on the inside with knowing yourself, accepting yourself unconditionally and learning to trust your intuition. A bit of courage combined with good decision-making and learning experiences eventually leads to wisdom. The experience of successes – even small ones – will support the strongest faith that a person can develop: the confidence in yourself. Starting now, consider it part of your unfolding destiny to make better decisions for yourself and your loved ones in order to play a healing role in the world. Let it work out that way right before your eyes!

It's normal to stumble as you learn to dance, but if you keep practicing, you will develop a better sense of rhythm as you go along. You will enjoy the dance of life more and more. Make it fun. Start by playing more of your hunches. Let yourself be willing to go through the fear of making some mistakes. Go ahead, it won't kill you! Let it be okay to embarrass yourself if that's what needs to happen for you to release a fear of judgment or disapproval. You will learn that a little embarrassment is not the end of the world and often well worth it in terms of educational value.

Feel the fear and go for it anyway, remembering that fear and excitement are two sides of the same coin. Remember that, no matter what predicament you've ever found yourself in, you've handled it, right? Get revved up to practice more frequent risk-taking in small ways, which makes the art of intuitive decision-making into a manageable adventure of self-discovery, evolution and progress. Take comfort in remembering that your own resourcefulness is the safety net that nobody can take away from you.

Begin with small risks. If you are someone who tends to be shy, you could start introducing yourself to strangers – perhaps by asking directions even if you don't need them. Or you might take a dance lesson or acting class where you are required to interact with others in a graceful way. If you are extroverted, you can risk some of your time and attention by the practice of focused listening, or by interviewing another person and not interrupting them before they complete their reply. In general, try testing your intuitive impressions. Allow yourself to be guided by them to get a deeper sense of people you encounter – even people you think you already know. Take the risk of interviewing them a little bit to see how often your intuitive hunches about them turn out to be right.

Acts of generosity and loving-kindness are excellent ways to take small risks (and contribute to social harmony at the same time). Make it a habit to perform at least one unconditional act of generosity every day, expecting nothing in return – not acknowledgement, credit, or even gratitude. Why is this a risk? Because giving can feel like depletion to our ego if we forget all of the resources that are on loan to us and stay mired in poverty consciousness or a pessimistic point of view. Also, to the extent that we are not accustomed to donating time, energy, or money, to freely give any of these can take us out of our comfort zone.

While the practice of generosity is meritorious in every stage of life, it practically defines Stage Three. Once I transitioned from the "builder" stage by selling my business, I founded the Divination Foundation as a "legacy non-profit" to express my creativity in the form of books, blogs, and radio interviews – all as a way of exercising my interest in helping people to make better decisions. (Note: All proceeds from the sale of apps and books, including this one, go to the foundation's non-profit projects.) In addition to my contribution of time and energy in the form of non-paid work, I also maintain a personal "giving budget" – a concept that has been around for millennia. Ancient Jewish law, for instance, mandated the tithing of 10 percent of one's income to charity. But giving isn't just about money, nor is that necessarily the best way. If you cannot afford to give support in a financial way, don't let anyone tell you that you should donate 10 percent or 5 percent – or any percentage – of your income. There are so many ways to support the collective good with a bit of time and energy. All generosity is good.

Let's Dance!

The more you trust your intuition around taking risks that will grow you, treating life like a game or a dance, the better your intuitive sensitivity will become. Your understanding of people, and human nature in general, will dramatically improve. You will discover that the more that you trust yourself, the more confident and happy you are. Change is inevitable and changes that happen outside your control can be frightening. But as you cultivate your natural intuitive intelligence, you will discover that you have the agility to ride unpredictable waves of change like a balanced surfer. Going forward, you may even be able to influence the shape of waves to some extent. Your creative influence will grow.

Situations fluctuate, opportunities expire, and relationships change form without asking permission. But armed with VDM practices and operating assumptions, you now have the creative power to influence the flow of change more than before. Even slight improvements in coordination and timing will compound to exponentially greater abundance and joy in your experience of life, facilitating both your individual and the collective healing. So, here's to co-creating good fortune – not only for your sake, but also for the good of humanity and the natural world upon which our survival itself depends!

Beyond getting survival needs met, another aspect of personal happiness is being securely connected – to a partner, family, and community, all of humanity, to nature and spirit. A secure attachment with family or community supports greater confidence and creative explorations. Beyond our needs for security and belonging, however, we deserve a chance to be successful or happy in ways that mean something to us. Many studies have found that seeking meaning rather than happiness is associated with greater life satisfaction. We thrive on meaning. In making an effort to live your life with a sense of purpose, your learning capacity will expand throughout your lifetime. Your beliefs will evolve and change as needed, based on what you learn.

Being true to who you are and what is most important to you – together with cultivated intuition – will give you the means to make great decisions and find your perfect timing in every stage of life. Through your willingness to take the risks involved in following your destiny, abundance and joy become will not only be more possible, but much more likely.

These days we are dealing with more rapid change than ever before. Let's develop our internal sense of security by becoming more resourceful and creative as we learn how to better manage change. Visionary Decision Making is the central skill to help us meet this challenge of a lifetime. May you awaken, activate and learn to trust your intuitive intelligence... and may you enjoy the adventure of your Hero's Journey!

Acknowledgements

The lessons in this book took forty years to learn and four years to write. Although I expect more learning (and writing) to come in this lifetime, a book that covers such a major part of my life and significant lessons is an important part of my legacy. Like a "legacy letter" that a person might write to a descendant that he or she will leave behind, I wrote the book to pass on teaching stories that encourage others to follow their hearts and live their dreams.

Great Decisions, Perfect Timing would have never come to fruition without the tireless support, project management and superb editing of the Divination Foundation's co-director, producer and chief editor, Nayana Jennings. She consistently tempered my flighty dalliances with the Muse to help me stay on task and complete this book.

There has been a lot of other help along the way. My gratitude goes out to editor Mahesh Mohan and editorial assistants Sandra Ferconio, Vanessa Lampson and Cecily Crow. In the proofreading department, we acknowledge Janice Hussein's unfailing attention to detail. And special credit goes to my niece, Jewel Mlnarik, who did a great job designing and developing the book's website: GreatDecisionsPerfectTiming.com.

The wise counsel and friendly encouragement of fellow author, Catherine Ingram, helped tremendously, as well as the support of several other friends who took a peek at the work in various stages and nudged me toward the finish line. And, of course, I am most grateful for the generous contribution of a Foreword by my brilliant friend, John Gray.

A year ago, when I was feeling stuck and having trouble motivating myself to finish this book project, my good friend, executive coach Michael Beck, reminded me that my ultimate goal was not sales or profits (even though all proceeds go to the Divination Foundation's non-profit work). The only goal for me has been sharing some hard-won wisdom with enough readers to make the effort worthwhile. So, no matter how you came across a copy of this book, dear reader, I thank you for being a receptive audience and thus helping to make this massive effort worthwhile. And, if there is an easy way for you to pass this book on, I invite you to do so!

This book is an effort to give something back to the commons that supported my ability to learn, be creative and prosper – all the accumulated learning, tools and infrastructure we have inherited that make any kind of success possible. Above all, I am grateful to be alive on a beautiful planet and to perceive more every day how Infinite Intelligence is backing us up. The presence of higher powers that can inform and guide us has been confirmed by my teachers and all profound teachers going back eons. I am grateful to them all. Benefitting from their legacy and learning to call upon archetypal resources has been a sublime blessing for me in this evolutionary learning adventure called a human life.

Note: Anyone who wishes to contact the author or the Divination Foundation may do so via Divination.com/contact/. Please review this book on Amazon if you have an account. Thank you!

Visionary Decision Making Practices

Hierarchy of Values (Chapter 2)

Dr. John Demartini uses the word "values" in a specific, practical, and measurable way. In the approach that he calls "Hierarchy of Values," the word "values" does not refer to ideals, moral codes, or entrenched beliefs. Dr. Demartini teaches a way to identify real values by simply analyzing how much time, energy, money, and thought you actually invest in them: make a list of your current four or five major activities or preoccupations. Once you have created your list, keep it as a file on your computer or smartphone, or keep a small printed copy in your wallet or purse. The idea is that you can glance at your list to always remind yourself of your top current values (just knowing that it is there helps even if you don't look at it). Edit and refine the list as you become more and more clear about your own unique hierarchy of values.

Tracking Synchronicities (Chapter 3)

Keeping a synchronicity journal will help you take full advantage of signs that the universe provides. Whether it's paper-based or in the form of a digital file, make a point to record the meaningful coincidences – as well as dreams, hunches, and good ideas – that occur to you every day. If you have a smartphone or regularly use a computer, I recommend setting up a Synchronicity Journal file on your smartphone, tablet, or computer. Make a habit of entering all your synchronicities whether you understand their meaning yet or not.

Just having such a journal will motivate you to notice synchronicities more often. You will more quickly capture the moment when a profound coincidence happens. Your physical sense of a "gut feeling" or that "feeling in your bones" will become sharper and more refined.

The synchronicities you record will change your perspective and lead to new insights, relationships, and opportunities. The meaning of your impressions, the significance of the people you meet and new potentials will become clearer as you go back and look them over. Add reflections and insights once a week as you attain a deeper understanding of their meaning over time.

Weighted Pros Logic Technique (Chapter 5)

In order to balance out the emotional impact of loss aversion – the fear of losing has greater power than the hope of winning – I use a variation of Ben Franklin's "Pros and Cons" technique that I call the "Weighted Pros." It is a practical approach that will help with every major decision you need to make. When faced with a decision, create a simple table with your three best options across the top. For example, if your decision has to do with finding the right place to live, you might boil it down to three options:
rent downtown condo buy house in suburbs   housesit for friends

Instead of listing pros and cons below each of the options, list only its advantages. There are two reasons for only listing positives and not tallying the negatives. First of all, a con is usually an inversion of one of the pros of what is one of the alternative choices. On an emotional level, the pro of one choice can seem more compelling when viewed as a con of another. It just seems to be easier for the human mind to focus on what it doesn't want rather than what it does want. We need to make a concerted effort to counteract that tendency and take the fear element out of the calculations. Give each of the positives a weighted value on a scale of 1-10 (10 being the highest positive score), and then add up the total values for each column. The option that offers the highest value is your best logical choice.

Mindfulness of the Body (Chapter 6)

Just take a minute right now. Pay a few moments of close attention to the feelings in your body. The feeling of your weight against the chair (if you are sitting), the feeling of your skin against your clothing, the subtle sensation of your nose hairs in the wind as you inhale and exhale. During the day, the practice of mindfulness also notes your physically felt responses to information, people, and events that come your way.

Progressive Relaxation (Chapter 6)

The technique works best when you're seated or lying down, but it can even be done standing. First, tighten the muscles in the calf of your right leg. Hold the tension for five to ten seconds, and then let the muscles relax. Repeat the process with the muscles in the lower part of your left leg, and do the same by isolating other muscle groups in different parts while moving up your body. As you release the tension in a particular muscle group, the muscle relaxes not only to its pre-tensed state, but actually relaxes well beyond that point. If you have time to tense and relax all your major muscle groups, you'll feel the stabilizing, grounding sensation throughout your whole body and clarity in your mind.

A Letting-Go Moment (Chapter 6)

Close your eyes for a few moments and let go of whatever thoughts arise – noticing them but just letting them float by like passing clouds. Just do this for a minute or two and see what happens in your mind. Thoughts will keep popping up whether you want them to or not. Sooner or later, if you sit still long enough, you will experience a quieter, more spacious aspect of the mind that is like a clear sky, but in the meantime thoughts come and go, seemingly on their own. Since you didn't invite them or even want them, what makes the thoughts that arise *yours* any more than the clouds passing in the sky? Once you slip into the natural mindfulness of our ancestors, you will free yourself from having to pay attention to obsessive thoughts and worries that do you no good.

A Beginner's Meditation Session (Chapter 6)

Here's an easy way to begin a meditation practice session: Find a spot where you can be alone and undisturbed for fifteen or twenty minutes. Sit comfortably in a chair or on a cushion on the floor, close your eyes and begin to concentrate on your breath. Bring your attention to the bare sensation of inhaling and exhaling. The point is not to produce any special kind of breathing – deep or otherwise – but quietly watch the rise and fall of the breath, noting the subtle physical sensation of air coming in and out of the nostrils. Or if it is easier for you, note the rising and falling of the abdomen with the breath.

Sit still long enough to allow the chattering of your mind to simmer down, which can take up to fifteen minutes. During this time, use an object of concentration like the breath and continue until stillness of the mind is achieved. I compare this slow settling down of the mind to how boiling water eventually settles after you take the pan off the burner. The flames represent the desires and attachments that stir up the mind. Even when you turn off the flames of desire, the boiling water will continue to churn before it simmers down to a tranquil state. It takes a little time at first. This process can be frustrating to a novice meditator, because he or she lacks confidence and wonders if the settling will ever happen. But after just a little bit of patient practice, you will find that you can slip into a meditative state more and more quickly.

When first starting a meditation practice, I suggest using a timer and committing yourself to *sitting still* – and only that – for 20 minutes. Forget about achieving any results (even though you will). Psychologically, letting go of attachment to outcome reduces a tendency to put pressure on yourself to do it right or to wonder if you are being successful at *meditating*. If you commit to just sitting still and stick to taking such a "time out" on a daily basis, you *will* start meditating – if only because as long as you are just sitting, there is nothing better to do! With enough practice, it can become second nature for you to meditate wherever you are.

Mindfulness of Breathing (Chapter 6)

Your breath is an excellent object of concentration because it is always there for you – when you are standing in line, riding an elevator, or during other in-between times throughout the day. It's discreet in that it is not obvious that you are meditating. While it is useful to also have a formal sitting practice, there is tremendous benefit from every possible instant of mindfulness. The technique is simple: let go of identifying with rapidly changing thoughts and feelings by concentrating on your breath (or other object), while being open to and mindful of whatever arises in the field of consciousness.

The Letting Go Mantra (Chapter 6)

Close your eyes and take a full breath, thinking the word *Letting* as you inhale and the word *Go* as you exhale. Repeat. When you reflect on the meaning of the two words, this mantra is reminding you (in English) to do what meditation is all about – the letting go of attachment to thoughts and feelings that arise. Use the *Letting Go* mantra anywhere and at any time. It helps instill inner peace and serves as a conscious reminder that letting go is the key to having a clear and open mind. In addition, letting go of "busy mind" creates an opening for intuitive insights to alight like butterflies settling onto a sunflower.

Make a point to note insights that come up during your meditation session. In order to do this, you are going to need a pen and paper or a recording device to quickly capture insights when they arise. Once you've recorded an insight, let go of thinking about it, or anything. Go back to focusing on your breath, mantra, or other object of concentration.

Harvesting Intuitive Insights During Meditation (Chapter 6)

Traditional meditation is aimed at letting go for the sake of cultivating a transcendent consciousness. But another major benefit is greater intuitive sensitivity. Considering the value of insights that might arise, it can be useful to interrupt your concentration efforts long enough for the left brain to record valuable insights. Rather than placing all the emphasis on just letting go of thoughts that arise – especially if you are facing a big decision – make a point to note insights that may come up during your meditation session.

To do this, you will need a pen and paper or a recording device to capture insights as they arise. Once you've recorded an insight, let go of thinking about it – or anything, for that matter. Go back to focusing on your breath, mantra, or other object of concentration.

Although this approach to meditation is somewhat unconventional, there is creative value in using meditation this way, since the practice of mindfulness helps to develop an ability to hear the voice of intuition, which can connect Infinite Intelligence to your best interests.

Tracking Your Dreams (Chapter 7)

There is more than one way to keep track of dreams. Jung kept a notebook at his bedside, as many people do. Immediately upon waking, he wrote down what he could remember of his dreams. If Jung could have recorded his dreams using a tape recorder – as I prefer to do – he probably would have embraced the technology. Once you've recorded your dreams, you can start to interpret what they mean. The key here is to avoid self-censoring or second-guessing yourself. Let your mind generate free associations based on images you recall from the dream and record these too.

Even if you're looking for help with an important decision, don't narrow your interpretation to that specific issue – at least not at first. Be open-minded and receptive. Answers and insights may emerge in an order that is different from what you had been seeking. Record them as quickly as you can, without dwelling on what you put down. First impressions are most useful!

Invocations and the Synchronicity Prayer (Chapter 7)

When you are going through major transitions, it is helpful to practice an invocative prayer ritual on a daily basis – not so different from the habit of saying the morning and evening prayers that many of us were taught as children. You can return to the ritual of morning and evening invocations in order to stay more connected to Infinite Intelligence during the day and in your dreams at night. After you wake up in the morning, welcome a greater awareness of synchronicities throughout the coming day. Depending on what you intend to create or build or preserve, you can summon and activate other powers as well. At night, your affirmative prayer calls forth the healing and awakening power of dreaming.

To be more receptive to insights throughout your day, use the Synchronicity Prayer: "May I notice synchronicities that arise during this day and pay attention to them. If I don't understand their meaning, I trust that it will be revealed in due course. In the meantime, I am grateful to be able to notice the signals."

No matter how you choose to word your prayers (I recommend composing them in your own words in a file that you can edit on a computer, tablet, or smartphone), it helps to create a routine like this:

Sit and breathe with your back fairly straight. If you need to lean against a cushion, wall, or back of a chair, that is fine. The mind tends to be sharper when we sit or stand in a balanced position rather than slumping or reclining. Take three deep breaths to let go of tension in your body. If I am not going to disturb anybody by doing so, I find it satisfying to make an audible "ah" or "om" sound with each exhale.

Read your invocation – preferably out loud to yourself – taking the time to understand each word as you recite it.

Breathe slowly, as you let yourself project into, and feel, the archetypal power and state of mind that you are invoking.

Feel the bliss of being mentally magnetic through the clarity of your intention – and emotionally magnetic through the infectious power of your desire. Sit still and stay in the emotionally magnetic state for as long as you can.

Make a resolution to notice this attraction consciousness sticking with you throughout your day.

Here are a few suggestions for how your invocative prayers might be phrased (feel free to borrow from these examples and customize your own as well):

Sample Morning Invocations
May I notice all the magical moments today, as life unfolds synchronistically and perfectly, according to Destiny's plan.

As I face an important decision, I wish to invoke an archetype of Courage, so that my choices will not be distracted by fear.

May Wisdom guide my decisions today; may the wisest choices become clear to me.

I am creating the mental and emotional space to tune in my intuitive sensitivity in order to make the best choice now. Direct me to the best path of action.

Sample Evening Invocations
May the Dreamer bestow upon me symbolic dreams that I will remember and record, which will shed light upon my life and true self.

Let my dreams flow tonight, and may their symbolic meaning bring a greater awareness of who I am, my best direction going forward, and the most enlightened choices I can make.

Creative Manifestation Process (Chapter 7)

Use this powerful technique to attract and attain whatever your heart desires. Again, find a comfortable but alert sitting position. Take a few deep breaths, making an "ah" or "om" sound with each exhale. When you are relaxed but alert and ready, read your treatment slowly to yourself, preferably aloud. After you are finished reading your one-page document, stay in place and breathe. Feel the bliss of being spiritually magnetic via the clarity and power of expressed intention, and emotionally magnetic through the infectious power of the feeling. Before you finish the manifestation meditation, make a resolution to take your attracting attitude with you throughout your day. Here is one template that I have used, which you can edit for yourself:

Step 1: Recognition. I acknowledge Creative Power, the universal magnetic energy that unites and makes things whole. Divine power expresses itself as love, wisdom, and courage. It is reflected in the vastness of space, the sun around which Earth revolves, the beauty of nature, the joy of love and miracles. This unlimited resource operates according to the law of cause and effect that begins with attraction: First the image, then the declaration, and then manifestation. I know there is no limit to Creative Power.

Step 2: Identification. I am one with Creative Power, which not only surrounds me but flows through me. My breathing reminds me of my interconnectedness with all of nature, and I can feel the connection any time I close my eyes. Divine love and wisdom surround me, and go before me, making my way easy and successful. I AM capable of facilitating any results I visualize and feel. I don't need to know what exact form the results will take, but solutions appear quickly and easily. I deserve what is good for me.

Step 3: Declaration. I declare that I am *now* enjoying the realization of [my desire]. This feels [liberating, joyous and pleasurable, etc.].

Step 4: Thanksgiving. I give thanks for the fulfillment of [my desire], the joyful anticipation of which I am feeling already. I feel strong on my path. I AM confident, full of faith, and my heart is filled with gratitude.

Step 5: Release. I let go of tendencies to worry or interfere by trying to make results take shape in any particular way. I know that the law of cause-and-effect is operating on this treatment right now, even if my senses have no proof as of yet. I am attracting [my desire], and [my desire] is attracting me. The manifestation of this, or something better, is in process. Creative Power is synchronistically producing the right results for me in a way and according to a schedule that is perfect. I am letting go of trying to control things and surrender to the good that is my destiny. My "faith" is my intuitive sense of the manifesting process that is happening behind the scenes right now.

Step 6: Emotional magnetization. I am letting myself *feel* the presence of what I have declared, which is in the process of manifesting. As I let this feeling radiate throughout my entire being, I become magnetic.

Step 7: Action steps. I make the right moves at the right time, starting with better decision-making that taps my intuition, intellect, and receptivity to good advice. I make and follow up on commitments to myself. In the two-steps-forward, one-step-back dance of life, I am taking good steps in a timely manner. As long as I am in connection with Creative Power, I know I can't go wrong!

You can look up and/or download the Creative Manifestation Treatment on Divination.com in the Resources section. If this technique resonates with you, edit it to develop a personalized version. Once you have the wording formulated in a way that feels powerful when you speak it aloud, print it out and read it every morning before you start your daily routines. The use of the Creative Manifestation Treatment draws on divine powers to help you stay focused on the fulfillment of your highest priorities, empowered by an optimistic and creative attitude.

Preparing for an I Ching Experience (Chapter 8)

Center yourself for a fruitful I Ching experience. Enter a meditative frame of mind that supports a sincere desire for truth and wisdom. Perform whatever centering technique or ritual works best for you prior to any I Ching consultation. Do your best to enter a state of focused relaxation.

It's also vital to be clear about what you hope to learn or achieve. Possible goals could be making an important decision or reducing stress around changes in your life that are currently beyond your understanding. These are not the goals of the ego that always wants to make things happen. A centering practice is an intentional process that will help move your ego out of the way so your mind can be receptive to guidance. This is valuable in and of itself.

After you relax, consciously let go of any attachment to receiving a specific answer or outcome. Commit yourself to caring only about truth. By giving the ego a "vacation" from its usual preoccupations, you increase receptivity to archetypes that can inform your conscious mind and support your decisions and actions.

Simply lighting a candle, burning incense, or taking a few deep breaths with your eyes closed can facilitate focused relaxation.

Choose what feels the most comfortable for you. The information you receive from a reading comes from within you, not from the external environment. Once you've entered into the proper frame of mind, you can begin consulting the I Ching.

Before you cast a reading, take a few moments to affirm your allegiance to what is real. Confidently adopt the attitude that everything will work out the way it is supposed to – for some reason or another. This will be true whether or not you understand the reason now. Only consult the I Ching when you feel balanced and clear enough to listen to the wisdom it provides and to tap into your intuition.

Formulating Your I Ching Query (Chapter 8)

It is not necessary to formulate your issue of concern as a question. You can hold a specific subject in mind at the beginning of the divination process or just write down the name of a situation or a person with whom you are in some kind of relationship. The extra clarity of writing down your subject of focus will produce a clearer reading.

Documenting Your I Ching Readings (Chapter 8)

It is helpful to take notes when consulting the I Ching, so have a pen and paper at hand, or be close to your electronic device of choice. (The *Visionary I Ching* app conveniently allows you to cast a hexagram using a smartphone or tablet, read about your hexagram and save it for later review.) Saving your readings in some kind of journal lets you evaluate and compare them in the future. Include comments on your *experience* – including the details of your divination ritual and approach – your *interpretation* (a sentence or two that summarizes what the I Ching is reflecting) and the *result* (the after-effect of the decision you made following your reading).

The VDM Meeting (Chapter 9)

If you feel stuck or virtually paralyzed, schedule a VDM Meeting with yourself every morning for as many days in a row as necessary. Consider your options around the important matter every day until you are ready to make a decision and commit to a course of action.

Always schedule a VDM Meeting as early as possible in the day. Make it your *first* item of business in the morning until you have had enough of them to get to clarity. There doesn't need to be a set length of time for your VDM Meeting, but 45 minutes to an hour gives you enough time to review and reconsider your options.

Below are some ideas for a VDM Meeting:

Review your viable options, as winnowed down by the Weighted Pros logic technique.

• Read a guided meditation script aloud to yourself. This will put you into a state of mind that is positive and receptive to Infinite Intelligence. If you are not able to do this because of interruptions or emotional interference, stop the process and reschedule a VDM Meeting with yourself early the next day.

• Invoke the *Sovereign* archetype to support yourself as the chief executive decision-maker of your life.

• Invoke the archetype of *The Sage* and summon forth a "letting-go" state of egoless mind. You may feel empty and vast, as you open yourself up to creative potential. (I am reminded of the fertile Void of Creation that existed before the Big Bang, when all things were possible.)

• Do a short I Ching reading for one last reflection, asking for perspective on your decision. You can use three coins and the hexagram lookup feature on Divination.com, *The Visionary I Ching* ebook or the *Visionary I Ching* app on a smartphone or tablet.

• Optional step: Meet with one or two of your most trusted and objective advisors and share your latest thoughts about the strategic idea with them. Keep the focus on your decision-making.

Commitment via Written Agreement with Yourself (Chapter 9)

Formalizing a decision that has become a commitment by creating a written agreement is a powerful and positive technique. I would suggest starting out by writing an Agreement with your Self (e.g., the Self archetype) that goes something like this:

Dear Self, I hereby make the following commitment to you:

[write a short description of your decision]

I am letting go of fear and doubt, and resolve to do my best to implement my decision with power and grace.

Signed: _____

How to Upgrade Beliefs (Chapter 11)

Write down one or more beliefs, especially including any that you take for granted and never think about, which could benefit from reevaluation. Across from each of them, write out what a revised, more productive assumption might be. It is helpful to keep a small sheet of such a list on your fridge, in your wallet, or on your computer desktop. Let it grow. Upgrading old beliefs is like training a puppy to go outside: consistent reminders on a regular basis.

Having a hard time coming up with ideas? The following lists areas of life where you may have a self-limiting core belief:

- Your talents and capabilities: "I'm no good at that stuff anyway, so why would anyone hire me?" Antidote: I am capable of mastering anything I am interested in learning.

- Your worthiness to be loved: "I'm only lovable if I... am perfect... make lots of money... look beautiful." Antidote: I accept myself unconditionally. I am my own best friend and will never abandon myself... I appreciate my own kindness and resilience.

• Your luck: "Nothing turns out right. Everything bad always happens to me, so I shouldn't even try." Antidote: I am far luckier than I know. I can improve my luck starting now.

• Your world: "People only take advantage of you; it's foolish to trust anyone you don't know very well." Antidote: By allowing myself to give others a chance to be good with me, I expand my circle of friends and supporters.

Share Synchronicities (Chapter 12)

Synchronicity Forum: Openly or anonymously share your stories of amazing synchronicities and be inspired by the stories of others – in an online forum where people can collaborate in the search for deeper meanings of their Hero's Journeys. To be part of the Synchronistic Lifestyle Community, visit: www. GreatDecisionsPerfectTiming.com

APPENDIX B

Visionary Beliefs

Change is Your Friend

There are two basic orientations toward change – fear or excitement. People who see change as friendly are more optimistic and more likely to enjoy the up-and-down flux of life. People who fear change, on the other hand, would like time to stand still. Change is a constant; there is nothing we can do about that. In order to embrace change, therefore, we need to develop a more fluid relationship to time. When we enjoy life, time seems to go fast; when we are in resistance to something, it seems to crawl. When we come to regard change as a friendly force, the success brought by our improving sense of timing will encourage us to cultivate our intuitive intelligence.

The Vast Reservoir of Infinite Intelligence is Always Available

Individual willpower, no matter how strong, is never enough by itself to effect constructive change. In order to evolve and grow, we need to seek and accept the help of a higher power. (VDM simply refers to that higher power as Infinite Intelligence or Creative Power.) Once we learn how to tune in via our intuitive sense, Creative Power provides everything we need to be creative, productive, successful, and happier. When I was a bootstrap entrepreneur and asked if I had investors, I would reply, "Yes... my backer has infinite resources." (Of course, I was referring to that higher power.)

I Deserve to Have What I Want (and What I Want is Good for Me)

If you believe you *don't* deserve to live out a meaningful and fulfilling destiny, your subconscious mind will not allow you to manifest it. Learning to trust yourself, your intuition, and your own interpretation of meanings does wonders for self-confidence. Self-confidence arises from having discovered your natural talents and then practicing them until you achieve a level of mastery. Then you are in a position to create your own luck. As Louis Pasteur put it, "Chance favors the prepared mind."

The Synchronicity Belief: There Are No Accidents

Living a synchronistic life involves cultivating acceptance and wonder while letting go of judgment and resistance to the way things appear. Recall the old expression, "Things are never as bad – or as good – as they seem," because it is essentially true. Be a warrior of acceptance and accept your own karma (substitute your concept of cosmic justice here), taking refuge in the belief that "what goes around comes around." You will understand that *there are no accidents – only occasional failures to discern aspects of a larger unfolding pattern*. A greater awareness of synchronicity will ease the bumps and transforms your experience of life – with its inevitable ups and downs – into a more rhythmic and meaningful journey. Enjoy!

ENDNOTES

1 Edward O. Wilson, *Consilience: The Unity of Knowledge* (New York: Vintage Books, 1999).

2 Jeff Bezos, "We Are What We Choose" 2010 Baccalaureate Remarks, May 30, 2010 http://www.princeton.edu/main/news/archive/S27/52/51O99/index.xml

3 Alvin Toffler, *Future Shock* (New York: Random House, 1970).

4 John Tierney, "Do You Suffer From Decision Fatigue?" *New York Times Magazine*, August 17, 2011.

5 Eileen C. Shapiro and Howard H. Stevenson, *Make Your Own Luck: 12 Practical Steps to Taking Smarter Risks in Business* (New York: Penguin Group, 2005).

6 Joseph Campbell and Bill Moyers, *The Power of Myth* (New York: Doubleday, 1988).

7 Marsha Sinetar, *Do What You Love, The Money Will Follow: Discovering Your Right Livelihood* (New York: Random House, 1987).

8 Steven Taylor, *The Fall: The Insanity of the Ego in Human History and the Dawning of a New Era.* (UK: O Books, 2005).

9 John F. Demartini, *The Values Factor: The Secret to Creating an Inspired and Fulfilling Life* (New York: Berkley Publishing Group, 2013).

10 Robert A. Johnson, *We: Understanding the Psychology of Romantic Love* (San Francisco: Harper, 1983).

11 Carl G. Jung, *Jung on Synchronicity and the Paranormal: Key Readings Selected and Introduced by Roderick Main* (London: Routledge, 1973).

12 David Richo, *The Power of Coincidence: How Life Shows Us What We Need to Know* (Boston: Shambhala, 2007).

13 Robert H. Hopcke, *There Are No Accidents: Synchronicity and the Stories of Our Lives* (New York: Riverhead Books, 1997).

14 Carl G. Jung, *Letters, Vol. 1: 1906-1950* Gerhard Adler and Aniela Jaffe (Eds.). trans. R.F.C. Hull (Princeton: Princeton Press, 1973).

15 Terence McKenna, interviewed by the author, Pathways Radio Show. Portland, 1997.

16 K. von Meyenn, (ed.). *Wolfgang Pauli. Scientific Correspondence with Bohr, Einstein, Heisenberg, a.o., Volume IV/Part I: 1950-1952* (Berlin: Springer-Verlag, Berlin and Heidelberg, 1996).

17 Napoleon Hill, *Think and Grow Rich* (New York: Random House, 1937).

18 Ralph Waldo Emerson, "The OverSoul," *Essays: First Series* (Boston: Houghton Osgood, 1879).

19 Carl G. Jung, *Collected Works of C. G. Jung: The Structure and Dynamics of the Psyche* (Vol. 8). Gerhard Adler, Herbert Read & Michael Fordham. (Eds.). (Princeton: Princeton University Press, 1969).

20 Carl G. Jung, *Collected Works of C. G. Jung: The Archetypes and the Collective Unconscious* (Vol. 9, Part 1). Gerhard Adler (Ed.) (Princeton: Princeton University Press, 1959).

21 Jung, *Collected Works of C. G. Jung: The Structure and Dynamics of the Psyche.*

22 Ibid.

23 Robert K. Merton, Ph.D. "The role of genius in scientific advance," *New Scientist* No 259. 2 Nov. 1961.

24 Bob Proctor, *You Were Born Rich: Now You Can Discover and Develop Those Riches* (Scottsdale: LifeSuccess Production, 1997).

25 Eagleman, David. *Incognito: The Secret Lives of the Brain.* New York: Pantheon Books, 2011.

26 Robert W. Firestone and Joyce Catlett, *Fear of Intimacy* (Washington, DC: American Psychological Association, 1999).

27 Garrett Hardin, "The Tragedy of the Commons," *Science* (Vol 162, No. 3859) December 13, 1968.

28 Herbert A. Simon, *Reason in Human Affairs* (Stanford: Stanford University Press, 1983).

29 Gary Klein, *Sources of Power: How People Make Decisions* (Cambridge: MIT Press, 1999).

30 Gerd Gigerenzer, *Gut Feeling: The Intelligence of the Unconscious* (New York: Penguin Group, 2007).

31 Carl G. Jung, *Psychological Types. Collected Works of C. G. Jung* (Vol. 6) (Princeton: Princeton University Press, 1923).

32 Caron B. Goode, "Intuitive Intelligence Comes of Age," http://www.pregnancy.org/article/intuitive-intelligence-comes-age

33 William Hermanns and Albert Einstein, *Einstein and the Poet: In Search of the Cosmic Man* (Brandon Press, 1983).

34 R. Joseph, *The Right Brain and the Limbic Unconscious: Emotion, Forgotten Memories, Self-Deception, Bad Relationships* (University Press Science Publishers, 2012).

35 Caron B. Goode, "Intuitive Intelligence Comes of Age," http://www.pregnancy.org/article/intuitive-intelligence-comes-age

36 Brigitte Stemmer and Harry A. Whitaker, *Handbook of the Neuroscience of Language*, (London/Burlington, MA: Academic Press, 2008).

37 Thomas Lewis, Fari Aminii, and Richard Lannon, *A General Theory of Love* (New York: Vintage Books, 2001).

38 Cliff Saran "Decision-makers rely on intuition over analytics," June 5, 2014. http://www.computerweekly.com/news/2240221902/Decision-makers-rely-on-intuition-over-analytics

39 Goode, "Intuitive Intelligence Comes of Age," http://www.pregnancy.org/article/intuitive-intelligence-comes-age

40 Lewis, Amini, and Lannon, *A General Theory of Love.*

41 Rick Beneteau, *Inside the Minds of Winners* (Charles Burke, 2001).

42 Susan Jeffers, *Feel The Fear...And Do It Anyway* (New York: Random House, 1987).

43 Adam Hadhazy, "Think Twice: How the Gut's 'Second Brain' Influences Mood and Well-Being," *The Scientific American,* February 12, 2010.

44 Malcolm Gladwell, *Blink: The Power of Thinking Without Thinking* (New York: Little, Brown & Co., 2005).

45 Edmund Jacobson, *Progressive Relaxation* (Chicago: University of Chicago Press, 1938).

46 David Harp, *The Three Minute Meditator* (Fine Communications, 1999).

47 Donald Altman, *The Joy Compass: Eight Ways to Find Lasting Happiness, Gratitude and Optimism in the Present Moment* (Oakland: New Harbinger, 2012).

48 Jolande Jacobi & R.F.C. Hull (Eds.) *Psychological Reflections* (Princeton: Princeton University Press, 1970).

49 Joseph Campbell, *A Hero With A Thousand Faces* (Princeton: Princeton Press, 1973).

50 Carl G. Jung, *Letters, Vol. 1: 1906-1950.* Gerhard Adler and Aniela Jaffe (Eds.). Trans. R.F.C. Hull (Princeton: Princeton Press, 1992).

51 Ibid.

52 Carl G. Jung, *Dream Analysis, Notes of the Seminar given in 1928-1930,* William McGuire (Ed.). (London: Routledge & Kegan Paul, 1984).

53 Robert L. Moore and Douglas Gillette, *King, Warrior, Magician, Lover: Rediscovering the Archetypes of the Mature Masculine* (New York: HarperCollins Press, 1990).

54 Paul O'Brien, "Creative Manifestation Treatment," http://www.divination.com/resources/manifestation

55 Richo, *The Power of Coincidence.*

56 Paul O'Brien, "Divination Verses in the Bible," http://www.divination.com/resources/articles/bible-verses

57 Paul O'Brien, *Divination: Sacred Tools for Reading the Mind of God,* (Portland: Visionary Networks Press, 2007).

58 Richard Wilhelm and Cary F. Baynes, trans. *I Ching: Book of Changes.* (Bollingen Series 19) (New York: Bollingen Foundation, 1950).

59 Jung, *Collected Works of C. G. Jung: The Structure and Dynamics of the Psyche.*

60 Ibid.

61 Richo, *The Power of Coincidence.*

62 Molly Gilmour, "Steves: 'Best souvenir is a broader perspective'" *The Olympian,* September 18, 2014. http://www.theolympian.com/2014/09/18/3321877/steves-best-souvenir-is-a-broader.html

63 Marco Della Cava, "'Jobs' author Isaacson tackles tech history," *USA Today.* October 6, 2014, http://www.usatoday.com/story/life/books/2014/10/06/walter-isaacson-the-innovators-new-book-on-computer-history/16644797/

64 Hermann Hesse, *Siddhartha* (New York: New Directions Publishing Corp., 1951).

65 Malcolm Gladwell, *Outliers: The Story of Success* (New York: Little, Brown & Co., 2008).

66 Stewart Blackburn, *The Skills of Pleasure: Crafting the Life You Want* (Pahoa, HI: Hale Onaona Publishing, 2013).

67 Catherine Pulsifer, "Believe in Yourself," http://www.wow4u.com/believeyourselfquotes/

68 Carol S. Dweck, *Mindset: The New Psychology of Success: How We Can Learn to Fulfill Our Potential* (New York: Random House, 2007).

69 Ibid.

70 Bruce H. Lipton, *The Wisdom of Your Cells: How Your Beliefs Control Your Biology* (Louisville, CO: Sounds True, Inc., 2006).

71 Shapiro and Stevenson, *Make Your Own Luck*.

72 Hopcke, *There Are No Accidents*.

73 Richo, *The Power of Coincidence*.

74 Marney K. Makridakis, *Creating Time: Using Creativity to Reinvent the Clock and Reclaim Your Life* (Novato, CA: New World Library, 2012).

75 Richo, *The Power of Coincidence*.

76 Ibid.

Other Books by Paul O'Brien

The Visionary I Ching
(Ebook or App)
An illustrated modern version of the Chinese *Book of Changes*,
available in Ebook or iPhone/Android App formats

Divination: Sacred Tools for Reading the Mind of God
(Print or Ebook)
A study of classical divination systems throughout history,
including an examination of how they work and how to put them
to best use as aids for intuitive decision-making.

Made in the USA
Middletown, DE
13 April 2016